AF604297

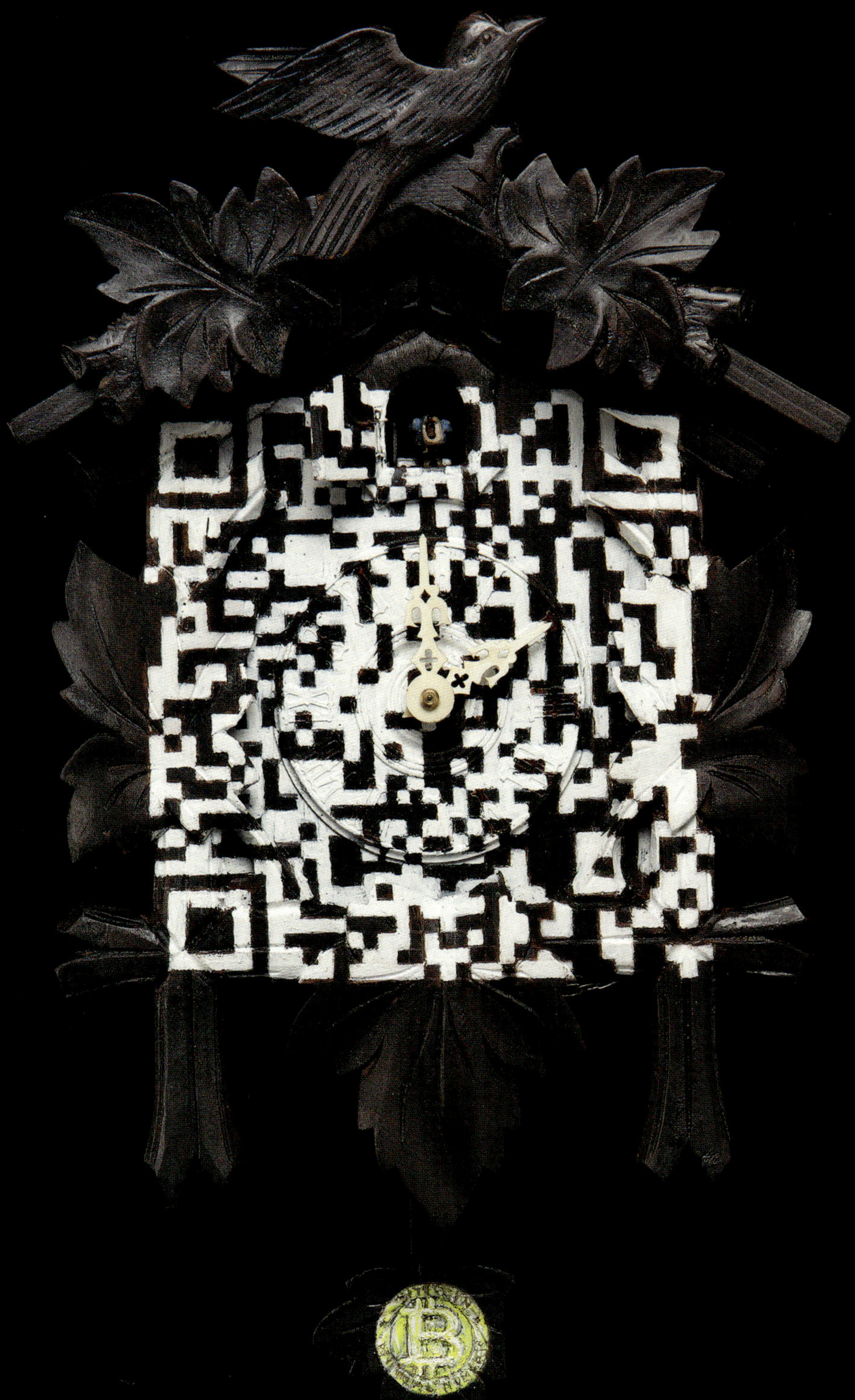

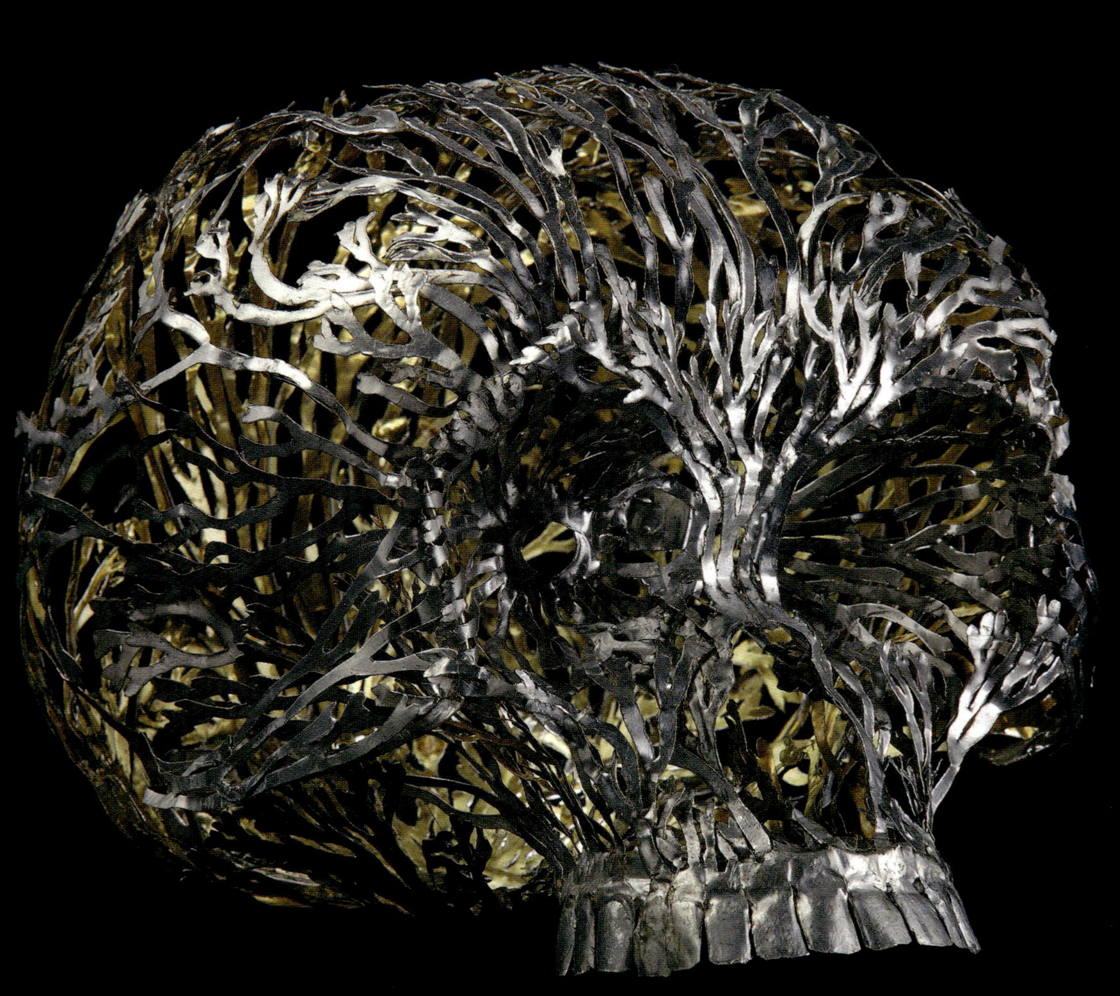

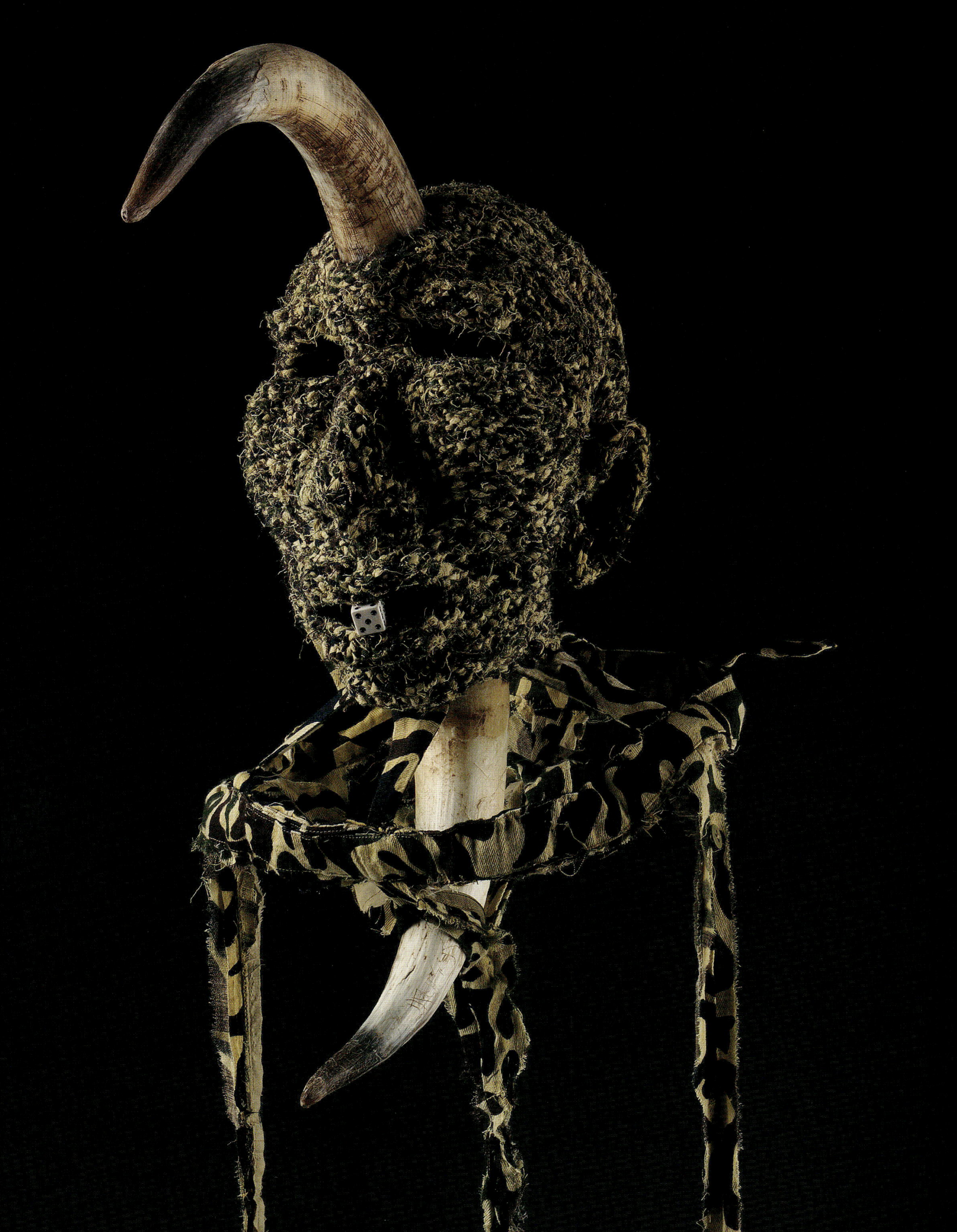

RTLY CLOUDY. 24°C TOM

YDNEY

ver

TERROR IN OUR HEART

Terrorism yesterday struck at the core of Australia's way of life when an Islamic extremist on bail over a murder case took innocent people hostage in a cafe. Reports, pictures P 2-13.

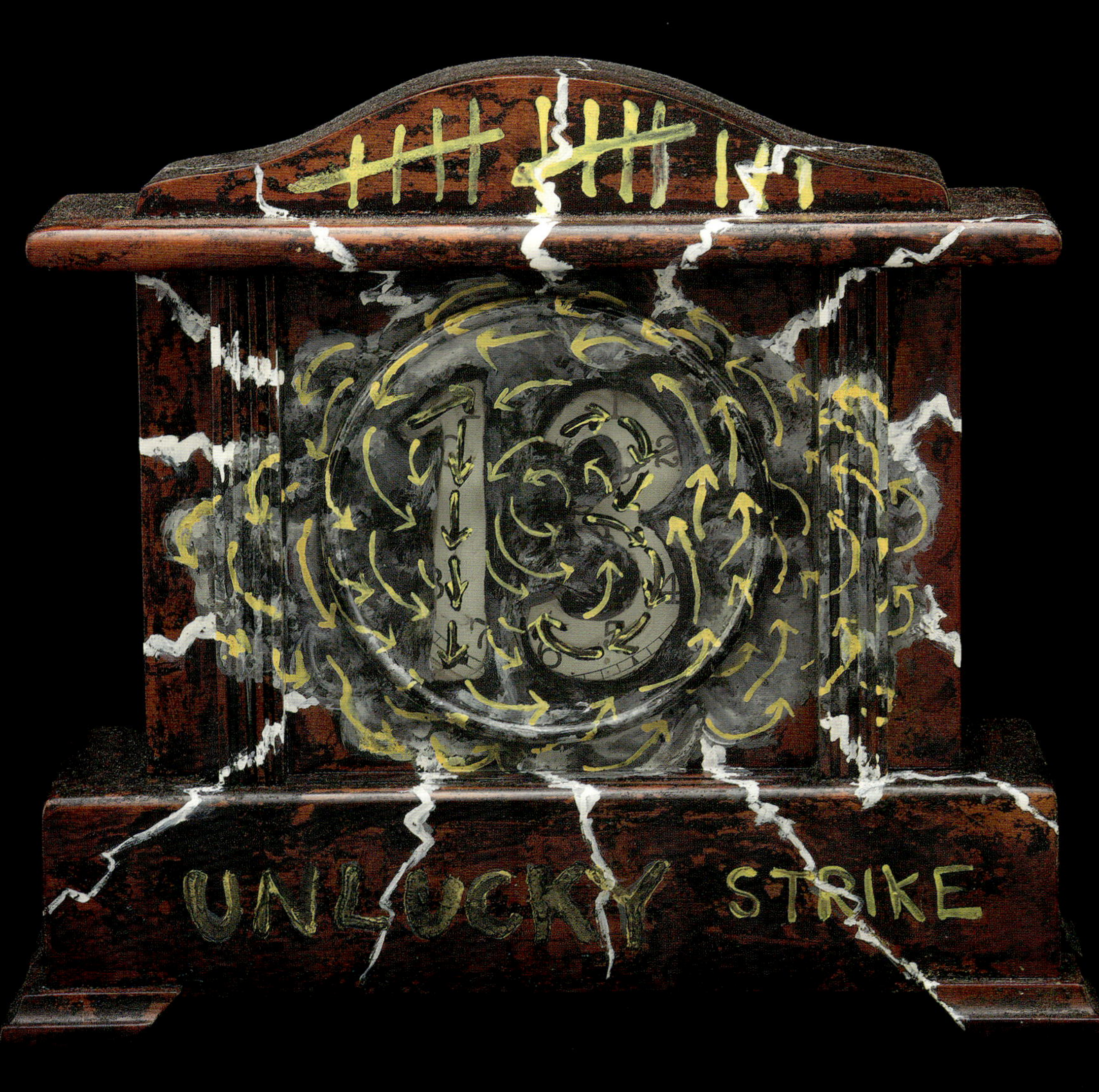
13
UNLUCKY STRIKE

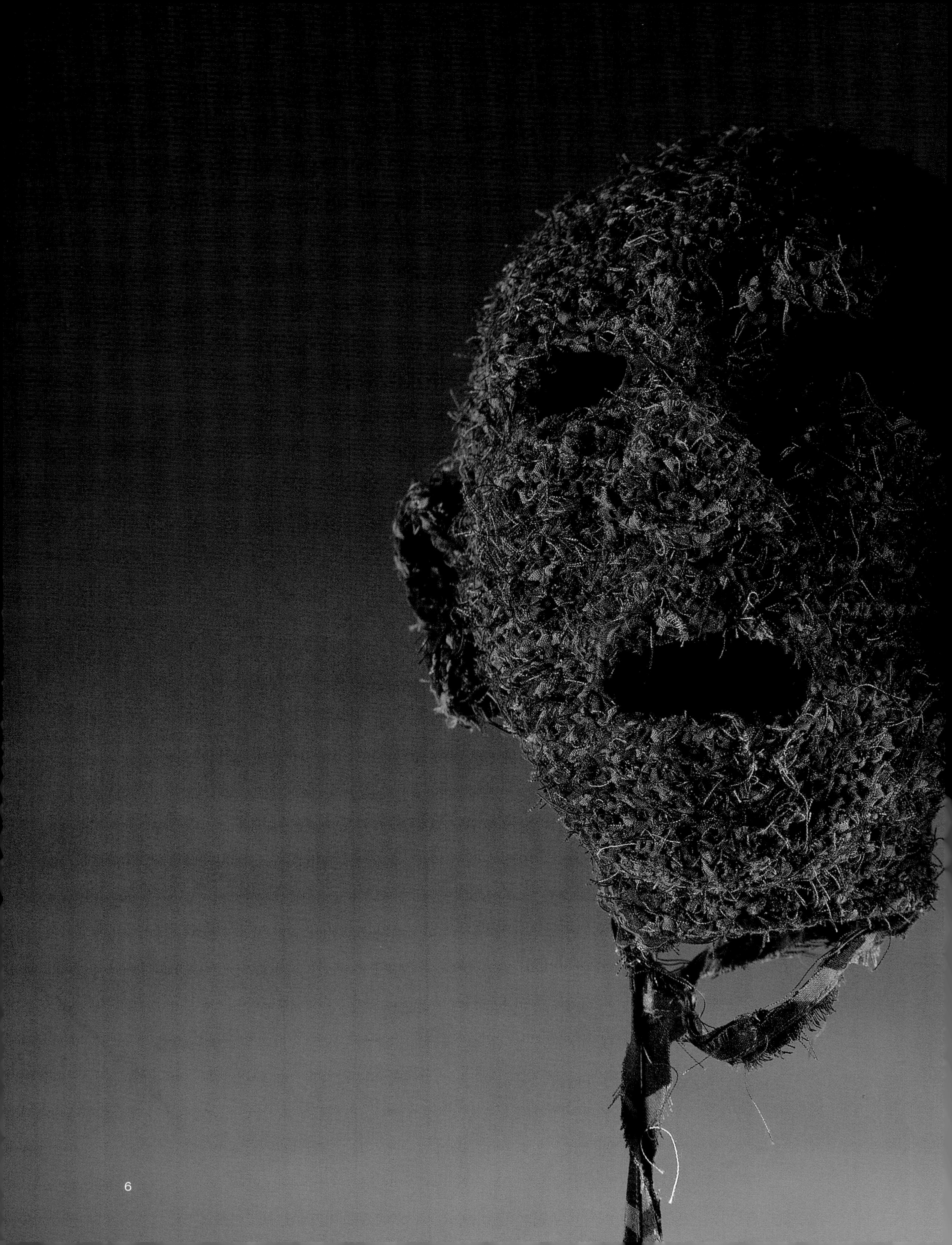

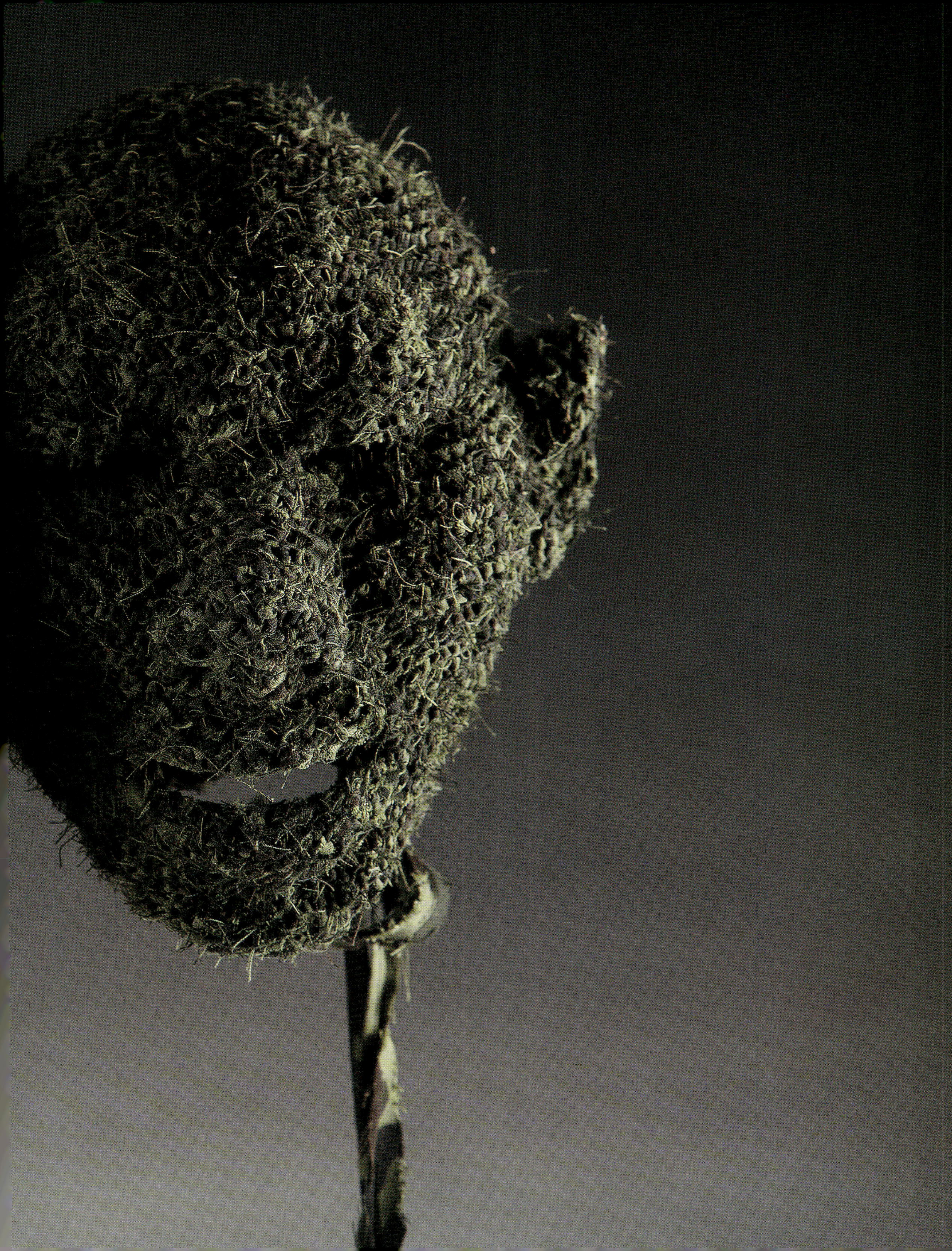

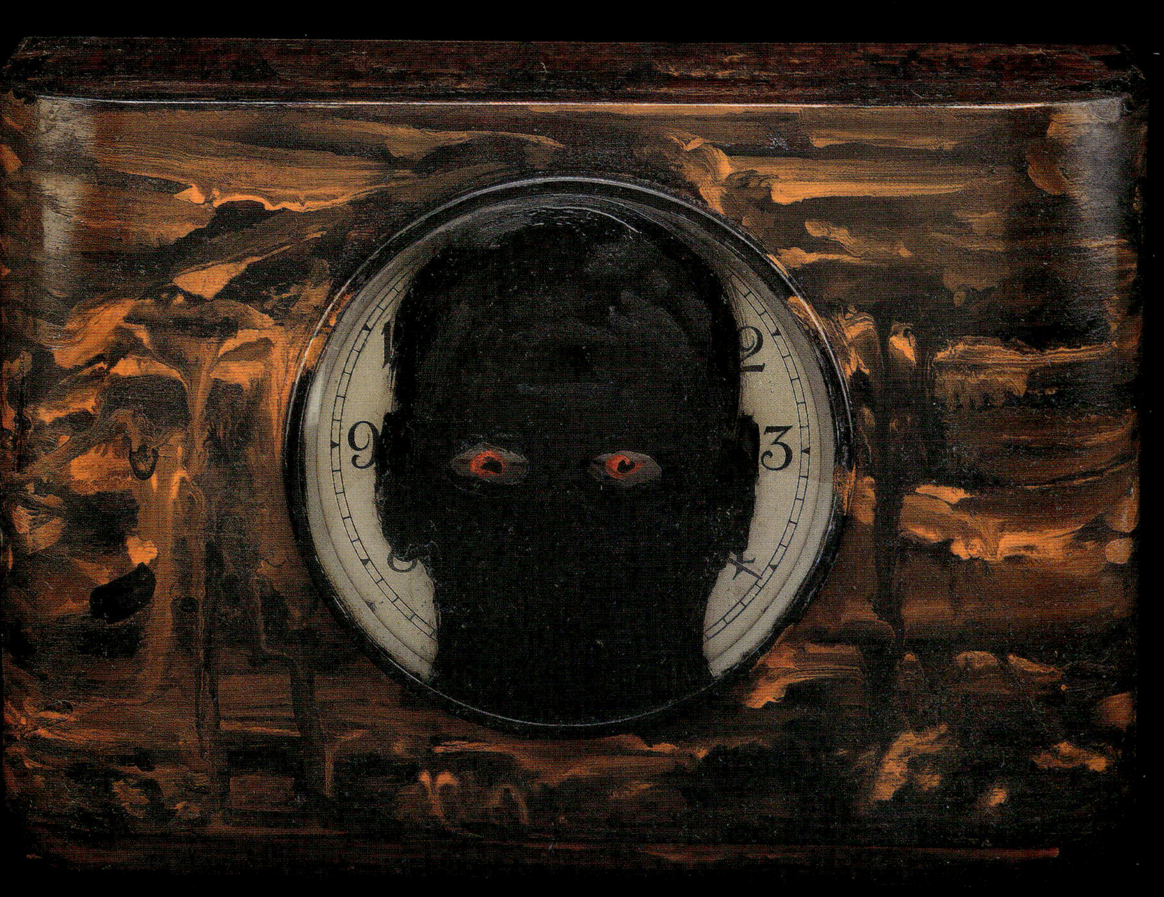

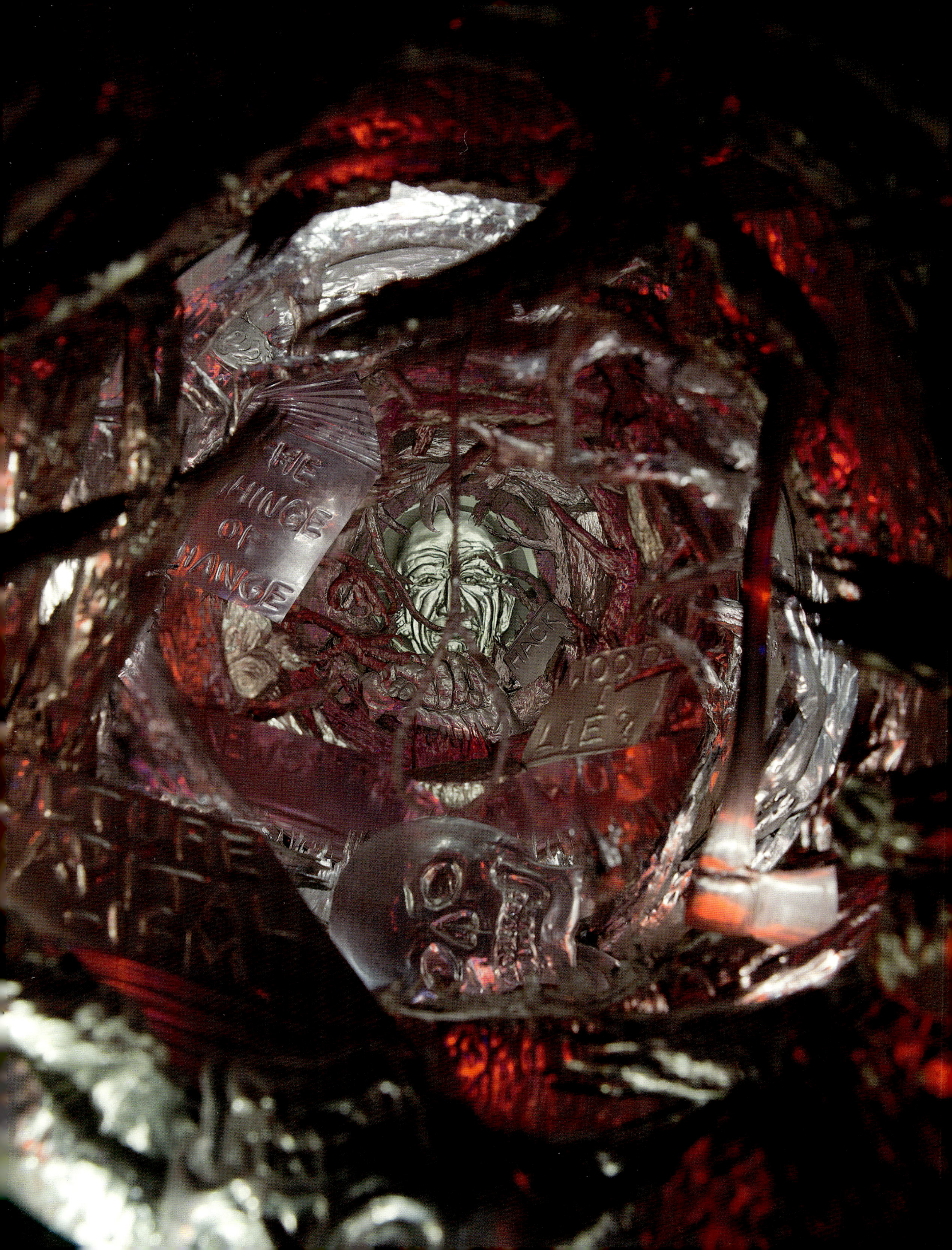
HINGE
OF
HACK
LIE?

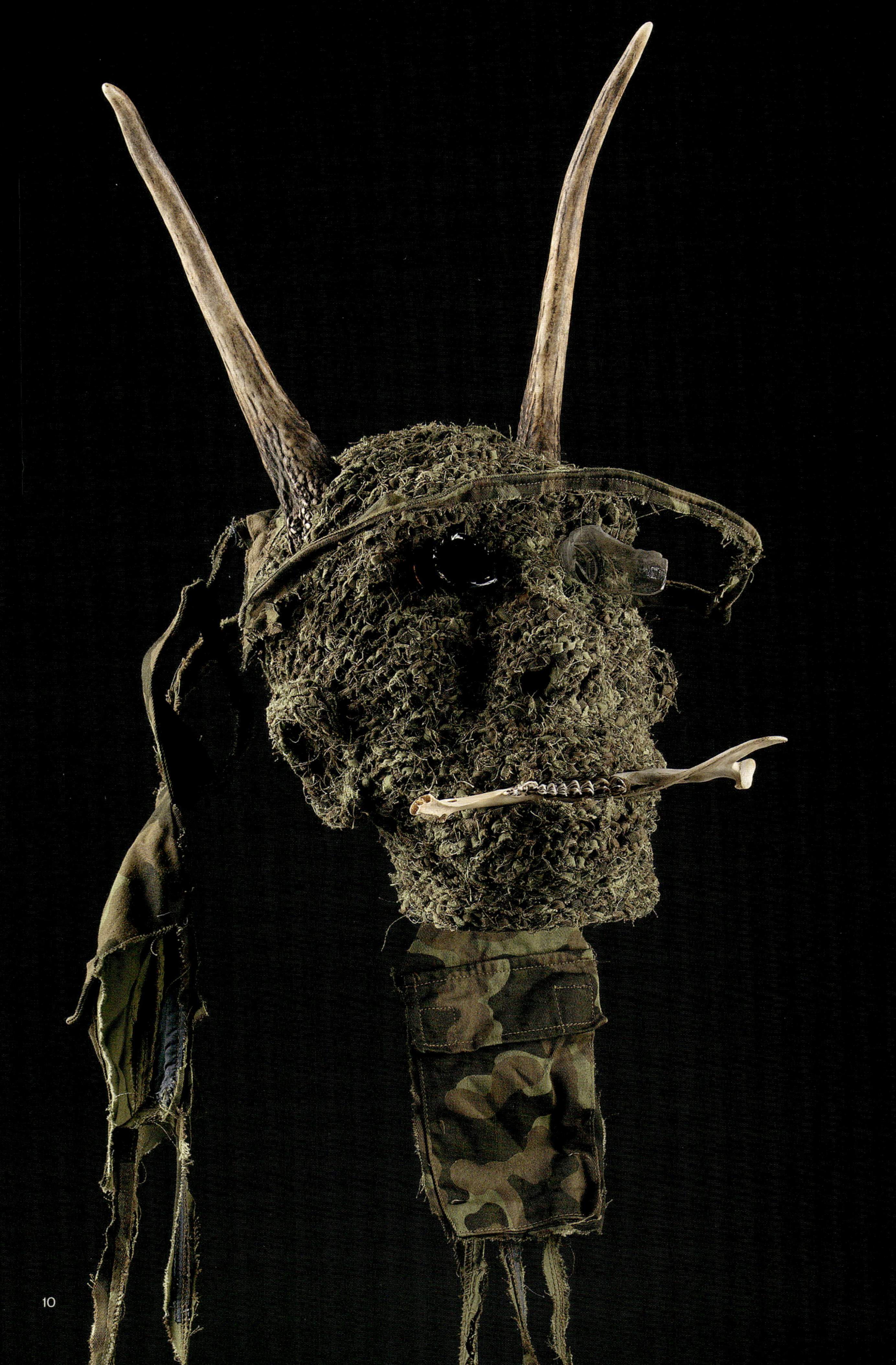

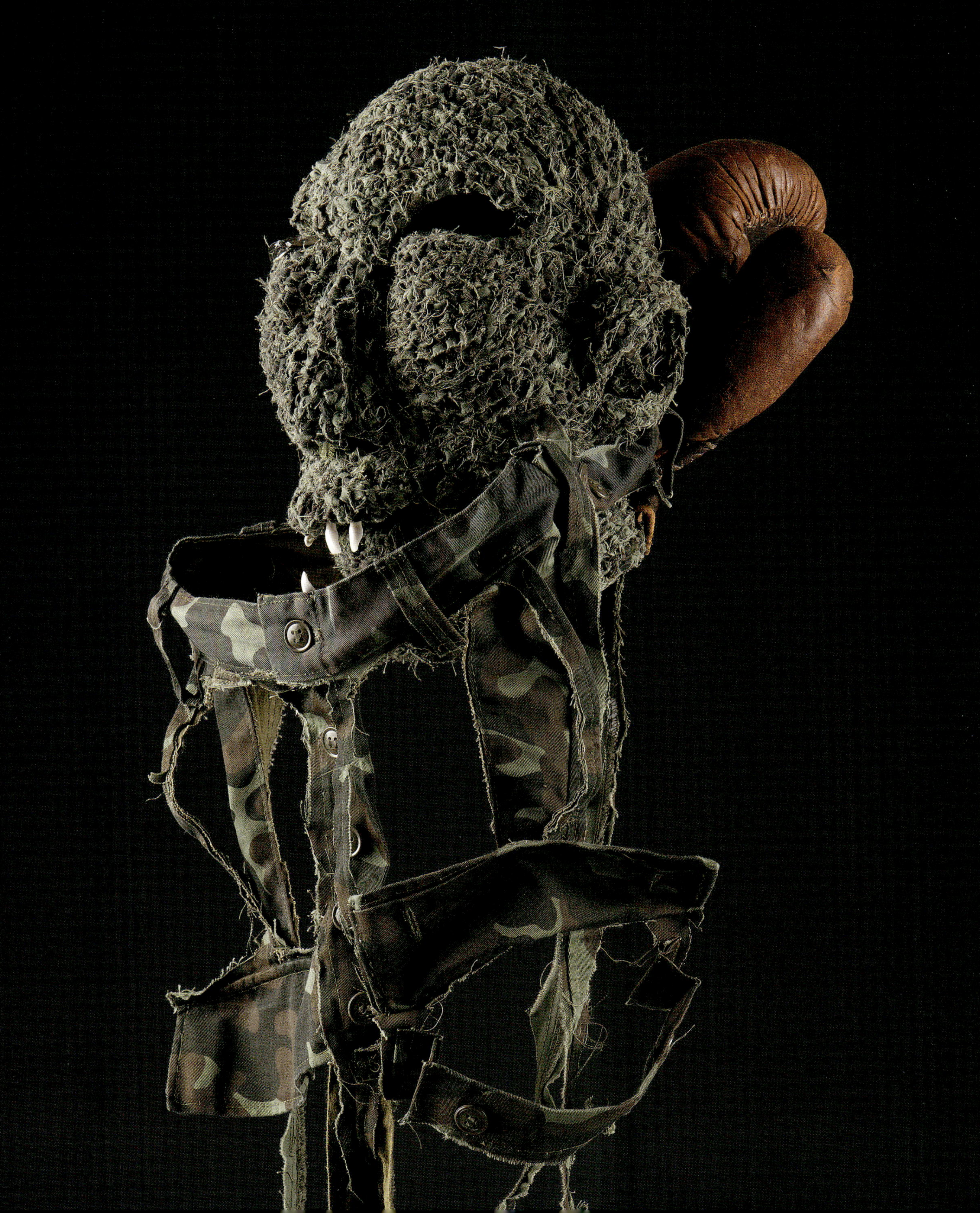

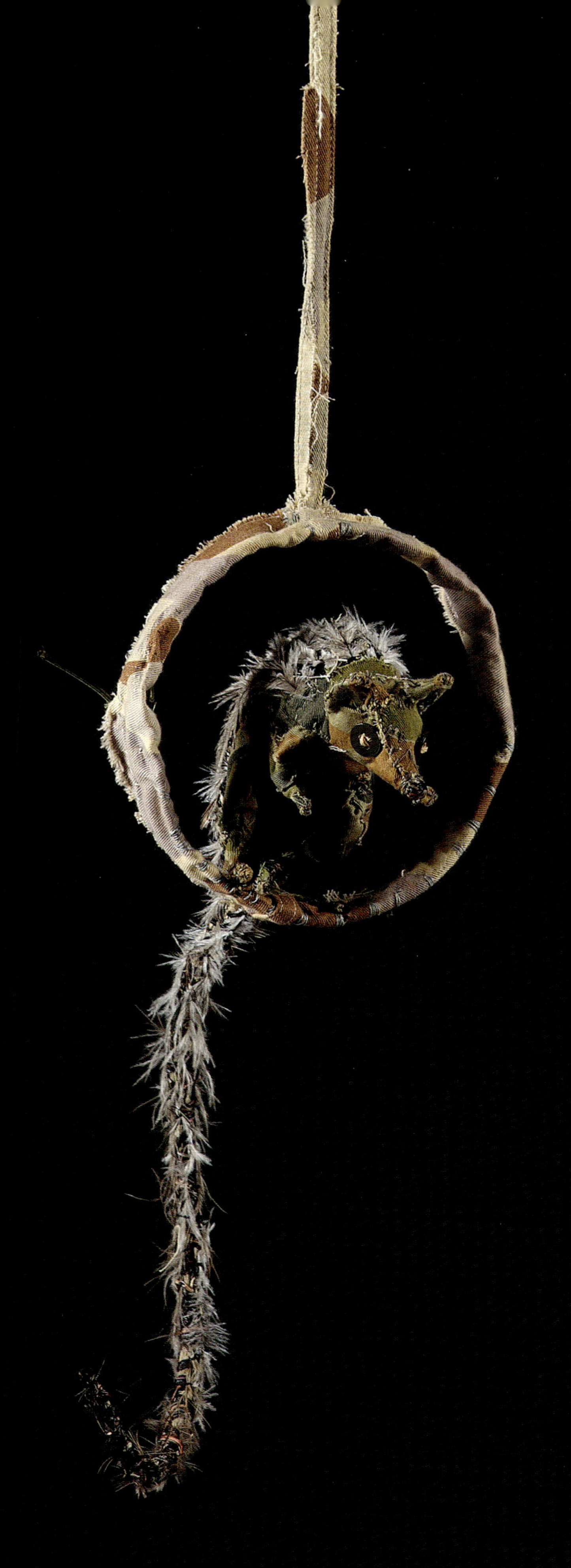

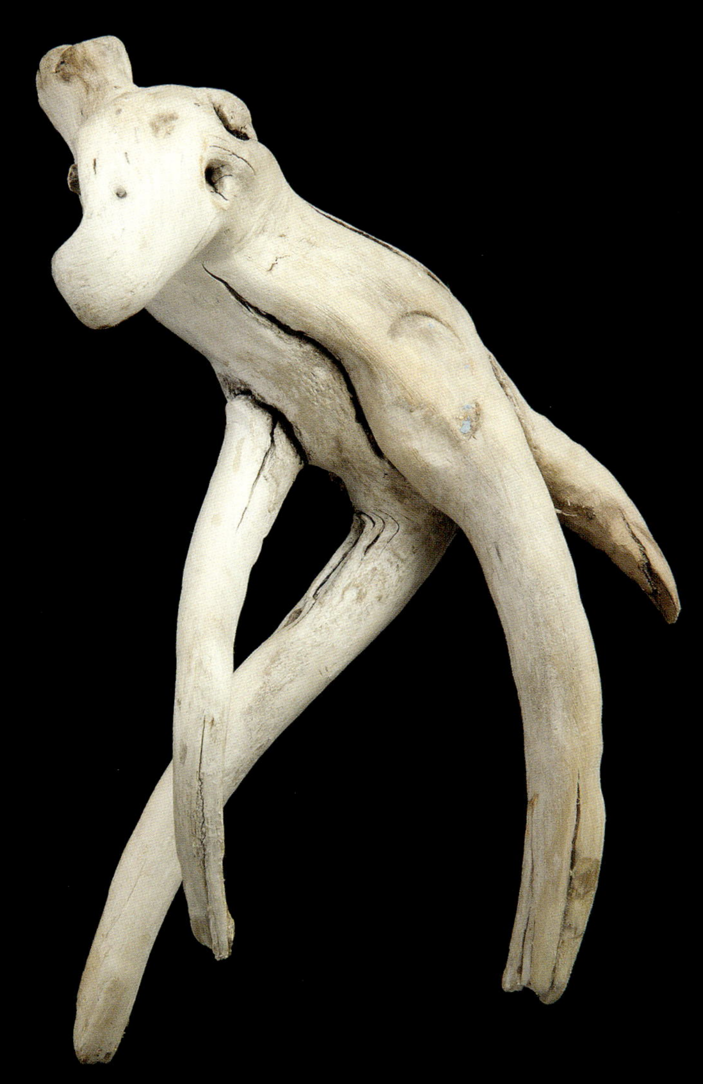

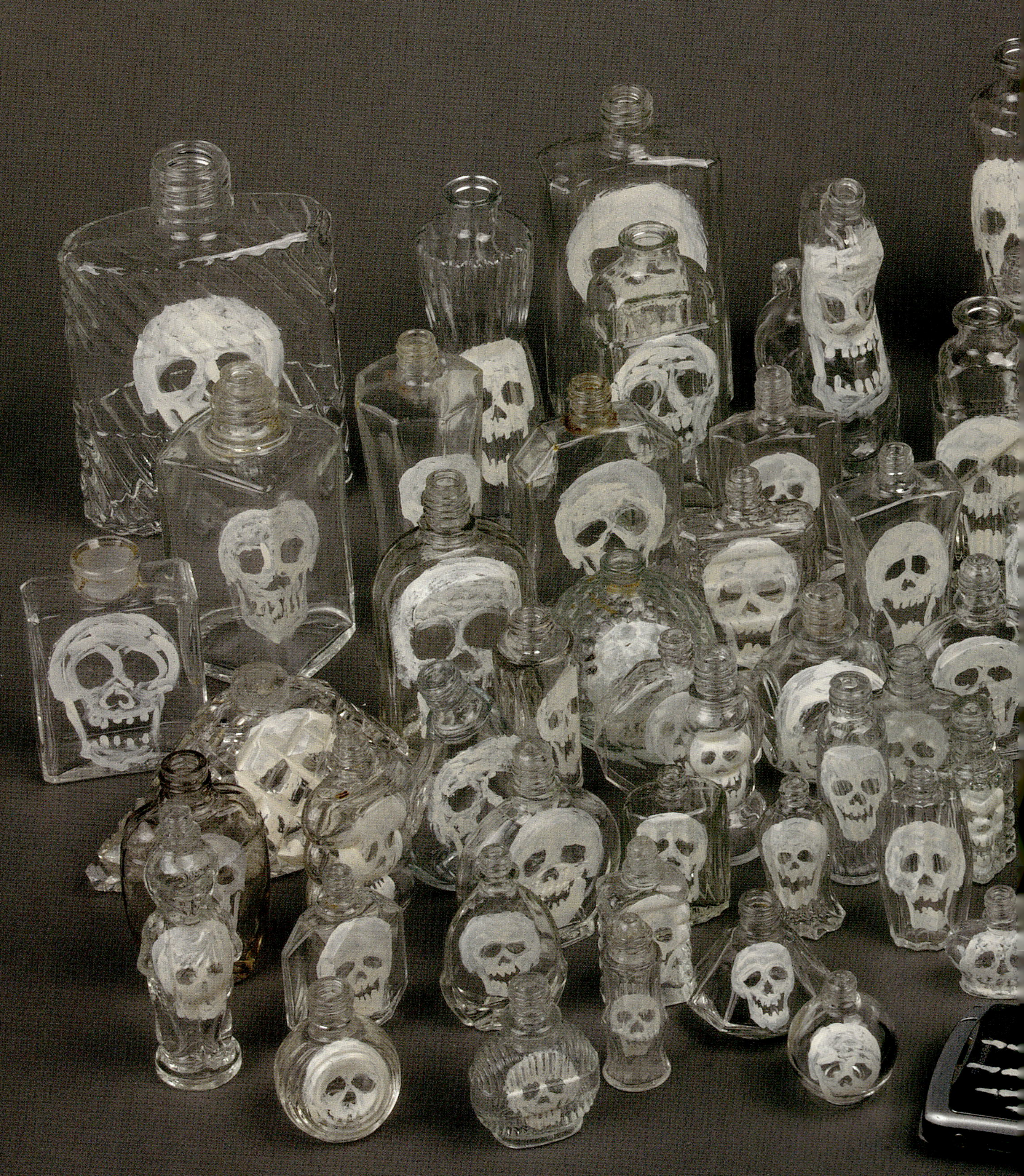

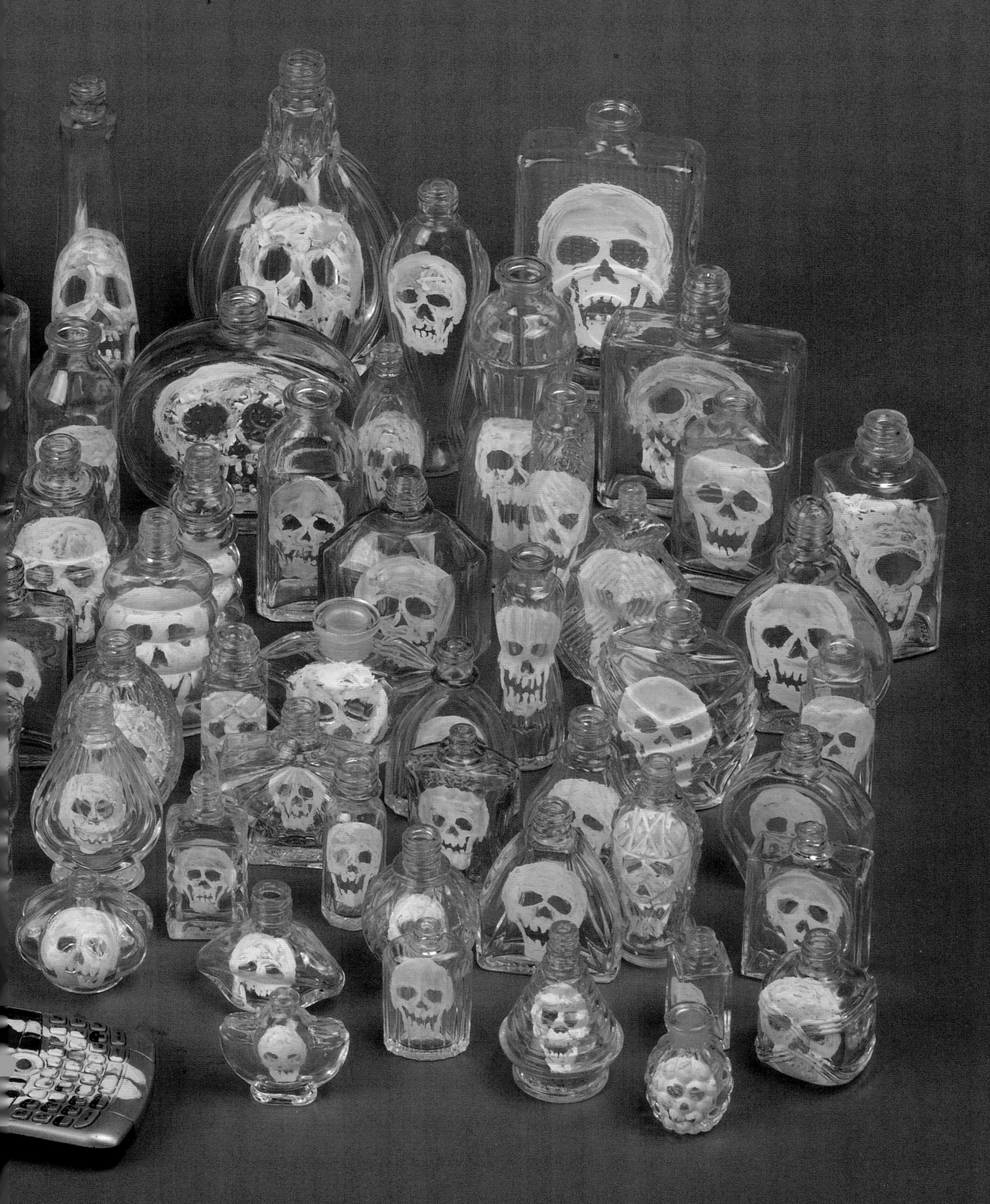

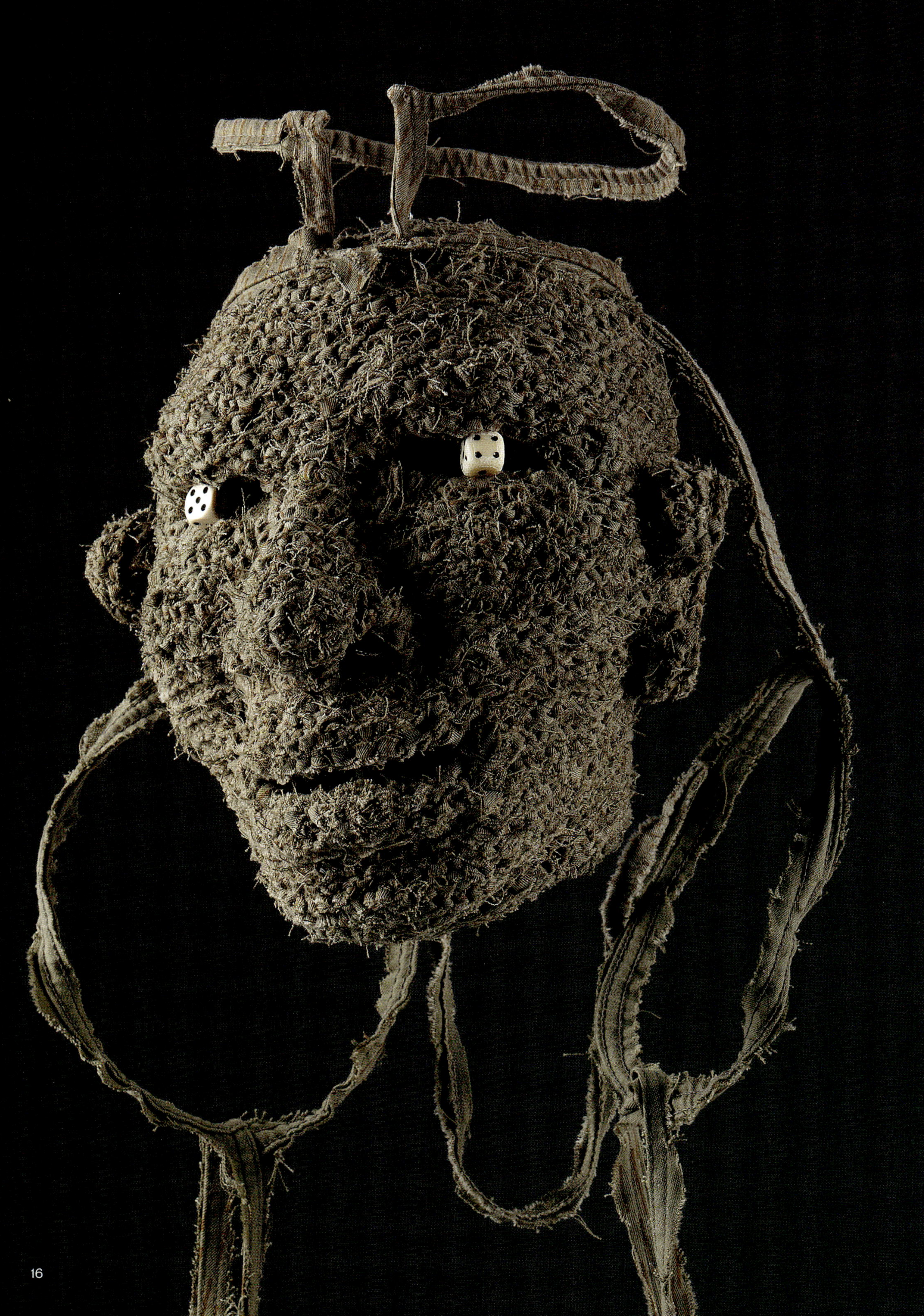

Fiona Hall
Wrong Way Time

Fiona Hall
Wrong Way Time

Edited by Linda Michael

Australia Council for the Arts
Piper Press

Fiona Hall: Wrong Way Time

First published by the Australia Council for the Arts in association with Piper Press on the occasion of the exhibition Fiona Hall: Wrong Way Time, curated by Linda Michael, for the Australian Pavilion at the 56th International Art Exhibition—la Biennale di Venezia, 9 May – 22 November 2015.

Edited by Linda Michael
Design by Mitch Brown and Andrew van der Westhuyzen, Collider
Photography by Clayton Glen, unless otherwise indicated
Typeset in FF Bau by Christian Schwartz
Pre-press by Spitting Image, Sydney
Printed in Hong Kong by Toppan

National Library of Australia Cataloguing-in-Publication entry
Hall, Fiona, 1953—author, artist.
Fiona Hall: wrong way time / Fiona Hall (artist, author);
Linda Michael (editor, author); David Hansen (author);
Tjanpi Desert Weavers (artists' statements).

ISBN: 9780980834734 (hbk: Piper Press)
9781920784799 (hbk: Australia Council for the Arts)
Hall, Fiona, 1953—Exhibitions.
Art, Australian—Exhibitions.
Michael, Linda, author, editor.
Hansen, David, author.
Tjanpi Desert Weavers.
709.94

Australia Council for the Arts
372 Elizabeth Street
Surry Hills NSW 2010
PO Box 788
Strawberry Hills NSW 2012
Australia
T +61 2 9215 9000
australiacouncil.gov.au

Piper Press
37 Lower Fort Street
Dawes Point NSW 2000
Australia
T +61 2 9251 8650
piperpress.com.au

Cover images: *Wrong Way Time* 2012–15 (details)

Plate pages 1–16; further information in List of Works
page 1: *Wrong Way Time* 2012–15 (detail)
page 2: *Wrong Way Time* 2012–15 (detail)
page 3: *All the King's Men* 2014–15 (detail)
page 4: *Untitled* 2015 (detail)
page 5: *Wrong Way Time* 2012–15 (detail)
pages 6–7: *All the King's Men* 2014–15 (detail)
page 8: *Wrong Way Time* 2012–15 (detail)
page 9: *Hack* 2014 (detail)
pages 10–11: *All the King's Men* 2014–15 (details)
page 12: *Helicopter and Sandhill Dunnart (*Sminthopsis psammophila*) / Ilikapatura munu mingkiri* from *Kuka Irititja (Animals from Another Time)* 2014
Page 13: *Manuhiri (Travellers)* 2014–15 (detail)
pages 14–15: *Vaporised* 2014
page 16: *All the King's Men* 2014–15 (detail)

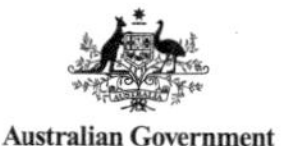

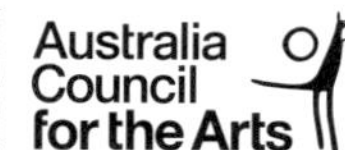

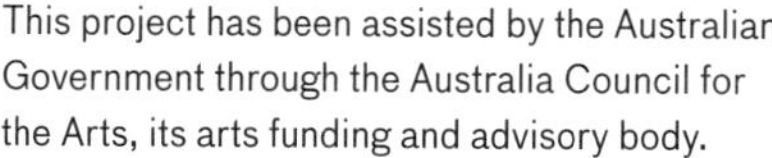

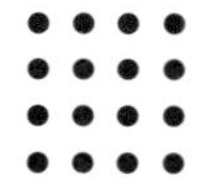

PIPER PRESS

Contents

Welcome

The Australia Council for the Arts is delighted to present Fiona Hall: Wrong Way Time at the 56th International Art Exhibition, la Biennale di Venezia.

For over sixty years Australia has celebrated our nation's contemporary visual arts at the Venice Biennale. This most prestigious and critical international forum provides Australian artists with a unique opportunity to exhibit their work and to raise the profile of Australian visual arts.

Australia is a culturally ambitious nation. Our culture is unique and is deeply shaped by more than 70,000 years of continuous Indigenous story-telling. It also reflects the settlement of Australia across two centuries by people from around the world. We are a diverse community of identities, faiths, individual differences and pursuits. As a nation we draw strength from this diversity and use it to expand the dimensions of our creativity.

We see 2015 as an especially exciting year for Australia and one that reflects our cultural ambition in the visual arts. Fiona Hall is one of Australia's leading contemporary artists and her exhibition is the first to be presented in the new Australian Pavilion, the newest permanent pavilion in the historic Giardini della Biennale and a significant work of architecture. The pavilion will enable Australian artists to realise their creative vision for years to come, as they claim the space for exhibitions as yet unimagined. It will give visibility not just to those artists selected to exhibit work but also, through the strong representation of our visual culture, to all our artists and the institutions and individuals that train and nurture them.

Australia's participation at Venice is made possible through the enthusiastic support of many individuals who contribute to the project in a myriad of ways. Our national community of supporters have been inspired by the leadership of the 2013 and 2015 Australian Commissioner, Simon Mordant AM. We extend our sincere gratitude to Simon for his unlimited energy and personal commitment to promoting Australian art to the world. We acknowledge the work and dedication of our exhibition curator, Linda Michael, whose experience and close collaboration with Fiona Hall has resulted in a truly mesmerising exhibition.

The Australia Council is pleased to acknowledge the Commonwealth Government of Australia, the Attorney-General and Minister for the Arts, Senator the Hon George Brandis QC, and the generous support and invaluable contribution of our many partners in making this project a reality.

As Chair of the Australia Council, I thank and acknowledge the role of the Council's Venice team, led by Elaine Chia, and offer sincere congratulations and appreciation to Fiona for her passionate and creative vision in realising this ambitious project.

Rupert Myer AM
Chair, Australia Council for the Arts

Commissioner's Foreword

I am honoured to introduce the work of Fiona Hall AO at the 56th International Art Exhibition, la Biennale di Venezia.

It is hard to imagine an artist more fitting than Fiona Hall to inaugurate Australia's new pavilion.

Wrong Way Time is a deeply immersive installation bringing together a multitude of works from her prolific practice. The idiosyncrasies of human nature, coupled with Fiona Hall's ongoing engagement with the environment and things 'counter and strange', underlie a multi-layered examination of intersecting concerns. The audience is enveloped in a minefield where the beautiful and grotesque merge in a poignant display of highly charged, emotive objects. Fiona draws visitors in through the allure of her meticulously crafted work, an enticement that sits in uneasy tension with the disturbing truths the exhibition conveys.

Throughout her career, Fiona Hall has grappled with some of the most complex issues facing society. Her art encourages a re-examination of consumerist behaviour and trends shaping our consciousness. Her interdisciplinary practice confronts environmental degradation, capitalism and political conflict, among other critical topics, and links them together in a range of works that evoke humanity's deep-seated concern over the state of contemporary life. A significant presentation of Fiona's practice has never been more relevant as these issues transcend borders and further embed themselves into our daily lives.

I acknowledge and thank Linda Michael, the curator of the exhibition, who has worked closely with Fiona Hall on the development of this extraordinary project. Linda's thoughtful approach and curatorial expertise in exploring and presenting the themes and trajectories present in Fiona's work provides us with a fascinating framework in which to experience the exhibition. I also thank Linda for her work on the exhibition catalogue in both curatorial and editorial capacities, Dr David Hansen for his insightful essay, and the Tjanpi Desert Weavers for their wonderful contribution to the catalogue.

Australia's representation at the Venice Biennale would not be possible without our many supporters and I would like to acknowledge the substantial support from our Sponsors, Partners, state government agencies and donors. Sincere thanks to our Major Partner, The Balnaves Foundation, for their ongoing commitment to Australia's representation at the Venice Biennale. Thanks also to our Supporting Partners: Anita Luca Belgiorno-Nettis Foundation, Arts NSW, Arts Queensland, Arts South Australia, Arts Victoria, Collider, Department of Culture and the Arts WA, ERCO, Heide Museum of Modern Art, Macquarie Group Foundation, Maddocks, The University of Melbourne and White Rabbit Gallery.

It has been a wonderful privilege for me to undertake the role of Commissioner and I have been most fortunate to have the support of Professor Charles Green as Deputy Commissioner. I am also deeply grateful for the generosity, contribution, commitment and advocacy of all members of the Commissioner's Council—Susan Armitage, Hamish Balnaves, Anita Belgiorno-Nettis, Dr Paul Eliadis, Adrian Fini OAM, Mark Henry, Roslyn Oxley OAM, Lisa Paulsen, and Nicholas Tobias.

This project would not be possible without our individual donors—our Champions. The Venice Biennale Champions share a passion for Australian art and a commitment to supporting our artists in Australia and internationally. Thank you.

We acknowledge the team at la Biennale di Venezia, in particular President Paolo Baratta and Manuela Lucà-Dazio, Executive Manager, Visual Arts and Architecture Department, for their valued assistance in ensuring the success of Australia's presence in Venice.

My sincere thanks to the Australia Council for the Arts for their leadership and management of Australia's involvement at the Venice Biennale, in particular, to Rupert Myer AM, Tony Grybowski, Elaine Chia, and the project team. Working with you has been a privilege.

Finally, I thank my wife Catriona—it has been her continued support, counsel and encouragement that has enabled me to pursue this wonderful project with energy and passion.

I congratulate Fiona Hall and everyone involved in presenting Wrong Way Time at the 56th International Art Exhibition, la Biennale di Venezia.

Simon Mordant AM
Commissioner for Australia, Venice Biennale 2015

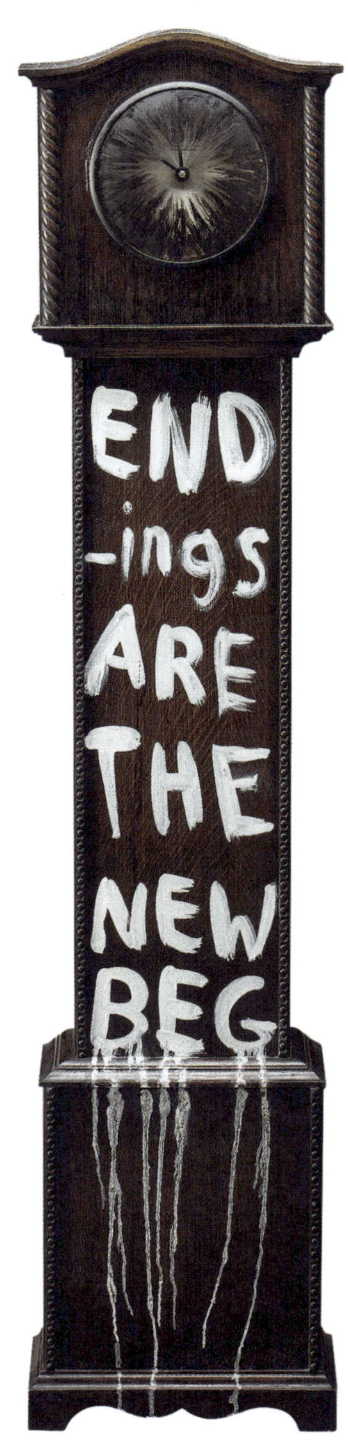

Wrong Way Time 2012–15 (detail)

Wrong Way Time
Linda Michael

> *Midway this way of life we're bound upon*
> *I woke to find myself in a dark wood*
> *Where the right road was lost and wholly gone*
> —Dante

In her ambitious installation for the Venice Biennale, Wrong Way Time, Fiona Hall brings together hundreds of disparate elements which find alignments and create tensions around three intersecting concerns: global politics, world finances, and the environment.[1] Like many of us, Fiona sees these as failed states, as 'a minefield of madness, badness, sadness, in equal measure', stretching beyond the foreseeable future. The ideas that underpin her work accord with those of writers in many fields who say anthropocentrism is coming to an end, who see nature as a nexus of references or an 'ecology of objects', and draw on so-called primitive beliefs in animism, the agency of non-living things, and sympathetic magic.[2] Fiona's lifelong passion for the natural environment can be felt intensely in works that respond to our persistent role in its demise, or to the perilous state of various species. Her work is one of many hoarse canaries in the mine. It is a corrective against mindless confidence in war and economic rationalism, or the denial of human agency in climate mutations that supports, at the time of this exhibition, an 'Australian political strategy of voluntary sleepwalking toward catastrophe'.[3] Increasingly, its underlying message is as described by writer David Hansen: 'that the planet Earth is going to hell in a handbasket, whipped and prodded by the apocalyptic monsters of ignorance, greed and self-interest'.[4]

Fiona's seemingly random conjunction of things in a *wunderkammer*-like installation appeals to our human impulse to make connections and see relationships, or perhaps to a paranoia born of the deep uncertainty and fear of our times. Yet despite the prevalent darkness—the gallery and cabinets are as black as her subject—her exhibition is fundamentally life-affirming, its own vitality in perverse distinction to the subjects it ranges across, which provide rich pickings for Fiona's extraordinary transformation of materials, images, and objects.

The dynamism of the installation comes from two forces at odds with each other. The first is a product of Fiona's curiosity and engagement with the present moment: her wish to explore the complexity and cruelty and terror of the world as it is thrust into daily consciousness—a world that is now global, wherever we live and however superficially we understand specific local situations. This exhibition is Fiona's response to her times, to the litany of war news, stories about terrorism, climate change, extinctions, environmental pillage, collapsing markets, and so on. Everything is grist to her mill.

The second registers an essentially very simple thing: her deep love of the world and all its wonder and variety and magic, a fundamental animism. The inherent challenge of the first to someone deeply versed in nature is the meaning of Wrong Way Time. Yet it is a challenge more than a verdict, as there is so much life here, indeed a profusion of creative riches that is hard to reconcile with the counting of the dead.

Fiona's work is therefore a chronicle of life in all its intricacy and diversity. Despite its professed agendas, it is not really message art or political art but a practice absorbed in the condition of living on this planet. Her outlook is tragicomic, a secular, even anarchic, vision of heaven and hell. It is not surprising that she loves the work of Dante, Blake, and Bosch, as well as Aboriginal, Oceanic, and African art, which imagine or emerge from complete worldviews and are not as confined in their focus as much contemporary art. There are echoes of this encyclopaedic approach in *The Whole Earth Catalog*,[5] the counterculture bible of the late sixties and early seventies, with its ecological, scientific, do-it-yourself approach to creating a more just society, one in which Fiona had been deeply schooled. Her art absorbs and reflects multiple currents from the world around her: what she hears or sees on various media, learns through conversation and research, or observes, touches, or hears in her daily rounds—from the minutiae of life in the garden to the geometry of constellations. As Julie Ewington writes: 'in the tensions between macrocosm and microcosm lies the charge of Fiona's work as an artist: making sense of now'.[6]

Although the expression 'wrong way time' suggests a pessimistic outlook—a 'now' wrenched from the flow of time—Fiona's approach is typically allegorical and alchemical, one that perceives the fundamental unity of good and evil, and therefore the potential for transformation. She can see constructive potential where one might see decay, or order where others fear chaos, likely gleaned from her understanding of natural cycles. Her piece of coal, for example, supports a diamantine creation with the same carbon substrate; her burnt cabinets are exquisitely illuminated. As Gregory O'Brien writes: 'Her work gathers and hoards darkness as it does translucence, bearing in mind that darkness has its fecundity just as the greenest of days has its rot'.[7] (Though her reformist passions are clear she doesn't believe that art can change the world and wonders if she might make just beautiful things in the manner of Sri Lankan architect Geoffrey Bawa, whose exquisite Garden Pavilion on his country estate Lunuganga, in which she has worked on several visits, was built in response to atrocities committed in his country.)

Yet Wrong Way Time seems to register an irreversible tipping point, such as scientists have warned has already passed with global warming, or economists in relation to unconscionable inequities. The exhibition certainly registers the *fear* we have, in its votive offerings, its ritualistic repetitions, its surrealistic excess. It cannot contain enough stuff to ward off death or emptiness, or divert us with mimetic skill or satiric wit. Hers is a gallows humour.

Nature and our relationship to it is the abiding theme of Fiona Hall's practice, its subject and its inspiration. Mimesis is its primary mode, fuelling the endless production of similarity, and cycles of growth and decay. If, as anthropologist Michael Taussig proposes, the mimetic faculty is 'the nature that culture uses to create a second nature', then Fiona is its master.[8] Her earliest works enacted a double mimesis, using photography to represent nature drawn by culture. She has since rivalled the facticity of photography in three dimensions, creating life-like natural and human forms out of soap, banknotes, uniforms, videotape, aluminium cans, plumbing tubes, cardboard—she can seemingly make anything out of anything. These 'copies' do not rely on trickery or deception—we can see the artifice—nor are they in any way naturalist or pictorial. Though abstracted, they have a fundamental verisimilitude based on acute observation, and the very energy of their making somehow inheres in the object and alerts us to the wonders of the original. Fiona's aim is that 'you look at the work and you think of the wonder of nature rather than pressures on the environment'.[9] Yet it is hard to imagine looking at a bird's nest in quite the same way after seeing hers in *Tender*, even though hers are mere 'copies' constructed from banknotes—perhaps because her objects reveal, in this case very literally, that the very act of representing is inextricable from the gainful destruction of nature. She is so attuned to this process that she can recognise when images or objects reveal the layered histories that tie nature to culture, a mimetic quality that she also picks up in language, often using punning or onomatopoeic titles.

The found driftwood pieces in *Manuhiri (Travellers)* (pages 91–94), for example, chosen by Fiona for their resemblance to living creatures, reveal nature's mimetic capacities. Conversely—or in parallel—*Tender* is a collection of more than eighty nests Fiona made from shredded US dollar bills, accurately replicating a great variety of avian constructions at a time when habitats have disappeared or are threatened by logging and development. The beautiful range of forms emerges from her research in ornithology collections; as she says, 'you can't just make a fictional idea of a nest'. Her work makes us attentive to real nests—her mimesis is extraordinary, but nest building is normal for birds. The empty nests, the valueless money, and the title converge to question what our society wishes to nurture and what we are prepared to lose (see further on page 45).

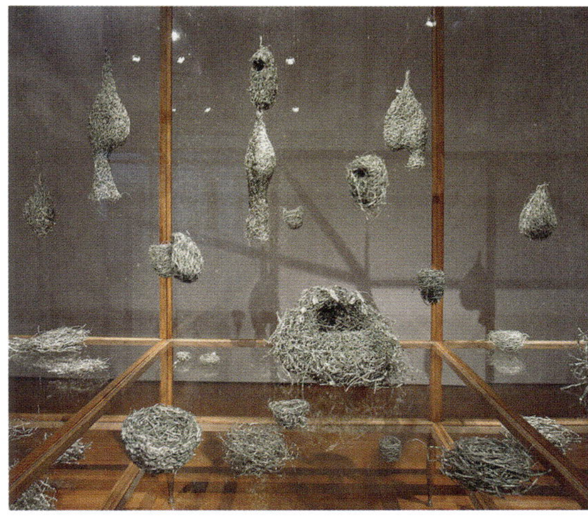

Tender 2003–06 (detail)
US dollars, wire, vitrines, vinyl lettering
86 nests, ranging from approx. 5 x 10 (diam.) cm to 108 x 17 x 13 cm; two vitrines, each 220 x 360 x 150 cm
Collection: Queensland Art Gallery
Purchased 2006.
The Queensland Government's Gallery of Modern Art Acquisitions Fund
Photograph: Greg Weight
Image courtesy: Roslyn Oxley9 Gallery, Sydney

For *Manuhiri (Travellers)*, Fiona collected the driftwood—pine and poplar, manuka and kanuka, and many other species—from the Waiapu River on the east coast of the North Island of Aotearoa New Zealand, where she regularly holidays. Before pastoralists cleared the region from the 1880s onwards, the river's catchment area was eighty per cent forest, and despite replantings it remains highly degraded, with erosion problems, runoff from agricultural chemicals, and a massive build-up of silt. It is one of the world's most sedimented rivers, and Fiona noticed a 'staggering' amount of debris after heavy rain. From this bounty, guzzled and spat out by the river (*wai* means 'water' and *apu* 'to cram into the mouth, gorge, glut, gobble up, wolf down'), Fiona has selected pieces that resemble living creatures, a poetic allusion to those lost as the result of the same process that brought the driftwood into being. She draws out their metaphorical or transfigurative potential—they possess animal spirit as well as evidential force. The collection is a kind of abstract bestiary: some pieces have the simplicity and grandeur of Cycladic sculptures. Their incomplete and lopsided features lend a vulnerability of expression. Some even seem to reach out for connection. Here, as Baltrusaitis wrote of 'pictorial stones':

> We are at the heart of the world of the visionaries, the surrealists, a supernatural, disturbed world brusquely revealed in an actuality of nature. Today's masters have not done better, even haunted as they are by the same play of paradox and surprise. Here we have geometry and abstraction decomposing and recomposing the shapes of life, forms pure in and of themselves.[10]

No less than the driftwood, the sculpted creatures from the adjacent display *Kuka Irititja (Animals from Another Time)* (pages 95, 97, 99–101) are those of the imagination. For this collaborative project, Fiona and twelve women from the Tjanpi Desert Weavers fashioned extinct and endangered creatures—and the odd feral or familiar animal—out of native desert grasses and materials including strips of camouflage fabric (see the artist statements, pages 49–54). All the artists had a history of making animal forms from materials at hand. The women collected grasses, while Fiona supplied contemporary British and Australian military uniforms to incorporate in the sculptures, in acknowledgement of the loss and displacement suffered by the Aboriginal women under colonial and subsequent regimes—including that arising from the secret British nuclear bombing on their lands in Maralinga in the 1950s. Interestingly, 'camouflage' derives from a French word that during the First World War replaced the use of the word 'mimicry' by naturalists such as Darwin. The women's quick uptake of the camouflage material, aside from responding to its numerous contemporary uses, reveals a close attention to and observation of animal behaviour—including the human, militarised variety. They understand mimicry and know to judge, and play with, appearances. Fiona had been schooled with the postmodern aphorism that 'the map is not the territory' but, as her work reveals, believes otherwise—like the Aboriginal women, she grasps the truth and magic of surfaces.

Everything represents something else; there is no ground. For Fiona, 'the pressures on the environment are very much linked with global finance, and camouflage is a pattern stolen from nature commandeered into warfare. The crossover is what makes the exhibition; it's that nexus of things.'[11] Here, as elsewhere in the exhibition, systems of description are overlaid on one another, enmeshing us within webs of connection.

On the way to the Tjanpi artist camp Fiona had been introduced—via a child's painting of a naughty classmate—to Mamu, the local devilish figure that appears in numerous guises in Pitjantjatjara culture. Like Satan, Mamu instils fear or caution, and is as seductive as it is scary. When the nuclear tests were carried out at Maralinga, the elders attributed the black smoke to the Mamu. In several of Fiona's sculptures this personification of evil appears with characteristic vitality, attended by the endangered creatures: a quoll atop a burnt dried-milk tin morphs into a toothy Mamu; and a frog jumps on a wild, feathery Mamu with a gaping mouth. The impact of white-man's food or nuclear testing on the environment is the sting in the tail—there in both material and subject but dominated by the lively

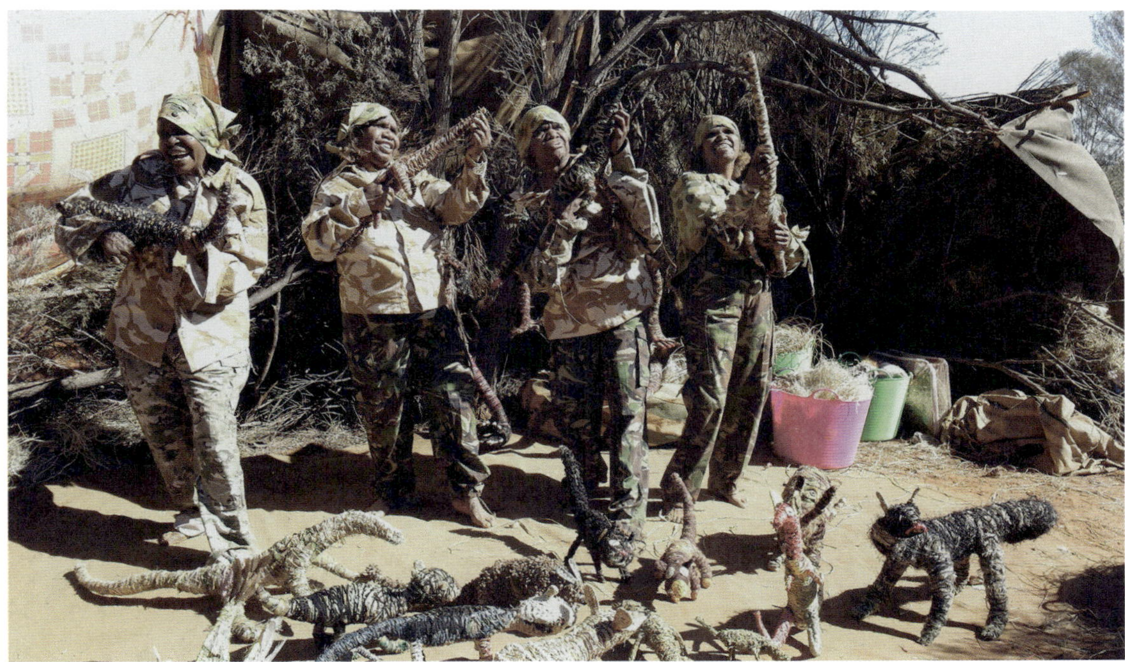

From left: Mary Pan, Roma Butler, Rene Kulitja and Angkaliya Nelson in military uniforms supplied by Fiona Hall for use as weaving material, artist camp near Pilakatilyuru, Western Australia, June 2014
Photograph: Fiona Hall

spookiness of the figures. In other sculptures an aeroplane, helicopter, or bat bomb displace the Mamu, conceivably in this context personifying the devil of colonisation. Here, however, all are overpowered (exorcised?) by the creatures, which dwarf the machines. Interestingly, the Tjanpi Desert Weavers' most animated sculptures are also the most devilish—not the lost native animals but the feral cats, the animals they know—fierce, hungry, and on the lookout.

Kuka Irititja (Animals from Another Time) and *Manuhiri (Travellers)*, among others, register the impact of colonisation and capitalism on a natural environment. Fiona is simultaneously a collector–scientist (on the side of culture, objectivity, rationality) and an artist–animist (on the side of nature, subjectivity, intuition), and the dynamic of her work reflects this. While science expands our knowledge of the world through the study of living organisms as objects, animism focuses on our relatedness to the natural world, so that rather than thinking *about* the world we are alive and responsive *to* it.[12] One side has clearly dominated in our world, at increasing cost. Fiona aims to get beyond the separation of these two ways of thinking, bringing them together in mutual dissonance and, in the words of Bruno Latour and many others, shifting from 'economy to ecology'—closer to the reciprocal and respectful relationships humans have with animals within Aboriginal culture, for example. She is drawn to the simplicity, unselfconsciousness and confidence of art from traditional cultures, or by outsider artists, and her own rituals and objects could constitute a reverse cargo cult, aimed at effecting such a shift. In her work there is an underlying mysticism that corrupts any scientific approach, however meticulously and logically applied. To paraphrase Walter Benjamin: 'Her gift of seeing resemblances is nothing other than a rudiment of the powerful compulsion in former times to become and behave like something else'.[13]

Fiona has an almost electrical sensitivity to currents in our world, an alertness to the not-quite-dead things that register histories and presage the future, coupled with an ability to create objects by hand with such dexterity and mimetic acuity that maybe, through the revivifying power of representation, they might redirect time the right way. It is as if her intense engagement with the world is transferred through collecting, making, and arranging, an obsessive and continuous process of warding off the sadness, madness, and badness this very engagement produces, or at least intensifies. The mimetic and memorialising functions of recent works extend earlier photographic forays, but their human scale and multi-sensorial elements bring the installation into the realm of experience as well as documentation.

Wrong Way Time is in part a compendium of the ashes of modernity, a residue literally represented by charred cabinets and encyclopaedias that act as plinths for several works. Material about to be consigned to history abounds—cash, clocks, newspapers, coal—the detritus of a capitalist world that thrives on redundancy. But her work's more profound subject is the casualties of the living. Drawing upon age-old iconography, she piles up the skeletons, skulls, and other remains; repetition and open sequences defer disaster and make us see our fear of the end. Her attraction to the Pitjantjatjara's Mamu is unsurprising and apt, as its devilish ability to take changing form aligns with the transformative impetus of her works.

Two large groupings in the installation are *All the King's Men* (pages 78–90) and *Wrong Way Time* (pages 57–62, 116–20). Fiona conceived *All the King's Men* as 'a field of free-hanging, three-dimensional heads—some figurative, some contorted into other states of being, or not being'—knitted from camouflage garments from many militaries, 'signifiers of the prevalence and omnipresence of warring forces'.[14] This nihilistic core of the exhibition presents the figures within a geometric structure resembling several earlier grids of hanging figures or part-bodies, which likewise responded to wars as we observe them on our screens. *Slash and Burn*, 1997, was Fiona's response to seeing television footage of the Rwandan genocide. Its black body parts made of videotape from war films 'hover *in memoriam*, challenging Hollywood's glamorisation of war with an image of indiscriminate destruction',[15] and, as it turns out so many times in Fiona's work, in memory of videotape itself. In *Scar Tissue*, 2003–04, she again knitted videotape unspooled from war movies into body parts and children's toys, mimicking the horrifying yet ultimately numbing images on our televisions at a time when Australia itself had become enmeshed in conflicts in the Middle East. As Fiona extrapolates from reading about the unity and disharmony in ant colonies according the degree of genetic variation within them, 'we are hardwired to be competitive and to fight ... It just goes on ... I think the whole 'wrong way time' thing is not just of the now, it is forever and a day, and it is part of biology, it is what Darwin calls the survival of the fittest.'[16]

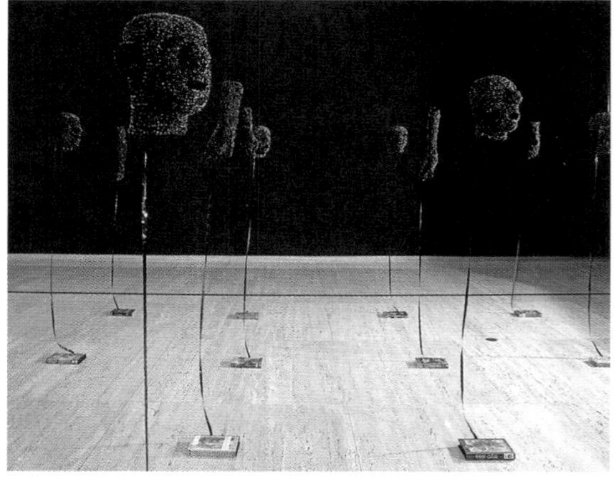

Slash and Burn 1997
36 video boxes,
36 videotape sculptures
and wire suspension-grid,
installation dimensions variable
according to room size
Art Gallery of New South Wales
Contemporary Collection
Benefactors 1997
Image courtesy:
Art Gallery of New South Wales

Yet an accelerating sense of unease about the future and the ramping up of global conflict has increased the urgency of Fiona's work. An intense, compacted energy characterises the ghoulish heads of *All the King's Men*, knitted camouflage forms over wire armatures that were painful to make. Some heads are riven with sharp deer horns or are glassed; all have missing or distorted features. The way of making carries the hope and the despair. As David Hansen has suggested, it is the artist's 'embrace of animal instincts', 'her constant, determined, even manic manual activity—all that cutting and shredding and knitting of post-industrial detritus—that lend this work its undeniable affective power'.[17] It is this power that Fiona recognises in African sculpture, which she has long observed and which has become an increasing influence, a power that gives form to the unconscious, as Picasso maintained was his aim in *Les Demoiselles d'Avignon*, 1907, when he described it as 'the first canvas of exorcism'.[18] Here, too, the faces are masks, life solidified into empty shells that we look through or that look at us. No longer foot soldiers but grief objects or spirit figures, they are made over and over in a kind of incantation or petition: one dead, one more, another, and another. Their bodies are mere vestiges articulated by raggedy seams, adorned with the occasional remaining button or epaulette—'*memento mori* for a world that continues to unravel politically and fray at its social and cultural edges'.[19]

These figures are not so much *about* the horror of war as *of* it. In this field of war camouflage both conceals and dazzles: conceals in that different camouflage patterns mimic each other as much as they do varying terrains, uniting the figures and their militaries (Iraq, Ukraine, Russia, Sri Lanka, Australia, Germany, Estonia, France, and Italy) in a variegated vegetal and animal field; dazzles in the magical power of its transformation and the remarkable energy of its making.

Another major component of the exhibition is a large group of clocks, *Wrong Way Time*, painted with images and texts on the installation's interlinked themes. It forms a wall of lament and animates the entire space with sound—an audio luminosity to match the beautifully lit cabinet of curiosities alongside. The sound is composed of resonant and melodious chimes on the hour, and parts thereof; the raucous sounds of cuckoo clocks; and recordings of crows that introduce a sense of space as their caws diminish in strength.

Masking the glass face of the title clock *Wrong Way Time*, a red U-turn painted anticlockwise over the growth rings of a tree conveys Fiona's feeling that we seem to be going backwards. As an index of past time, the log's rings also reveal a future literally lopped off. This metaphor extends into allegory as Fiona replicates media images, such as those of the Islamic State propaganda video from September 2014 depicting the beheading of a journalist. The masked assassin appears on several clocks, joining a graveyard of painted skulls and skeletons, dramatised by the resemblance of the long-case clocks to coffins and the circular faces of mantle clocks to disembodied heads. They stand like so many memorial totems—in the Australian context not dissimilar to the hollow log coffins of *The Aboriginal Memorial*, 1988, at the National Gallery of Australia—and in a typical overlaying they memorialise the analogue clock itself.

Some clocks are painted with texts that have the directness and incantatory quality of protest signs—there is little of Fiona's characteristic craft here.

Graffiti she saw in Adelaide inspired *Endings Are the New Beg* (page 26), poetic in its economy: its blunt end just like losing a job, to start begging or to begin with the future in doubt. It accords with a general sense of urgency, even mania, which is heightened by the contrast of the texts with the sober, upright, bourgeois objects they are painted on.

Fiona's crude handwritten capitals press the point amid the rows of tally marks counting the dead, coiled barbed wire, felled logs, skulls, and skeletons: COUNTING FOR NOTHING, NO MAN'S LAND, UNLUCKY STRIKE, WRONG WAY TIME, MELTDOWNS, ZERO HOURS. Curiously, clocks have no zero, so keep the ultimate end at bay. Their passing regular beat is set against the cumulative and random events of history; as Fiona says, 'it just goes on'. The resonant chimes of floor and mantle clocks offer a strange calm and certainty, but the cuckoos and caws unsettle as much as the images, evoking the sense that time is running out.

At the same time the exhibition requires us to slow down, to somehow enter the slow time of its making (for Fiona there is never enough time; though there is a shift to more spontaneous works many are supremely intricate). As noted by Gregory O'Brien, time is *crafted* in much of her work, and folds back in on itself through repetition.[20] Through a continuous process of making, the present is stretched out so that both the past and the future may enter. Fiona conceived Wrong Way Time as 'an odd archaeology that's dug out of the recesses of my take on the "now"'.[21] Her 'now' is as much spatial as it is temporal, not an evanescent moment, but what one theorist has described, characterising a digital world in which the past cannot be forgotten, as a 'broadening present of simultaneities'.[22] Her collections of found materials register movements of people, plants, and capital across the globe, as well as her own explorations or travels (the driftwood, the banknotes, a giant lump of coal literally dug out of the ground), or give presence to contested borders and issues of our time (atlases, newspapers). Other elements of the installation recall works by contemporary artists (Kader Attia, Narelle Jubelin, Colin McCahon, Giuseppe Penone and Ricky Swallow are some that come to mind), though they have become Fiona's own and seem also to emerge from the history of her own practice; or tap into general artistic trends—the 'archaeological turn', the 'curatorial turn', the new Bronze Age, a focus on ecology, animism, outsider art—as well as drawing on a wide range of social and scientific disciplines, including anthropology, archaeology, botany, and ornithology. Fiona harnesses all this and more into her evocation of a present constantly pulled back by the prospect of catastrophic change.

A surfeit of connectivity is partly an effect of Fiona's implosive mimetic layering, which replicates the inextricable ties between nature and culture, and partly an effect of time, as the world comes to meet Fiona's longstanding artistic concerns. The sheer multiplicity of potential relationships between things defines an installation imagined as 'a matrix in which varied and disparate elements and their underlying emotive forces can find alignments and create tensions in multiple (and hopefully unexpected) ways'.[23]

Conceived as a single work, Wrong Way Time contains a mind-boggling array of objects: found, constructed, cast, woven, and knitted; natural, handmade, and hi-tech. Many form extended sequences. There are sardine tins cut and fashioned into delicate sculptures of plants, figures, and endangered marine creatures from the Kermadec Trench in the South Pacific; skulls painted on empty perfume bottles and a mobile phone; burnt cabinets and encyclopaedic volumes; bread sculptures on atlases; lead sculptures of potatoes morphing into Platonic solids, or acting as bases for a strange array of votive offerings, from a credit card to a shellfish carapace; a bronze tree cast from toilet rolls; a video of a spider in a Chinese cork-landscape diorama and real spiders weaving webs around a collection of such dioramas; a painting on tapa cloth; metal car badges; bronze casts of fortresses fashioned from packaging and military model kits; zoomorphic and phallic driftwood; a central group of knitted heads and figures made from military camouflage garments, bones, teeth, and dice; dozens of working cuckoo, mantle, and long-case clocks painted with a variety of texts and images of war and finance; a kaleidoscopic peep-show, *Hack*, focusing on the world of Rupert Murdoch; newspapers of the day and bronze crystal formations; a bifurcated bronze brain; economically valuable plants and isobars of sperm drawn across groups of banknotes; further collections of banknotes sporting images of tractors, dams, and oil rigs; endangered animals, devils, feral cats, and flying machines woven from camouflage fabric and dried desert grasses; lists of plant taxonomies and banknote serial numbers; wasps' nests; a huge lump of coal; and more. This list details the small, and often exquisitely beautiful, parts of a bigger picture. In the abstract the whole is impossible to take in, let alone decipher. Excessive and obsessive, this constructed world is one that can only be experienced. Though Fiona is interested in classificatory systems, she doesn't impose one, instead allowing the sights, sounds, and smells to elicit discoveries where they will.

The profusion of things is contained by geometry and chromatic restriction, with an overall palette dominated by black and earthy grey-green and silver-white tones. Much of it is housed in more than twenty metres of tall, charred cabinets that form a large open square, enclosing the figures in *All the King's Men*. Fiona has a penchant for geometrical metaphysics, for instance Jain cosmologies, and indeed the exhibition plan is like a mandala, though her central gods are not enlightened beings but rather those from a secular pantheon that dramatise the extremes of human folly. The formation of driftwood is echoed by another cosmological diagram constructed from car headlamps lit up like stars. Numbers from the Fibonacci sequence are painted on a clock conveying both the exponential rise of deforestation and natural growth patterns. In *Platonic Underground* (page 76) lead potatoes have been shaped as the five Platonic solids, of interest to Fiona for their history of representing perfection since ancient times, the mathematical substructure of the world. Her solids retain their lumpen potato-ness, a bizarre and beautiful melding of the ideal and the real, culture and nature.

In turn these 'potatoes' link with other staples and products of the Earth—bread, crystals, coal. The indubitable geometrical structure of a crystal is offset by the vagaries of the daily news in a multilayered cabinet filled with bronze crystals emerging from layers of newspapers—representing the precious and the expendable too, a pairing with resonance across the exhibition. These crystalline forms retain the channels, ridges, and imperfections of the corrugated cardboard they were cast from, as if the substructure of our world is being eaten away. Or are they just aberrations that mimic natural variation? In a matching cabinet, pieces of bread shaped into bones, brick walls and other formations that suggest conflict are laid over open atlases—a source of sustenance atop sites of conflict, the beautifully rendered contours of borders past and present.

These and other curiosities invite speculation about the resilience of our planet, and draw attention to what we have lost, or need to protect. *Untitled* comprises a collection of vintage Chinese cork dioramas in a cabinet with live spiders. If all goes to plan, these handmade miniature landscapes will gradually be overtaken by an equally intricate network of spider webs. Used for Feng Shui placements and given names such as 'Long Forgotten Land', they are in effect mini-museums, remnants of exotic landscapes—replete with storks, tea houses, pagodas, pandas, and willows—destroyed or threatened by massive urban development. Fiona consigns them to the deadening space of the museum cabinet and lets nature take its revenge.

Throughout Wrong Way Time, clusters of objects, images, and words—each element of which has its genesis in a particular political event or personal experience that could be unravelled in detail—point to the way we objectify and manipulate nature or to the reality of our own animal nature. Fiona Hall's work aligns with the views of those who approach non-human environments through what is now called a 'relational' stance. It is ecological and future-oriented; everything is interconnected—words and actions here have repercussions there. Both warning and inspiration, Fiona's proliferating display paradoxically wills a future of restraint and austerity rather than growth, one described by Bruno Latour:

> 'Tomorrow,' those who have stopped being resolutely modern murmur, 'we're going to have to take into account even more entanglements involving beings that will conflate the order of Nature with the order of Society; tomorrow even more than yesterday we're going to feel ourselves bound by an even greater number of constraints imposed by ever more numerous and more diverse beings.'[24]

Notes

1. As such, this commentary is a general one on the ideas of the exhibition and some of its components, not a reading of an installation whose complex interconnections will become apparent only at the time of exhibition.
2. References to such ideas abound in discussions of the Anthropocene, the term widely used to describe a new geological era, one in which human actions drive accelerated change to Earth systems, breaking down any separation between nature and culture, a concept visualised in Fiona's art for many years.
3. Bruno Latour, 'On some of the affects of capitalism', lecture given at the Royal Academy, Copenhagen, 26 February 2014, http://www.bruno-latour.fr/sites/default/files/136-AFFECTS-OF-K-COPENHAGUE.pdf, p. 1.
4. David Hansen, 'Cryptoserendipitous palimpsestery, or, seeing the wood for the trees', in Kendrah Morgan (ed.), *Fiona Hall: Big Game Hunting*, Heide Museum of Modern Art, Melbourne, 2013, p. 39, writing of Fiona's installation *Fall Prey*, in dOCUMENTA (13), 2012.
5. I am indebted to Julie Ewington for the reference. Fiona was raised in a home of conservationists with leftist leanings.
6. Julie Ewington, *Fiona Hall*, Piper Press, Sydney, 2005, p. 125.
7. Gregory O'Brien, 'A narrow road, a green night', *Fiona Hall: Force Field*, exh. cat., Museum of Contemporary Art, Sydney and City Gallery, Wellington, 2008, p. 43.
8. Michael Taussig, *Mimesis and Alterity: A Particular History of the Senses*, Routledge, New York and London, 1993, p. 250.
9. Fiona Hall, conversation with the author, 2 March 2014.
10. Jurgis Baltrusaitis, *An Essay on the Legend of Forms: Aberrations*, trans. Richard Miller, MIT Press, Cambridge, MA and London, 1989, p. 100.
11. Fiona Hall, conversation with the author, 8 July 2014.
12. See Tim Ingold, 'Being alive to a world without objects', in Graham Harvey (ed.), *The Handbook of Contemporary Animism*, Acumen, Durham, 2013, p. 214.
13. Walter Benjamin, 'On the mimetic faculty', in Peter Demetz (trans.), *Reflections*, Schocken Books, New York, 1986, p. 333.
14. Fiona Hall, unpublished proposal for the 2015 Venice Biennale, October 2013.
15. Julie Ewington, *Fiona Hall*, p. 140.
16. Fiona Hall, conversation with the author, 31 January 2014.
17. David Hansen, 'Cryptoserendipitous palimpsestery', p. 44.
18. Pablo Picasso, cited in Jack Flam with Miriam Deutch (eds), *Primitivism and Twentieth-century Art: A Documentary History*, University of California Press, Berkeley and Los Angeles, CA and London, 2003, p. 33.
19. Fiona Hall, artist statement on *Scar Tissue*, Third Moscow Biennale of Contemporary Art, 2009, http://www.moma-art.ru/Mediashare/view/aid/9/mid/93.
20. Gregory O'Brien, 'A narrow road, a green night', p. 39.
21. Fiona Hall, proposal for the 2015 Venice Biennale.
22. Hans Ulrich Gumbrecht, in conversation with Joe Gelonesi, 'Finding presence in a digital age', *The Philosopher's Zone*, ABC Radio National, 22 October 2014.
23. Fiona Hall, proposal for the 2015 Venice Biennale.
24. Bruno Latour, *An Inquiry Into Modes of Existence*, Harvard University Press, Cambridge, MA, 2013, p. 10.

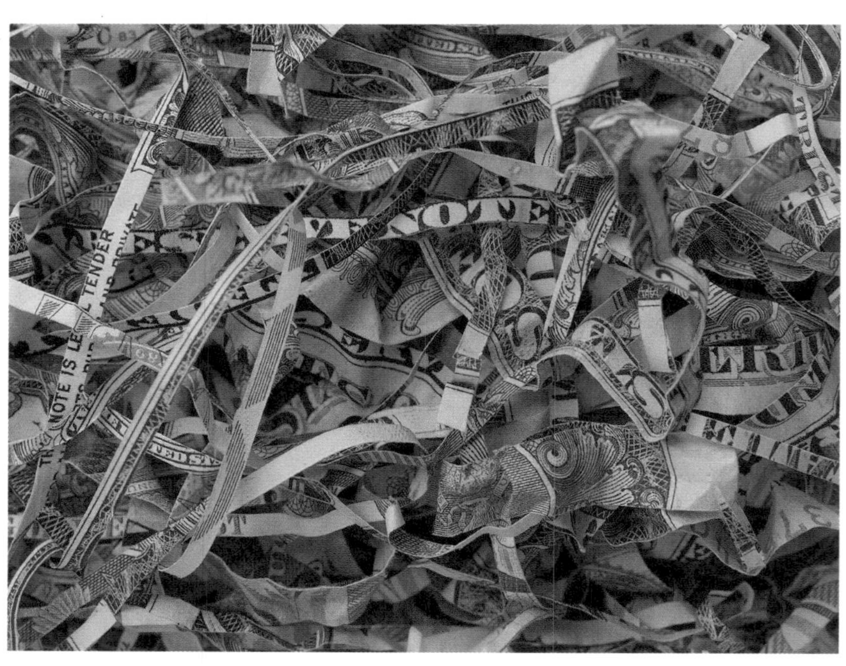

Tender 2003–06 (detail)
US dollars, wire, vitrines, vinyl lettering
86 nests, ranging from approx. 5 x 10 (diam.) cm to
108 x 17 x 13 cm; two vitrines, each 220 x 360 x 150 cm
Collection: Queensland Art Gallery
Purchased 2006. The Queensland Government's
Gallery of Modern Art Acquisitions Fund
Photograph: Natasha Harth
Images courtesy: Queensland Art Gallery | Gallery of Modern Art

The Folding Stuff
David Hansen

> *A rising tide lifts all boats.*
> —popular saying, often attributed to J.F. Kennedy

According to Title 18, Chapter 17 of the U.S. Code, that section which deals with currency crimes, anyone who 'mutilates, cuts, defaces, disfigures, or perforates, or unites or cements together, or does any other thing to any bank bill, draft, note or other evidence of debt issued by any national banking association, or Federal Reserve bank, or the Federal Reserve system, with intent to render such bank bill, draft, note or other evidence of debt unfit to be reissued' can be liable to a fine or imprisonment.

Fiona Hall need not be concerned. The works of art in which she employs banknotes do not entail criminal intent, but are rather means of value-adding. In her various money sculptures the flat sheet of the currency is not so much mutilated or defaced as it is converted: from a simple, regular plane surface into the perceptual paradox of a Möbius strip, from a signifier of national identity and personal wealth to a mordant critique of political economy. She takes the banknote into the domain of metaphor, treating its physical, material form in the cavalier, perspective-busting manner of Piranesi's architectural fantasias, its pictorial-symbolic decoration in the teasing political manner of Dread Scott's *What is the Proper Way to Display a U.S. flag?* 1988.

In the context of Hall's total oeuvre, such transfiguration is nothing new. In the mid-1980s she participated in an Australian Centre for Photography project with the American Polaroid Corporation, working with the large-format camera in Polaroid's New York 24 x 20 Studio. Recalling that experience, the artist later commented that 'the technical restrictions of the Polaroid large-format camera for extreme close-up work—the depth of field is reduced to almost zero—made me look for ways of creating images that appeared to have a greater depth than was actually possible.'[1]

This statement, as well as the low-relief tin tableaux to which it alludes, points to a subtle but distinctive aspect of Hall's practice, her attention to or articulation of complex spatialities. Behind or beneath the direct and compelling imagery of her objects and installations lie various topological revisions or re-imaginings, which transform her chosen media through a kind of dimensional sleight-of-hand.

In *Medicine Bundle for the Non-Born Child,* 1993, for example, a typically rich cultural commentary devolves on that typical figure of modern America, the Coke can. Beginning with this familiar pop-culture, Pop-art motif, Hall's longstanding botanical interests led her to explore the resonances of the coca leaf and the cola nut (two of the beverage's original ingredients, and the source of its famous brand name): the ritual narcotic use of each by indigenous peoples in South America and Africa, and in the case of the former the wrapping of magical 'medicine bundles' in coca leaves. Reinforcing this First World–Third World antinomy, she collapses the historical into the contemporary, introducing the fact (gleaned from a Harvard Medical School report) that Coca-Cola is a remarkably (ninety-one per cent) effective spermicidal douche, particularly useful in developing countries, where other forms of contraception may not be readily available. From here it is a short but significant imaginative and conceptual step to the making of a complete baby's layette from shredded aluminium Coke cans, to an irony as sweet and as corrosive as the drink itself.

Yet behind these central scientific and social narratives, the work has a formal or rather structural backstory. The circles of *Medicine Bundle*'s teething ring-rattle are made from the top and bottom discs of Coke cans. Moving then from line and plane to solid geometry, Hall adds a six-pack of cylinders: rubber-teated baby-bottle cans. Finally, she goes back to line, cutting other cans into thin strips of aluminium, which are then knitted into the soft, irregular, flexible forms of a jacket, a bonnet and a pair of bootees.

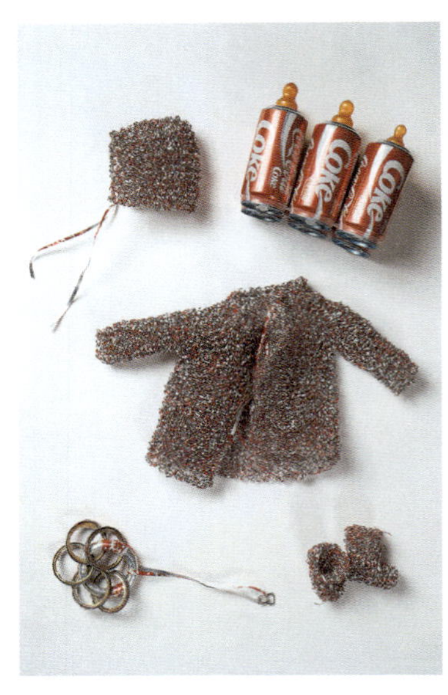

Medicine Bundle for the Non-Born Child 1993
aluminium, rubber, plastic
layette comprising matinee jacket: 27.5 x 47.5 x 10 cm, bootees: 7 x 5 x 8.5 cm and bonnet: 13 x 13 x 6 cm; rattle: 32 x 8.5 x 6 cm; six pack of baby bottles: 17 x 20 x 13 cm
Collection: Queensland Art Gallery | Gallery of Modern Art
Purchased 2000. Queensland Art Gallery Foundation Grant
Image courtesy: Roslyn Oxley9 Gallery, Sydney

A similar process can be seen in a work from ten years later, *Scar Tissue*, 2003. Here the artist addresses the horrible televisual spectacle of contemporary armed conflict by knitting children's soft toys, severed heads, limbs and torsos from half-inch videotape, which spools out and up from war movie cassettes on the floor, rising like smoke from Iraqi oil well fires, like black Rwandan genies released from quadrilateral lamps. With our attention held by the force of the nightmare iconography, we can easily miss the work's protean material aspect, the fact that *Scar Tissue*'s original, motive source is the flat, rectangular screen image, which is stored on a 400-metre ribbon of magnetised mylar that is in turn rolled onto cylinders and contained in a rectangular plastic box before being pulled out and knitted into three-dimensional body parts.

Form and flux, substance and shift: Hall's subliminal but consistent conceptual-constructive method is at the core of her works' often disturbing, unbalancing, vertiginous affect. It is not just a matter of things being made from unlikely, unexpected materials, as, for example, sardine cans becoming botanico-erotic votive offerings (*Paradisus Terrestris*, 1989–2005), or fruit and flowers, bones and body parts being constructed with gorgeous, shimmering coloured beads (*Understorey*, 1999–2004), or military camouflage dress being reshaped as threatened animal species (*Fall Prey*, 2012). After all, art has always been essentially a metaphorical operation, by which base matter—coloured earth mixed with water, eggs or oil, or lumps of metal, stone and wood—is transmuted into something else entirely: a spirit, a person, a place, an idea. Rather, Hall's material transformations have a more fundamental aspect, the rigorous scientific logic of mathematical theorems or the periodic table. Her media bloom and expand physically and sensually, intellectually and apperceptively, like the unfolding definitions of Linnaean binomial nomenclature.

In an age when much art is concerned, even obsessed, with the found object, with the unmade thing she, too, employs the most commonplace, quotidian materials: not only aluminium cans and videocassettes but also soap, Tupperware and PVC piping. And yet, as we have seen, her chosen media are not random selections but bear specific conceptual loads. At a time when much art is concerned, even obsessed with revealing process, with celebrating incompleteness or contingency, the material humility of plywood and plaster and/or low-tech obsessive-compulsive repetition, she, too, leaves technique exposed on the surface of the work. And yet her finely detailed carving, cutting, knitting and beading is not just reified labour, but necessary craftsmanship in the service of the idea and image she has in mind and in hand. At a time when much art is concerned, even obsessed, with message, with 'addressing' and 'referencing' and 'interrogating', she, too, engages with real-world issues of politics, social justice and in particular the manifold threats to the natural environment. And yet her skulls, clocks and camouflage, plants, birds and animals are not crusade branding devices, but elements in a thoroughly researched, carefully considered, complex, nuanced and often (when it is not utterly depressing) witty discourse.

So when she uses money as a medium, it is not in the manner of that legion of American dollar doodlers who decorate, fold, cut and collage the greenback in order to achieve instant recognition and some sort of meaning-by-association. Neither do her banknote works have the flat, flattering manner of Andy Warhol's dollar-bill paintings, where the deadpan satire is somewhat muted by The Factory's complicity with the art market. By the same token, nor does she employ the Futura Bold oppositional strategies of Barbara Kruger, in works such as *Untitled (Money Can Buy You Love)*, 1985, or *A Rich Man's Joke is Always Funny,* 2010, works which despite their polemical bite are still essentially framed by authority, by the modernist notion of the artist as autonomous creative subject. Hall's installations exemplify a more subtle practice, the kind of work described by Canadian academic Max Haiven as that which 'draws specific attention to the deep affinity of both art and money as forms of mediation under capitalist totality.'[2]

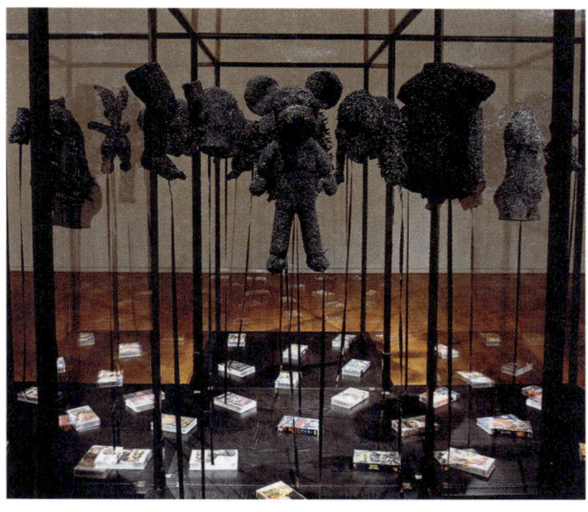

Scar Tissue 2003–04
videotape, video boxes, vitrine
vitrine dimensions:
210 x 330 x 330 cm
installation view, Roslyn Oxley9 Gallery, Sydney, 2005
Collection: Museum of Old and New Art, Hobart
Image courtesy:
Roslyn Oxley9 Gallery, Sydney

That is to say, here is an artist who engages with the ramifications of global economics. Neither art nor money is simple, linear, causal; both are in fact signs of social relations, with all the complexities and contradictions inherent therein. Often they are not even actual. Neo-Dada, post-conceptualism and relational aesthetics are as every bit as obscure, as recondite, as recherché as derivative securities, credit default swaps and collateralised debt obligations. Both sets of operations, the artistic and the economic, depend on a certain level of communal desire or consensus or tolerance (or perhaps only false consciousness) for their maintenance.

Hall gets this, and gives it.

She came to the use of money some time after she had begun to explore in her work the dynamics of markets and empires, with banknotes first appearing in *Cash Crop*, 1998, a sculpture which is primarily concerned with the intertwining of the worlds of nature, science and trade. This vitrine installation presents eighty plant products carved from soap arrayed across five glass shelves, all of them as precisely rendered as the late nineteenth-century *papier-mâché* models preserved in the artist's beloved Santos Museum of Economic Botany in her home town of Adelaide. The choice of material is deliberately allusive; the specimens are carved from soap; some, not surprisingly, golden yellow, others (Caucasian) flesh pink. Soap also implies water, signifying maritime trade's potential softening, blurring and even total dissolution of the natural ecosystems in which the plants originate and of the traditional uses and economic interests of the indigenous people of their source countries. Inscribed on the glass adjacent to each fruit or vegetable or seed pod is a label giving its Latin botanical and English common names, punningly matched against a term from the jargon of economics: thus the cola nut (*Cola acuminata*) previously encountered in *Medicine Bundle for the Non-Born Child*, here stands for 'global liquidity' and, similarly, a grape (*Vinis vinifera*) is a 'liquid asset'; seaweed (*Ascophyllum nodosum*) is inscribed 'offshore trading', and the water chestnut (*Trapa bicornis*) 'currency plunge'; a bitter lemon (*Citrus limon*) denotes 'tax reform', while 'tax return' is, in keeping with common experience, a peanut (*Arapis hypogaea*).

These sharp-edged double-entendres refer variously to the appearance, growth conditions, natural and processed form, geographical-environmental origins and human usage of each of the plants represented. Indeed, as curator and art writer Julie Ewington has observed, 'despite the simple structure of the work, the codings of *Cash Crop* are complex. Hall play[s] with conjoined systems of classification, purposefully slip-sliding ... botanical classifications interact with economic terms and rich plays of meaning.'[3] What is not so elusive is the unavoidable term in the semiological and economic equation: capital. On the very bottom of the vitrine, below the shelves, at the base of the transparent trapezoid–prism, as foundation or residue of the commodity trade, lies an opaque carpet of banknotes, each one decorated in ghostly white gouache with an image of a leaf of the plant whose fruit is represented above.

In her second sequence of currency works, *Leaf Litter*, 1999–2003, we see once again that subtle engagement with geometric structure, with 'creating images that [appear] to have a greater depth than [is] actually possible.' Here the 'trading floor' of *Cash Crop* is turned through ninety degrees to a vertical, pictorial orientation, and the perceptual play is very much with the flat surface. In this suite of collage-gouaches, Hall paints exquisitely detailed *grisailles* of individual leaves or sprays of foliage (their monochrome rendering inevitably recalling eighteenth- and nineteenth-century deluxe botanical engravings), each leaf set on a ground of banknotes from the plant's country or region of origin.

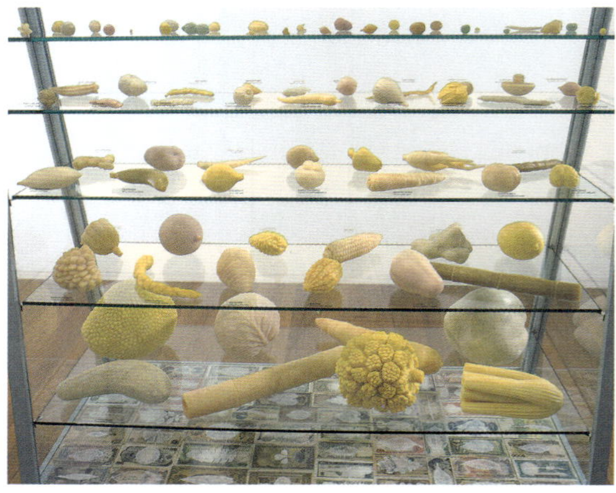

Cash Crop 1998 (detail)
carved soap, painted bank notes, vitrine
174.0 x 132.2 x 57.2 cm overall
Collection: Art Gallery of New South Wales
Contemporary Collection Benefactors 2000
Image courtesy:
Roslyn Oxley9 Gallery, Sydney

The leaves seem to float on top of or rather in front of the bills, in some cases in deliberate counterpoint to some aspect of the design, but always simultaneously reflecting and contrasting with their rectilinear supports. Reflecting, in that the leaves' complex vein or rib structures parallel both the rich linear surface patterns of the notes and, more abstractly, the branching flow patterns of imperial-colonial wealth. Contrasting, most obviously in the discrepancy between organic and rectangular shape, between nature and culture, but also in the discrepancies between the black and white image and the chromatic variety of the money, and between the image repertoire of the plant kingdom and that of the kingdoms of men, with its portraits of heads of state, national heroes and patriotic symbols. Most noticeable, if not most significant, are the differences of scale. Each leaf is painted at its actual, natural size, requiring the artist to increase her rectangular expenditure to accommodate the larger species; her spectacular lotus (*Nelumbo nucifera*) leaf covers no fewer than eighteen Cambodian 1000 riel notes.

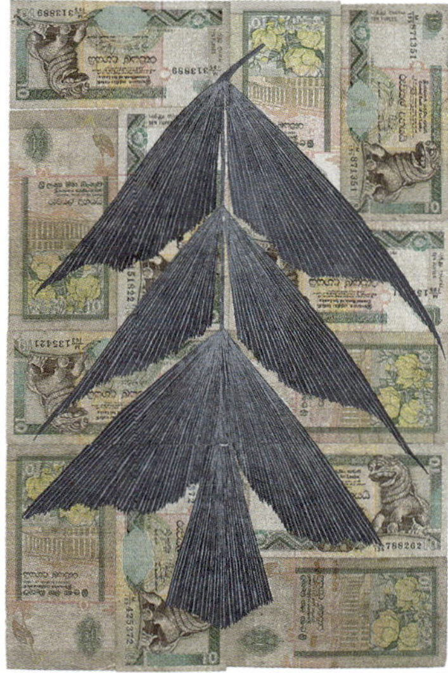

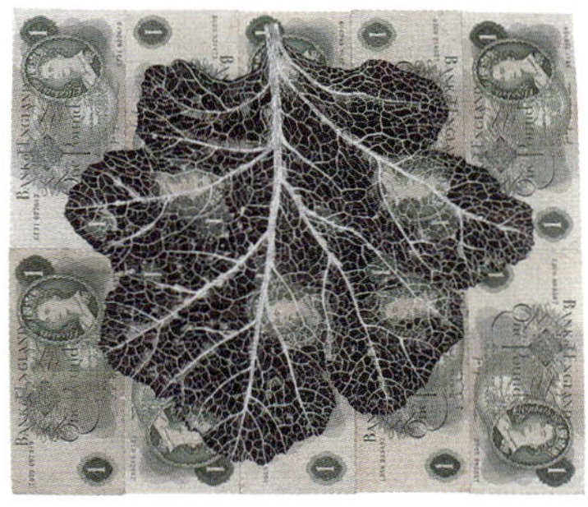

Caryota urens; Kitul palm
(Sri Lankan currency)
36.0 x 23.9 cm
Crambe maritima; sea kale
(British currency)
30.2 x 35.3 cm
from *Leaf Litter* 2000–02
gouache on banknote
National Gallery of Australia, Canberra
Purchased 2003
Image courtesy:
Roslyn Oxley9 Gallery, Sydney

In the following money series, one of her most intriguing, the spatial frame of reference segues from the one-to-one ratio to the global scale. *When My Boat Comes In*, 2003– (pages 107–11) is based on a simple but brilliant conceit: the matching of national banknote images of various marine or riverine vessels, of 'anything that floats, really'[4]—Peruvian reed canoes and Chinese junks and Egyptian dhows; clippers and steamers and container ships; galleons and frigates and submarines—with plants of economic value to be found in those countries.[5] Cotton (*Gossypium hirsutum*) from Mexico, rubber (*Hevea brasiliensis*) from Brazil, kauri pine (*Agathus australis*) from Aotearoa New Zealand, haricot beans (*Phaseolus vulgaris*) from Peru—each specimen (and plant) has its own rich and complex story. Given the imperial ambition of the series, and its temporal continuity, it is clearly not possible here to give details of each one.[6] Equally, however, given the Venice Biennale's traditional function as a site of national cultural representation, and given Hall's interest in colonial histories, it is appropriate to consider one example of particular relevance to Australia, an English note decorated with an oak leaf (*Quercus robur*).

Historically, given that metal currency bore the image of the king or queen on the obverse, the crime of 'coining' was deemed to be an offence against the crown, and therefore punishable by death. From the end of the seventeenth century, the inexorable logic of jurisprudence saw the capital penalty also being applied to the forgery of Bank of England paper notes. During the Revolutionary and Napoleonic wars, Britain's gold bullion reserves were severely depleted, and following a run on the provincial banks, the Bank of England suspended specie (gold and silver) payments, with its banknotes becoming de facto currency. Furthermore, throughout the ensuing so-called 'Restriction Period', from 1797 to 1821, it also issued low-value £1 and £2 notes, of dubious quality and security. These measures led to a virtual epidemic of forgery; in 1801 more than £15,000 worth of forged notes was discovered; by 1817 that figure had risen to £37,000. The Bank was assiduous in pursuing the criminals, and while an 1801 law allowed offenders the option of a plea bargain to the lesser crime of possession (punishable by fourteen years' transportation), between 1800 and 1827 over 350 people were hanged.

Part of the problem was the ease with which the notes could be reproduced, and while the Bank's search for a technical solution was at best dilatory, the wider community was clearly concerned; in 1819 we find a report from a committee of the Society of Arts 'Relative to the Mode of Preventing the Forgery of Bank Notes'.[7] From the same year comes Hall's bill, a political satire by George Cruickshank published by William Hone in the form of a 'Bank Restriction Note', with eleven men and women on the gallows, prisoners' shackles, a noose, a cameo of Britannia as Saturn eating her children and other relevant images, the note bearing the mock-signature (on behalf of the Bank's governors) of the notorious seventeenth-century executioner Jack Ketch Behind the figure of Britannia, lightly etched, are four ships, each with a pennant fluttering from its mainmast labelled 'TRANSPORT.'

This is where Australia's boats came in. In the late eighteenth and early nineteenth centuries, hundreds of convicts were transported to New South Wales and Van Diemen's Land for forgery, uttering or possession. Much of settler Australia's early visual culture was based not just on the imperial lie of *terra nullius*, but on the individual falsehoods of colonial painters such as Thomas Watling, Joseph Lycett, T.G. Wainewright, Joseph Backler, George Peacock and Knut Bull, and the architects Francis Greenway and James Blackburn.

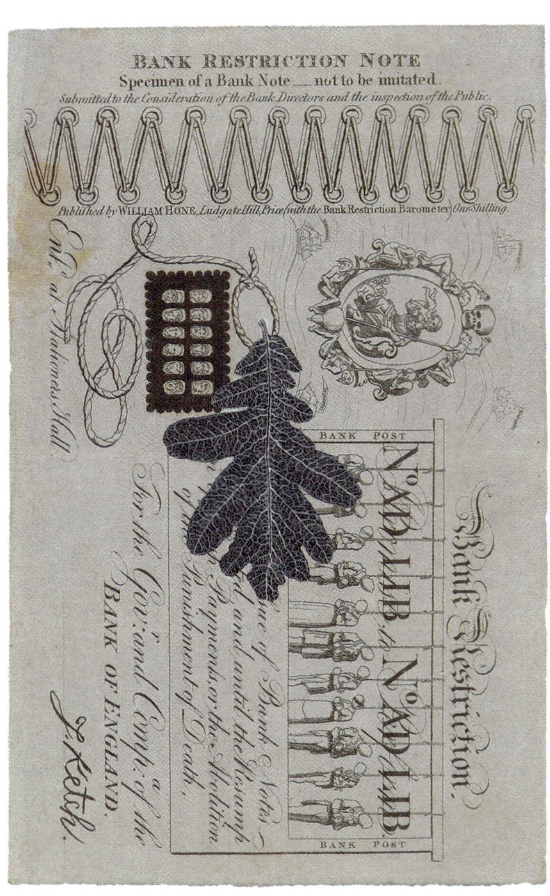

Quercus robur; English oak
from *When My Boat Comes In*
2003–
gouache on banknote
20.5 x 12 cm
Image courtesy:
Roslyn Oxley9 Gallery, Sydney

The chorus of the Royal Navy anthem *Hearts of Oak* includes the line: 'We'll fight and we'll conquer again and again.' The empire of money always prevails, even over itself. In pursuit of appropriate combinations of image and nation, since she started work on *When My Boat Comes In* Hall has become gradually enmeshed in, even obsessed by, the world of numismatics and its sub-discipline of notaphily. Employing the same methodology that she uses for her ship money, Hall has more recently embarked on several new series, working with other motifs symbolic of economic or political power. *Untitled*, 2015, features banknotes showing the tractor, emblem of broad-acre agricultural modernisation, of Soviet-inspired five-year plans and commodity exports. *Triumph of the Damned*, 2015, focuses on hydroelectric or agricultural dams, those high profile, capital-intensive, multinational-rewarding development projects so beloved of both Third World autocrats and the debt-mongers of the World Bank. A third current sequence, *Spill*, 2015, explores oil rigs and petroleum refineries, those wellsprings of foreign exchange in our carbon-hungry world. Finally, in *Where the Wind Blows*, she has selected notes bearing the portraits of sundry dictatorial generals and presidents, which she decorates with flowing curves, map contours or isobars described in dotted lines

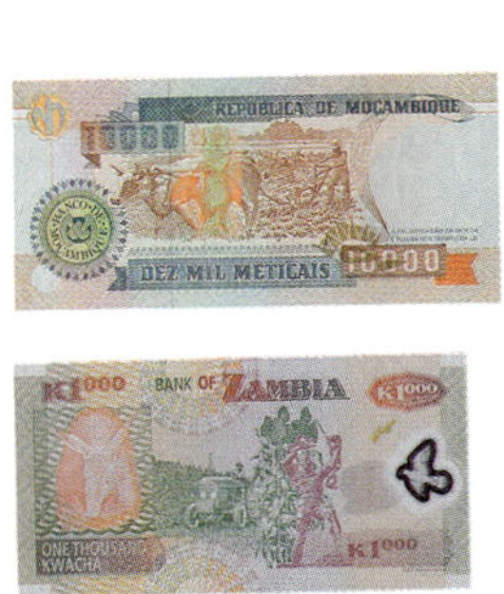

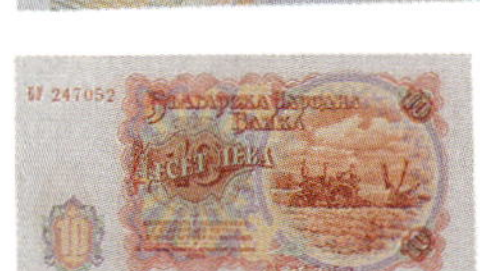
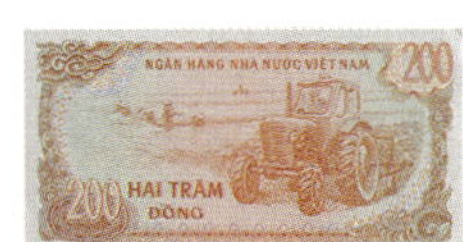

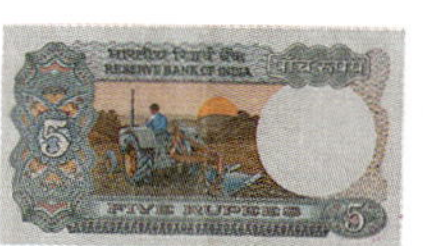
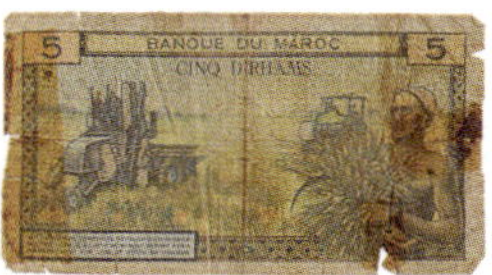

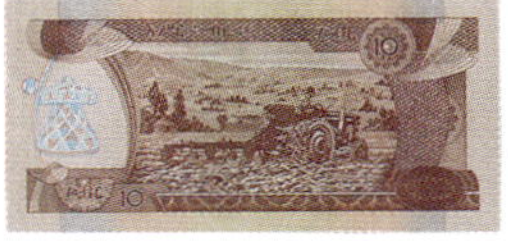
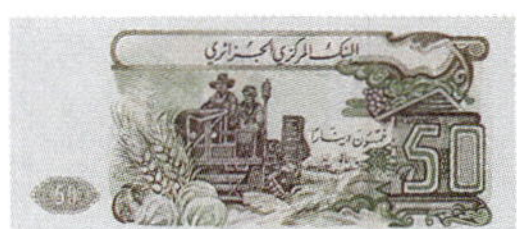

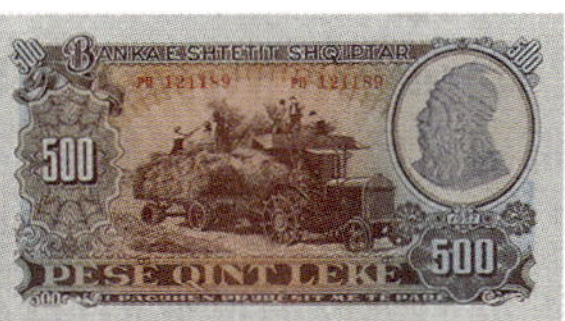

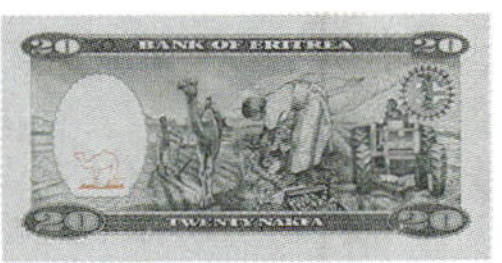

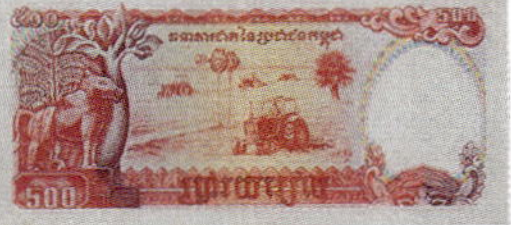
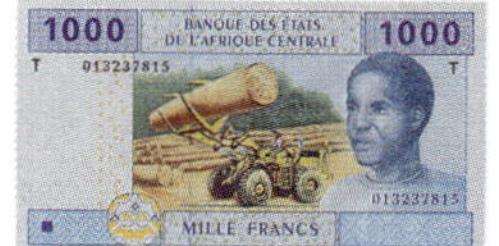

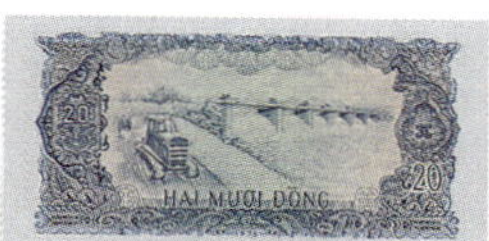

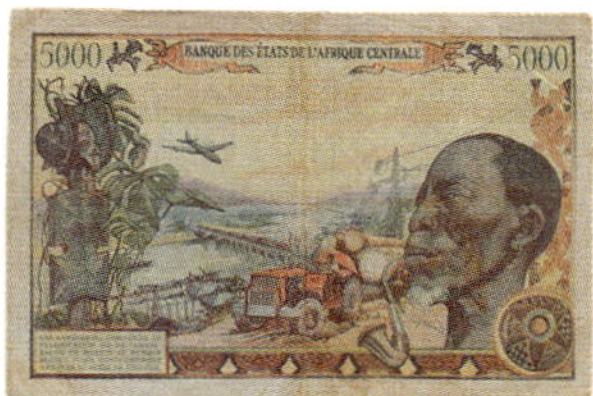

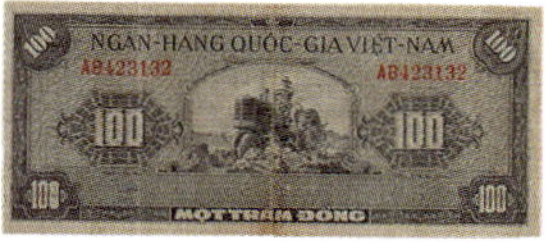

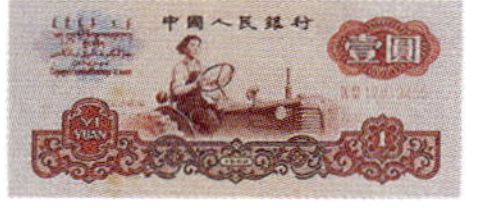

Untitled 2015 (detail)

of swimming sperm, diagrams of the primal natural forces of the earth and the weather and the masculine will to power.

In her exploration of the world of banknotes, Hall experiences and re-presents to the viewer that strange electricity, that tension—well-known to collectors and curators alike—that arises between the individual object or artefact or work of art and the field from which it arises, between the type specimen and the entire classificatory system, between William Blake's grain of sand and the universe, between John Ruskin's one leaf and the world.[8] This incommensurable gap is the space of connoisseurship, the locus of value, and the site of socio-economic and political consensus. Not coincidentally, Hall's complaint of the difficulties of the numismatic hunt makes her sound like a merchant banker: 'Money has become so much more expensive ... the Chinese are buying a lot ...'[9] Between the necessity of our monthly pay packets and the baffling abstractions of the nightly news' stock market report lies an act of faith; god and capital inhabit the gap.

But there is nothing there.

In one of her most moving vitrine installations, *Tender*, 2003–06, Hall uses sliced up American dollar bills to weave elaborate, scientifically accurate models of the nests of dozens of different bird species. At one level this work is a characteristically overdetermined play on words, matching the term 'legal tender' that appears on the banknotes with the instinctive tenderness associated with reproduction and the nurture of the young. It is also an expression of the artist's longstanding interest in the similarities and contradictions between different systems of classification, different systems of knowledge, the vitrines being inscribed both with lists of the avian genus and species responsible for each type of nest, and with the two-letter, eight-digit serial numbers of the notes used to create them. Here, too, she employs that idiosyncratic topological-transformative method described above, first dissecting rectangular plane surfaces to make linear strips, then reassembling them into fully three-dimensional, curving concavities.

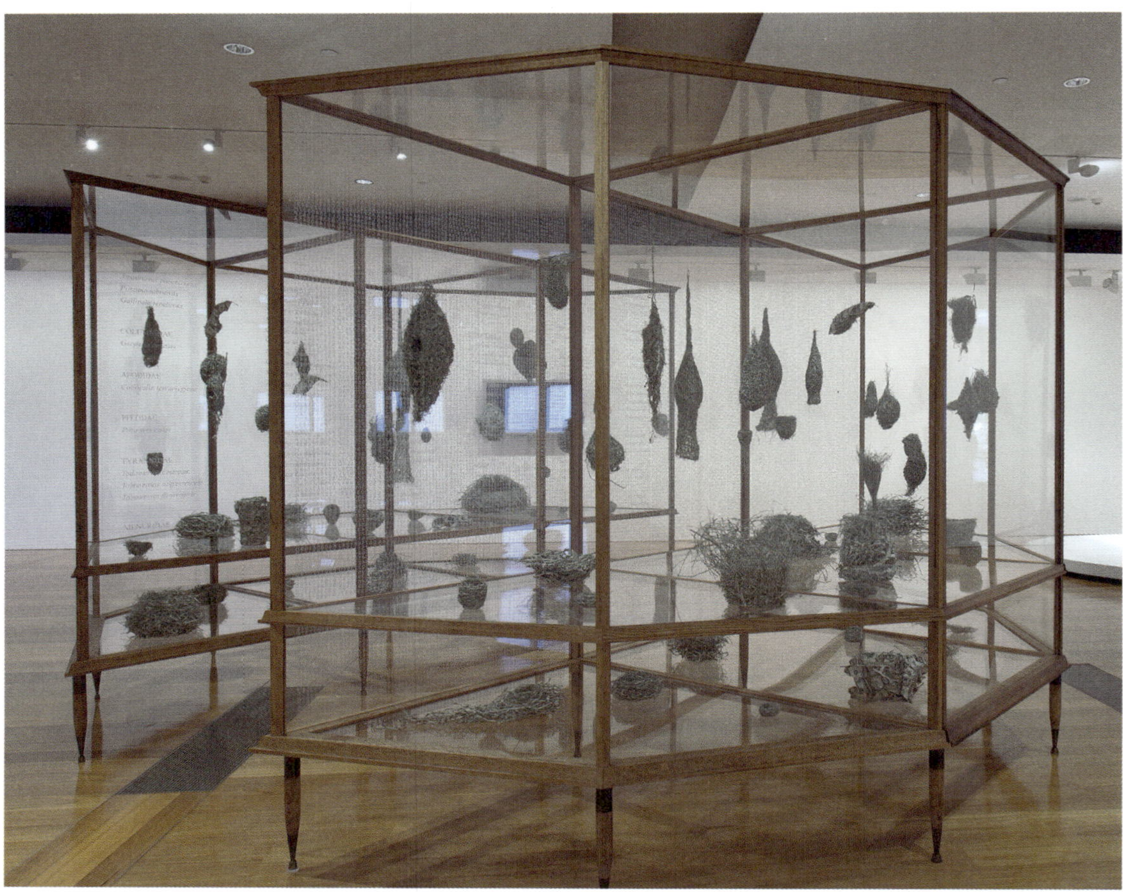

Tender 2003–06
US dollars, wire, vitrines, vinyl lettering
86 nests, ranging from approx. 5 x 10 (diam.) cm to 108 x 17 x 13 cm; two vitrines, each 220 x 360 x 150 cm
Collection:
Queensland Art Gallery
Purchased 2006.
The Queensland Government's Gallery of Modern Art Acquisitions Fund
Photograph: Natasha Harth
Images courtesy:
Queensland Art Gallery | Gallery of Modern Art

But the key to the work is not its artifice, but its emptiness. Not only are there no birds—no parents, no chicks, no eggs, even. There are no trees—no protection, no photosynthesis, no oxygen respiration. Just the faintest echo of faded chlorophyll in the lichen or lawn-clipping green of the paper currency itself. There is, in fact, no environment, other than the abstract museum space of the vitrine. The vacancy is terribly affecting. Ewington writes of the 'deep melancholy' of the work: 'This village of empty nests is indescribably sad. It speaks to me of loss, of remembering, even of haunting'.[10] At the same time, however, through the use of the banknotes Hall not only indicts transnational monopoly capitalism for the current planetary ecocide, but also points out the internal contradictions of the system. Shredded, the notes are worthless. Even in its own terms, the global economy, like the art world, is full of holes, whether the $34.4 trillion of capital lost through the Global Financial Crisis of 2007–09, the more than $3 trillion annual cost of worldwide tax evasion, or the sixty-five per cent of stock market trades that are now fully, algorithmically automated.

No nest egg is secure. The boat never comes in.

Notes

1. *Fiona Hall*, in 'Undermining the systems of a post-everything world: Timothy Morrell interviews Fiona Hall', *Art Monthly Australia*, no. 68, April 1994, p. 8.
2. Max Haiven, 'Money as artistic media: coins of the realm', Art and Money symposium, Dunedin School of Art, New Zealand, 30 August 2013; see http://vimeo.com/79456679.
3. Julie Ewington, *Fiona Hall*, Piper Press, Sydney, 2005, p. 142.
4. Fiona Hall, telephone conversation with the author, 7 November 2014.
5. It is particularly appropriate that the work should be seen in Venice. Firstly, because of La Serenissima's historic role as a maritime and mercantile capital, a key vector in the trade between Europe and the East. Secondly, because it is currently a site where both environment and community are threatened by the ongoing depredations of capital: not only by the rising sea levels that are the result of global warming from 200 years of industrial-age carbon emissions, but also by the Magistrato delle Acque's present plan to further degrade the lagoon's fragile ecosystem by dredging the Canale Contorta Sant'Angelo, a convenient channel for Costa's monster cruise ships.
6. For a detailed account of her treatment of the gingko, see David Hansen, 'Fiona Hall', in Victoria Lynn (ed.), *turbulence: 3rd Auckland Triennial*, Auckland Art Gallery Toi o Tamaki, Auckland, 2006, p. 78.
7. *Report of the committee of the Society of Arts, &c., together with the approved communications and evidence upon the same, relative to the mode of preventing the forgery of bank notes*, Royal Society of Arts, London, 1819.
8. In 'Trade: Fiona Hall' (*Artlink*, vol. 21 no. 4, 2001), Stephanie Radok finds an apt and intriguing resonance in Ruskin's dictum 'If you can paint one leaf you can paint the world' having been quoted by Bernard Smith in the concluding paragraph of his *European Vision and the South Pacific* (Oxford University Press, Oxford, 1960, p. 257)
9. Hall, telephone conversation with the author, 7 November 2014.
10. Ewington, *Fiona Hall*, p. 169.

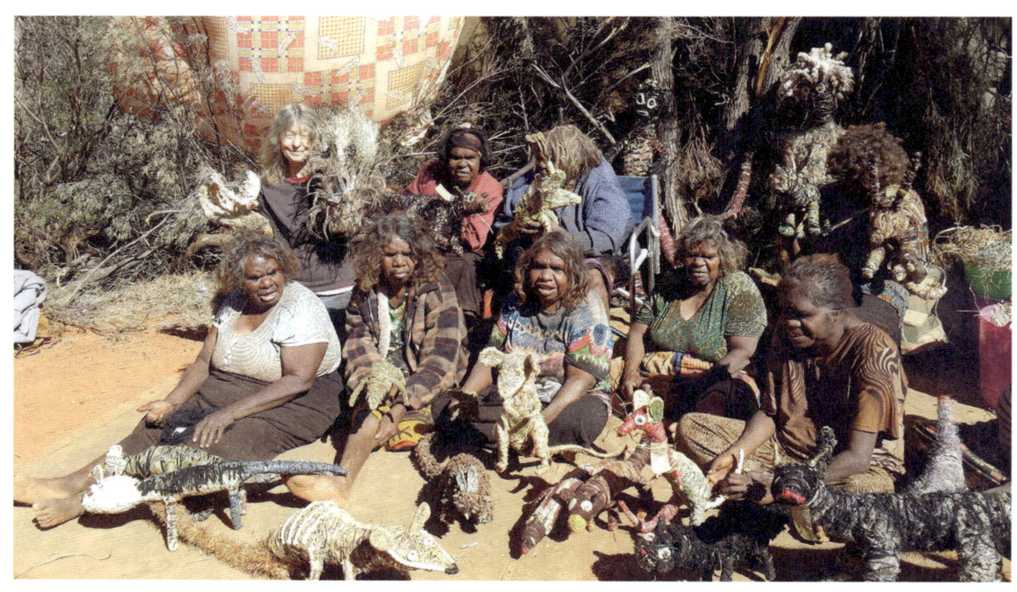

Fiona Hall and Tjanpi Desert Weavers with their work at the end of camp near Pilakatilyuru, Western Australia, June 2014
Back row, from left: Fiona Hall, Mary Pan, Nyanu Watson, Angkaliya Nelson
Front row, from left: Niningka Lewis, Yangi Yangi Fox, Roma Butler, Molly Miller, Rene Kulitja
Photograph: Joanna Foster

Tjanpi Desert Weavers

Wrong Way Time incorporates a group of works made by Fiona Hall and eleven women from Tjanpi Desert Weavers from the Central and Western Desert region of Australia—Roma Butler, Yangi Yangi Fox, Rene Kulitja, Niningka Lewis, Yvonne Lewis, Molly Miller, Angkaliya Nelson, Mary Pan, Sandra Peterman, Tjawina Roberts, and Nyanu Watson—as part of a project commissioned for the TarraWarra Biennial 2014: Whisper in My Mask, curated by Natalie King and Djon Mundine.

Extending the Tjanpi Desert Weavers' history of making animals in local grasses and other materials, and her own explorations about the effects of colonisation, Fiona suggested they work together to make endangered or extinct desert animals. The women drew upon their intimate and intricate relationship with animals, embedded in the interrelatedness of people, place, story, ancestral and lived experience that they call *Tjukurpa* (Dreaming), and arising from their knowledge of hunting, tracks and animal behaviour—including that of the predatory feral cat.

An artists' camp was held for this collaborative project in June 2014 at a place near Pilakatilyuru (about thirty kilometres from the community of Wingellina in Western Australia, in the tri-state border region close to South Australia). The women collected local *tjanpi* (grass), while Fiona brought Australian and British military garments. They used each other's materials as well as incorporating found objects to create *Kuka Iritija (Animals from Another Time)*, inspired by the plight of endangered species.

The women spoke about the collaboration in an interview with Jo Foster and Linda Rive in October 2014. Translations are by Linda Rive.

Takiriya Tjawina Roberts
Kuruntu kulira ngalturinganyi, Australiaku titu.

In our heart of hearts we worry deeply about the whole of Australia.

Paluru tjana kumpinu, ngaltutjara tjuta. Irititja tjuta kumpintja, animals tjuta. Ka ngananana mankurpa mankurpa kanyini kuwari.

Our animals have hidden themselves away, the poor things. The animals of old are now hiding somewhere. We now have only a few animals left.

Ngurpa ngayulu kuka walputi. Tjinguru tjitjingku. Tjamulu kamilu ngunytjungku mamangku kuka irititja kuka walputi ngalkupai. Katjalu tjana. Tjana kuka ngalkupai. Tjana wangkapai.

I have never seen a *walputi* (numbat). I may have possibly seen one when I was a small child but I don't remember. My grandfather, grandmother, mother and father would have hunted and eaten *walpuṯi*. My great-grandfather certainly. They all hunted and ate those animals. They always used to talk about them.

Katjalu, kamilu tjana kuka mala ngalkupai. Irititja, mai wiyangka. Nganaṉa rantjangka warkaripai munu kanyilpai.

Great-grandfather and great-grandmother and their generations always hunted and ate *mala* (rufous hare-wallaby). Back in the old days, before white flour. Nowadays we work as rangers, caring for our land.

We find it easy to make animals that we see on a daily basis and know. We know what their feet and paws and mouths look like, and we replicate them in *tjanpi*. We have been told all about those old animals. What kind of fur they have. What their fur patterns are. But we don't intimately know what their paws look like in detail.*

Yangi Yangi Fox
People in the outside world do not know about our animals. Our *tjanpi* animals are *kurunpa tjara nguwanpa*—it is as if they have their own spirit energy.

Rene Kulitja
We all carry skin names and totemic ancestors, like emu. For me, my totemic ancestral *tjukurpa* is an experienced sensation, not just an animal or an object that I can point at and experience as a physical thing.

Mary Pan
These animals are our *kuka irititja* that we used to hunt and eat, but which have now disappeared. They have all died and are no more. We don't know why. It could be because of fallout from the atomic bombs. It could be from bushfires. It happened a long time ago. A big fire can wipe out whole colonies of animals. But we suspect the bomb killed many of our animals. The bomb was responsible for a lot of deaths. Not many people in Australia understand this. Yes, there have been bushfires too, and yes, I know foxes and feral cats have wreaked untold havoc on our animals, but today I want to focus on the damage that the bomb has done. We lost a lot after that bomb fallout. Some of our animals have been saved and placed on remote islands to breed back up again, but we people living out here have lost our animals from our own country, which disappeared when we were children. The bomb was detonated when we were children and we were all forcibly moved to places like this. We were moved to the Fregon area, and we then lived in Ernabella. Many of us became terribly ill. My mother died from that bomb fallout. I had to grow up without a mother. I only had my father to look after me. My older sister and my older brother looked after me too, after the bomb killed our mother, and all those animals.

* This paragraph and other artists' comments were recorded in English only so do not appear in Pitjantjatjara.

Talking about the bomb upsets me terribly because I have never got over losing my mother. I don't like to be reminded of it. We never got to eat any of those animals that our grandmothers' generation ate regularly. All we have are these *tjanpi* animals that we have made. Our lands have been emptied of our *tjukurpa* animals. Some of us have seen *tjakuṟa* (great desert skink lizard) and *nganamara* (mallee fowl) but only very rarely. Most of our small mammals disappeared when we were just tiny children.

Our family was supposed to be safe in Ernabella, but people died in Ernabella. People died on Witjinti, Granite Downs. People died at Mimili. People died in many other places. I can't keep this story inside. Sometimes I have to talk about it. Put this story in the catalogue because not enough people know about it. I can never forget what happened to us. I remember what happened. It stays with me always. At night when I am lying down, trying to sleep, I see my mother's face. She died from the fallout from the bomb. I can never forget her. I can never forget why she died. She and many other people all died from the *puyu* (fallout). All those animals died too.

Niningka Lewis

Kuka irititja nganaṉa palyaningi ninu, wayuṯa munu tjalku. Palunya tjana nganaṉa palyaningi. Walpuṯi, partjaṯa, murtja, mitika, tarkawaṟa. Mitika puḻkanya, pitingka nyinapai, kuka puḻka. Tjanpi ngurangka tjanpingka nyinapai, tjanpi palyaṟa nyinapai, pitingka, tjanpingka tjunkula ngura ngarinytikitjangku. Kuka irititja uwankara.

At the workshop we sculpted *ninu*, *wayuṯa* and *tjalku*. We made all of those animals for this exhibition. We made *walpuṯi*, *partaṯa*, *mitika* and *tarkawaṟa*. We made *mitika*, which is a large animal, which burrows deep holes, and which was once an important meat animal. They lived in the *tjanpi* grasses, and they carried grasses into their burrows to make nests in which to lie. All these animals are part of our past heritage.

Tjungu wiṟu. Ngapartji ngapartji nintinu. Paluṟu palatja army tjara nintinu, ka nganaṉa tjanpi nintinu.

Our workshop was a shared space, where we taught each other. Fiona Hall brought out army clothing and showed us how she works with them, and we showed her how we work with *tjanpi*.

Ngayulu mala palyanu. Paluṟu tin-meat nguṟu palyanu munu milk tin, tjampita alatjiṯu, kaṯanu nipa-nipangka. Tjuḻpu nyaḻpi, tjungura wantingu, wiṟunya mulapa. Billycan-ngka nganaṉa palyaningi.

I made a *mala* (rufous hare-wallaby). She worked with tin-meat tins, and milk tins, all sorts of *tjampita* (tin cans), cutting them up with scissors. She used bird feathers, placing them on the pieces, which looked really good. She worked with old billycans.

Wayuta munu ninu, palunya pulanya ngayulu palyanu. Kulirana palyanu. Ngayulu ngurpatu nyara palumpa, ngurpa wiya, ngayulu nyangu kutju ara, wayuta panya, nganala, mala paddockngka. Kutjupa kutjupa changearinyi. Ngayulu kulilpai tjukurpa, wayuta panya.

I have made a *wayuta* (possum) and a *ninu* (bilby) for our exhibition. I really had to think really hard about them, to be able to make them. I have never seen them. Well, I have seen possums once, in the *mala* paddock. Our animals have changed completely. I always used to hear stories about *wayuta*.

Kuka tjana palunya panya mungangka pungkupai, kinarangka. Tjitji kunkuntjaraya wantikatira, munu ankupai, munu tjana kinara ngalya pakanyangka, tjinguru kinara ngalya pakalpai kaya ankupai munuya nyakupai, punungka, ngalta, palula kunyu nyinapai, paluru tjana. Kutjupa tjuta, punu muurmuurpangka, kutjupa tjuta nyinapai.

The old people used to hunt them at night, killing them in the moonlight. While the children were fast asleep, the hunters would go out in the moonlight, or in the light of the rising moon, and hunt *wayuta* in the *ngalta* (kurrajong) trees, where the *wayuta* would be hiding.

Ngayulu wiya palu paluru ninti. Paluru ngalkupai kuka irititja ngalkupai. Paluru tjukurpa wangkapai. Paluru wangkapai munu ngayuku ngunytjungku wangkapai, ka ngayulu kulilpai.

I have never eaten *wayuta* but my older sister has. She would eat the meat back in the old days. Everybody used to talk about it. My older sister always talks about these old days, and so did our mother, and I remember all those old stories clearly.

Tjinguru paluru ninti. Pina, tjina ma pitjala tatintja.

My older sister probably knows about their ears and their feet that were good for climbing.

Ka ngananana panya kuwari malu kutju ngalkupai, imiyu, kipara, ngintaka. Nyara palunya tjananya kutju ngananana malatja tjutangku ngalkuni. Kuka irititja tjuta ngaltutjara. Tjanala mirangka nyinantja.

So today all we have to eat are *malu* (red kangaroos), *imiyu* (emu) *kipara* (bush turkey) and *ngintaka* (perentie lizard). Those are the only meat animals we modern people of today get to eat. We feel a great compassion towards the *kuka irititja* (early-days meat animals) of yesteryear. Our forebears lived alongside them and saw them every day.

Ngayulu kulilpai, tjinguru mai nguru tjunkunyangka tjana wiyaringu. Kutjupa kutjupa tjuta tjinguru bombangkunti wampa ngayulu ngurpa.

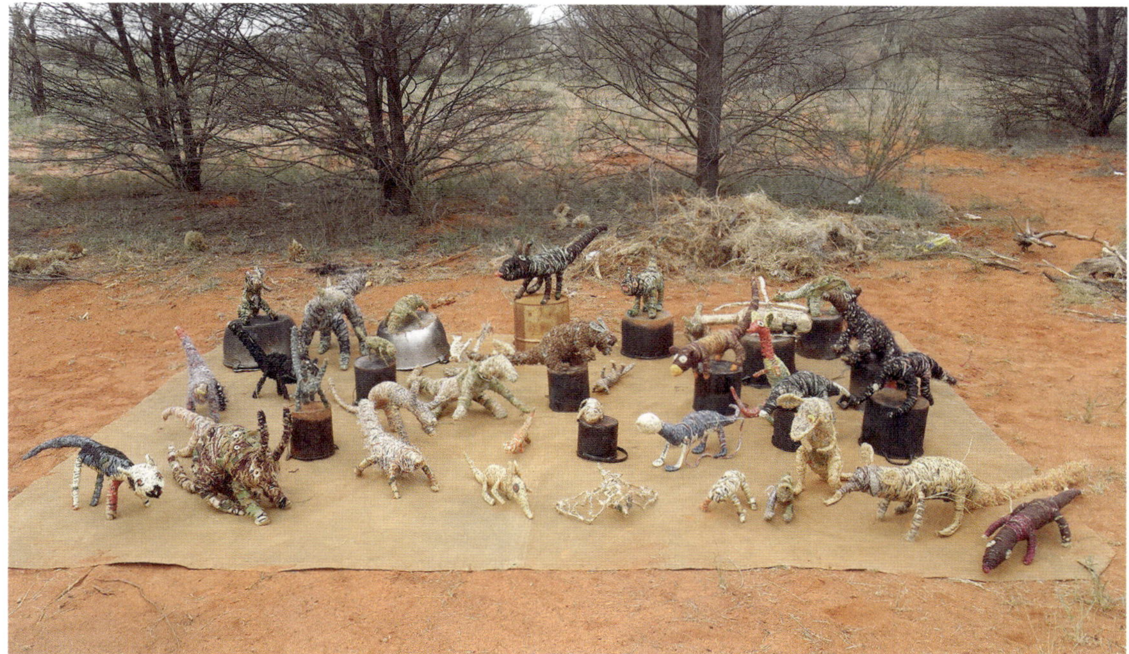

Kuka Irititja (Animals from Another Time) June 2014
near Pilakatilyuru,
Western Australia
Photograph: Fiona Hall

I have a theory that our meat animals disappeared when we started to eat *mai* (white flour, sugar and tea). Another theory is that the bomb killed them all off, but I just don't know, I am not sure.

These were our foods and as soon as we switched foods to white peoples' foods, the animals all disappeared.

Jo Foster

That is interesting too, Niningka, because when you think about it in the exhibition those tins the animals are sitting on, they are flour drum, sugar drum, *tjampita*...

Niningka Lewis

Wiya palya!! Uwa. True story. *Ka tjana nyara palunya tjananya palyanyangka tjana wiyaringulta.* Flour *katingu wati piranpa tjutangku. Ka paluru tjana ngalkuningi wakati, ngaltatjiti, kaltukaltu, mai tjanampa, walytjangku mantjilpai wirangka kilinira munu rungkalpai, munu mai pauni warungka munu ngalkuni. Kapi tjikini. Alatji tjana kanyiningi wirangka, mai tjanampa. Pulka, ka kutjupa tjuta kampurarpa, wirinywirinypa, tawaltawalpa, kulypurpa, palunya tjanaya ngalkupai. Pulka mulapa. Kanyiningi munu ngalkukapai, kuka putitja. Tjanmata, wayanu, ngantja, witjinti, ultukunpa, kalinykalinypa, ngapari.*

Interesting! Yes. True story. Flour drums, sugar drums, tins and drums represent the changes in our diet that came at the same time as the disappearance of our traditional meat animals. White flour was brought into our lands by white men. Our people had been eating traditional seeds such as *wakati* (inland pigweed seed), *ngaltatjiti* (kurrajong seed) and *kaltukaltu* (desert millet). Those were the traditional flour seeds that our forebears had always gathered in their wooden dishes, cleaning and winnowing them, then grinding them and cooking them in the coals of the fire, before eating their seed cakes. They drank only fresh water. That is how they lived, threshing and winnowing their seeds. Such good food it was, and such a variety, including *kampurarpa* (desert raisins) *wirinywirinypa* and *tawaltawalpa* (bush tomatoes), *tulypurpa* (bush gooseberries) and other delicious fruits. Important and sustaining fruits. Staple foods, along with bush meat animals.

Tjanpita unngu, tjama, wirkanulta, ka tjana nyangu. Whitefellangku katingu kamulangka munu ungangi mai kutjupa tjuta, tjama, tjuka mai flour. Tjana ngalkula munu tjana witungingi, 'Ara! Ernabellaku! Ernabellakuya ara!' Kaya Ernabellaku ngalya pitjanyi munu kutjupa tjuta ma katinyi Warburtonku, ka kutjupa tjuta katingi Pupanyiku. Katingi, nyanga alatji alatji, tjananya witungingu, wati piranpa tjutangku, 'Nyaratja mai pulka, Ernabellala, Warburtonta.' Alatji. Kaya uwankara pitjangi. Tjitji kutjutjara kutjutjara. Pika wiya, uwankara wiya tjara nyinangi, ngaltutjara. Nganana pikatjararingu kuwari. Diabetes. High blood-pressure. *Kapulpa.* Renal failure. *Uwankara pikaringanyi, ngura winkingka.*

Inside the tins and drums came jam, which our forebears saw for the first time. White people brought it into our lands on camel back, and were handing it out to our people. They gave them different foodstuffs, white flour, jam, sugar and more flour. They gave them the foods and then said, 'Go! Go to Ernabella! Go to Ernabella!' So some people were taken to Ernabella, and some were taken to Warburton and others were taken to Papunya. They were brought here and shown all the new things, this and that. They had been told by the white people, 'At Ernabella there is abundant food. Ernabella and Warburton.' That's what they were told. So everybody went there. Most couples only had one child at the time. Nobody had illnesses, everyone was in excellent health, bless them. Not today though, today we are all sick people. Diabetes. High blood-pressure. Kidney problems. Renal failure. Everybody is sick now, in every community.

Palu nganana pika wiya nyinangi palu puyu kutjungku.

We were not sick before the nuclear fallout landed on us.

Fiona Hall

On *Manuhiri (Travellers)* 2014

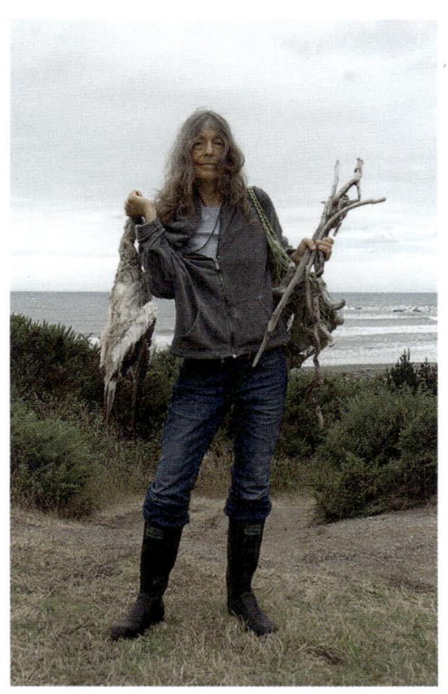

Fiona Hall at Awanui Beach, 2012
Photograph: Natalie Robertson

I collected the driftwood from the beach at Awanui on Aotearoa New Zealand's North East Cape, where the Waiapu River flows out to the sea. Storms and landslips bring fallen trees down from the forests upstream; years of intensive farming have caused large-scale erosion that is now silting up and reshaping the river at its mouth. When the Waiapu (which means rushing water) finally reaches the sea its cargo of fallen timber is thrown back onto the beach by the tide, piled up like bones from a forest graveyard. Scattered among them you can find the creatures of the woods and water, travellers from a former forest life, reshaped by the ocean currents and now journeying to another life back in the world of the living.

Ngā kōrero i roto i te reo Māori

*I kohia te tāwhaowhao mai i tāhuna ki Awanui, ki Te Tairāwhiti o Te Ika a Māui, Aotearoa ki te takiwa e rere te Waiapu ki roto i Te Moana-nui-a-Kiwa. Ka haria atu ngā rākau o uta ki te moana e ngā āwhā me ngā horo whenua. Nā te maha o ngā tau e whakamahia ana te whenua mo te ahuwhenua i horo nei te whenua, kei te kikī haere te ngutu awa i te parahua, ā, ka rerekē haere te āhua o te ngutu awa. Kia tae atu ngā wai o te Waiapu ki te moana, ka kawea ngā rākau kua hinga ki uta e ngā tai, ka whakaputangia ki tāhuna pērā i ngā kōiwi o te urupā rākau. I roto i te āhua o ngā tāwhaowhao, ka kitea ngā rauropi o te ngahere, o te awa me te moana kua hoki mai ki te ao hurihuri.**

* Translation by Makere Atkins

Wrong Way Time 2012–15 (detail)

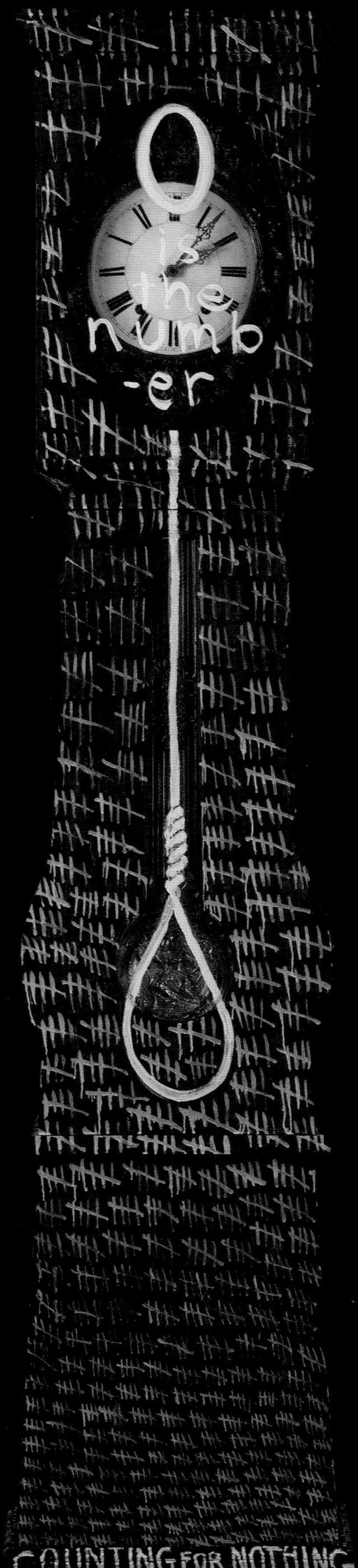

0
is
the
numb
-er

COUNTING FOR NOTHING

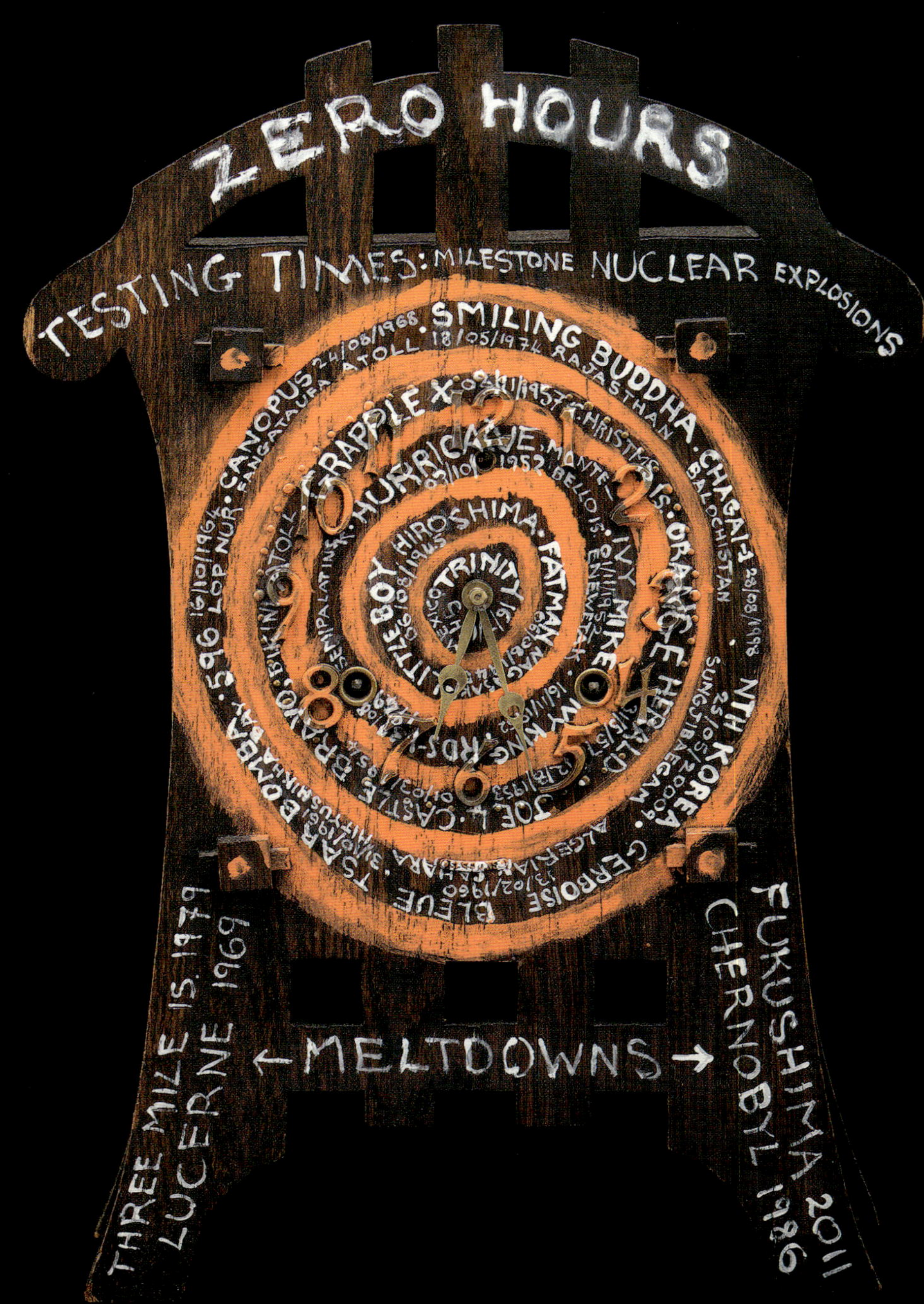

ong Way Time 2012–15 (details)

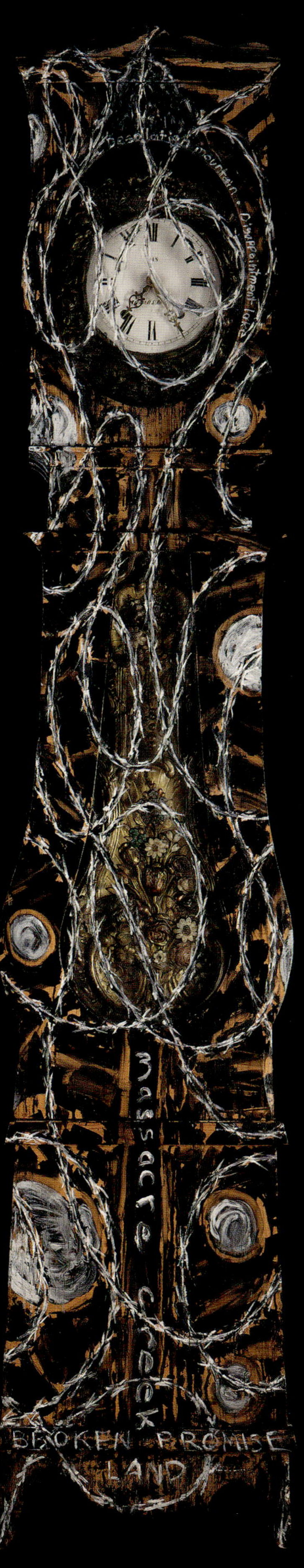
Desolation mountain
Disappointment lake
Massacre Creek
BROKEN PROMISE
LAND

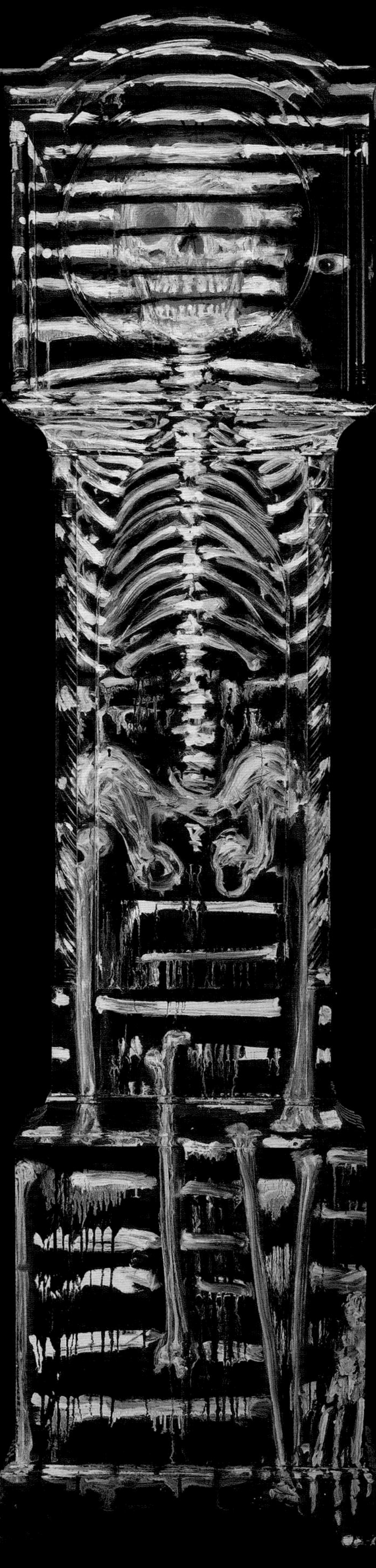

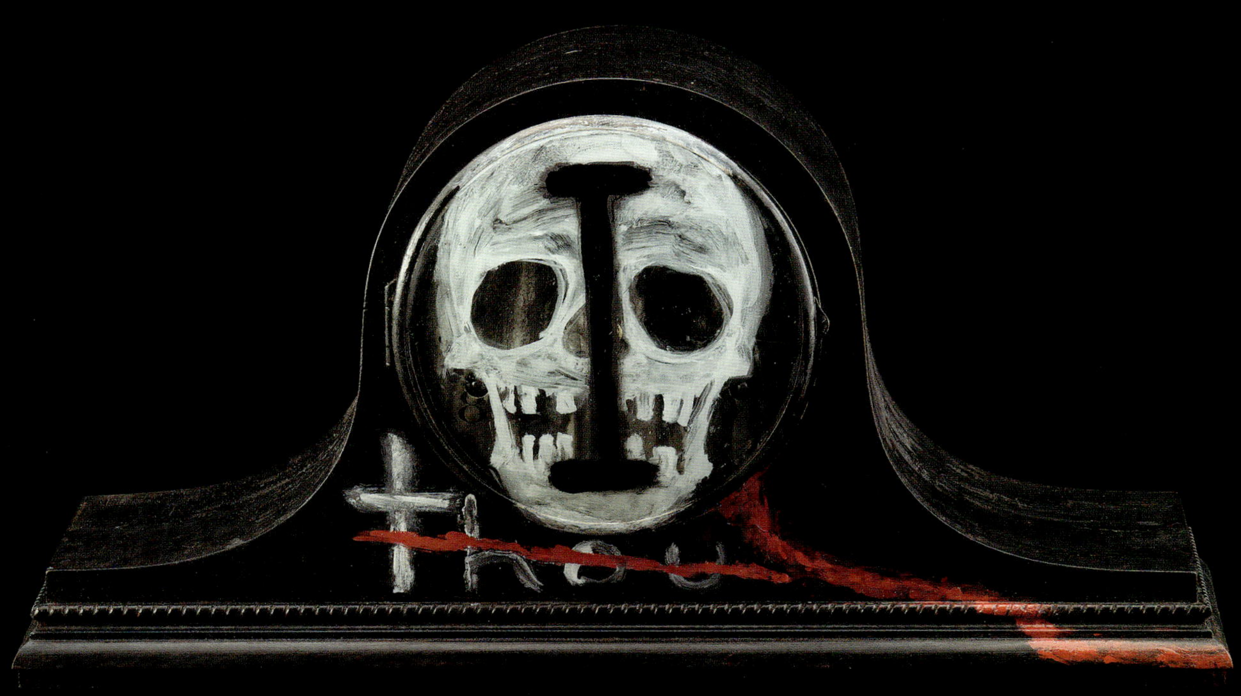

Wrong Way Time 2012–15 (details)

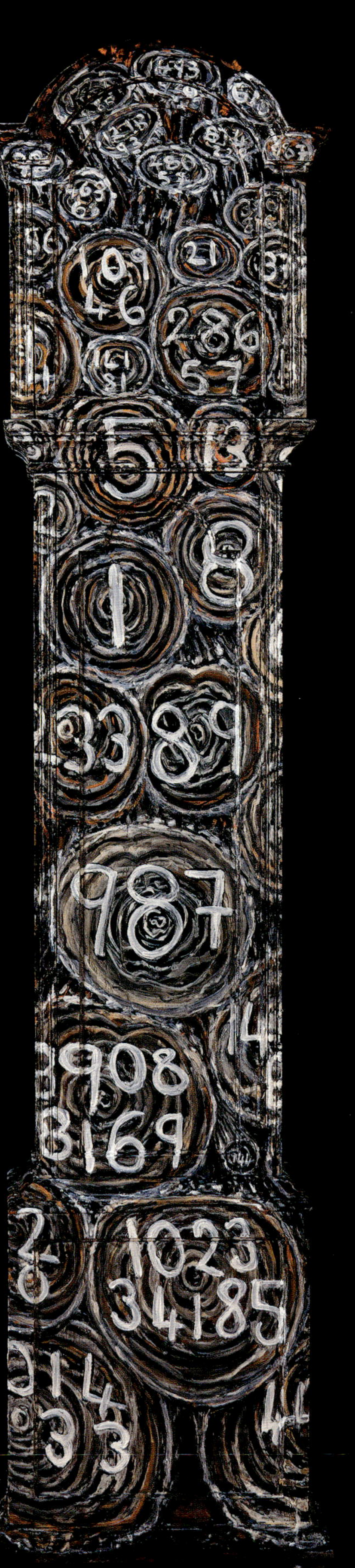

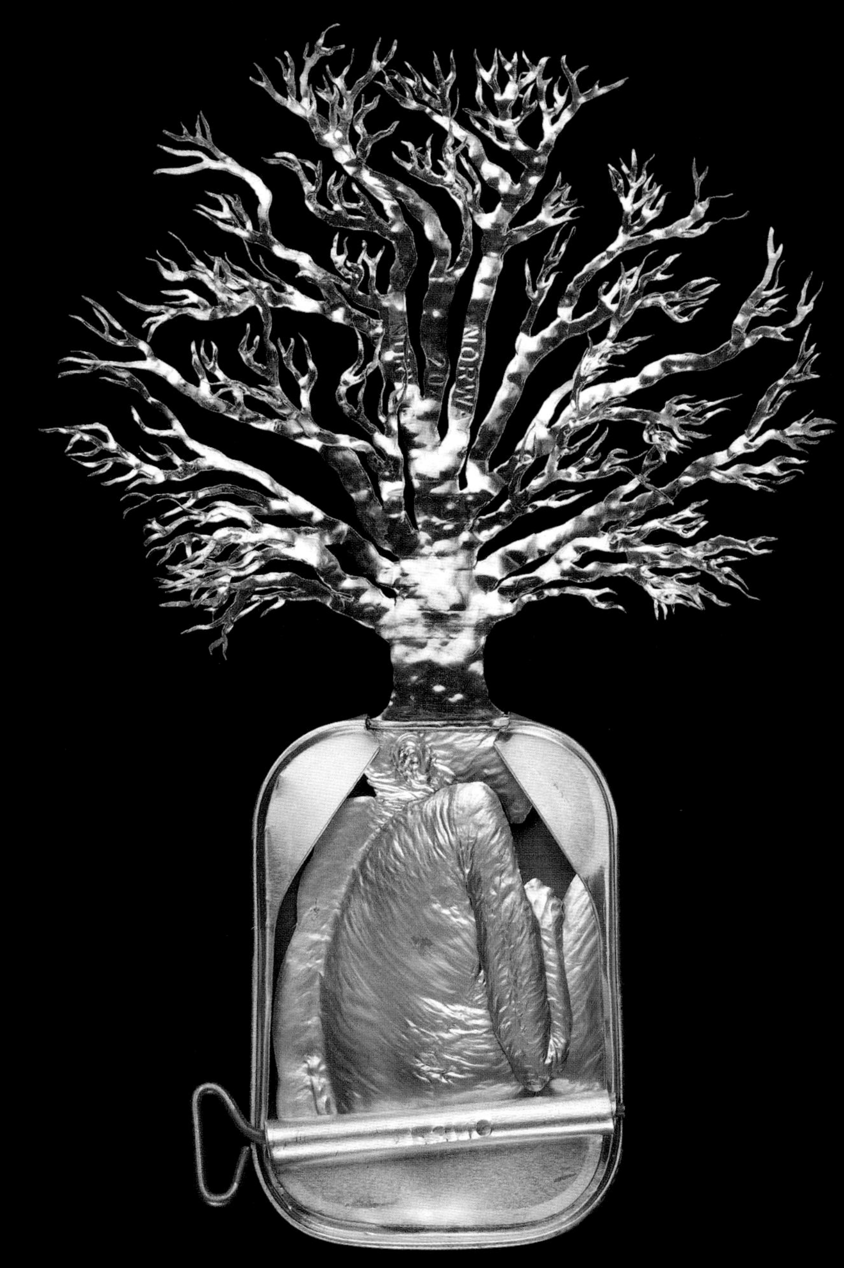

Quercus robur; English oak
from the series *Paradisus Terrestris* 1990–2005

Opposite
Wrong Way Time 2012–15 (detail)

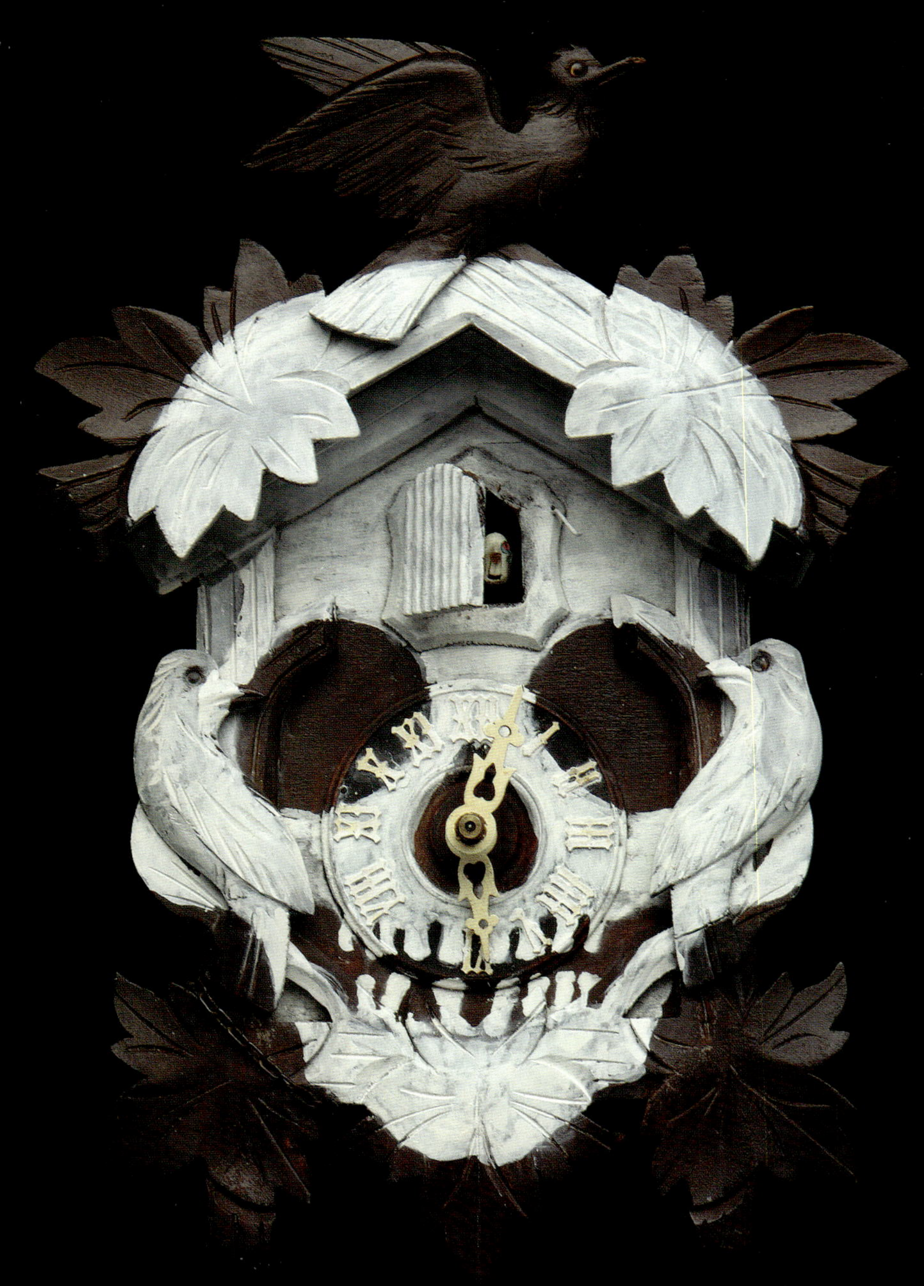

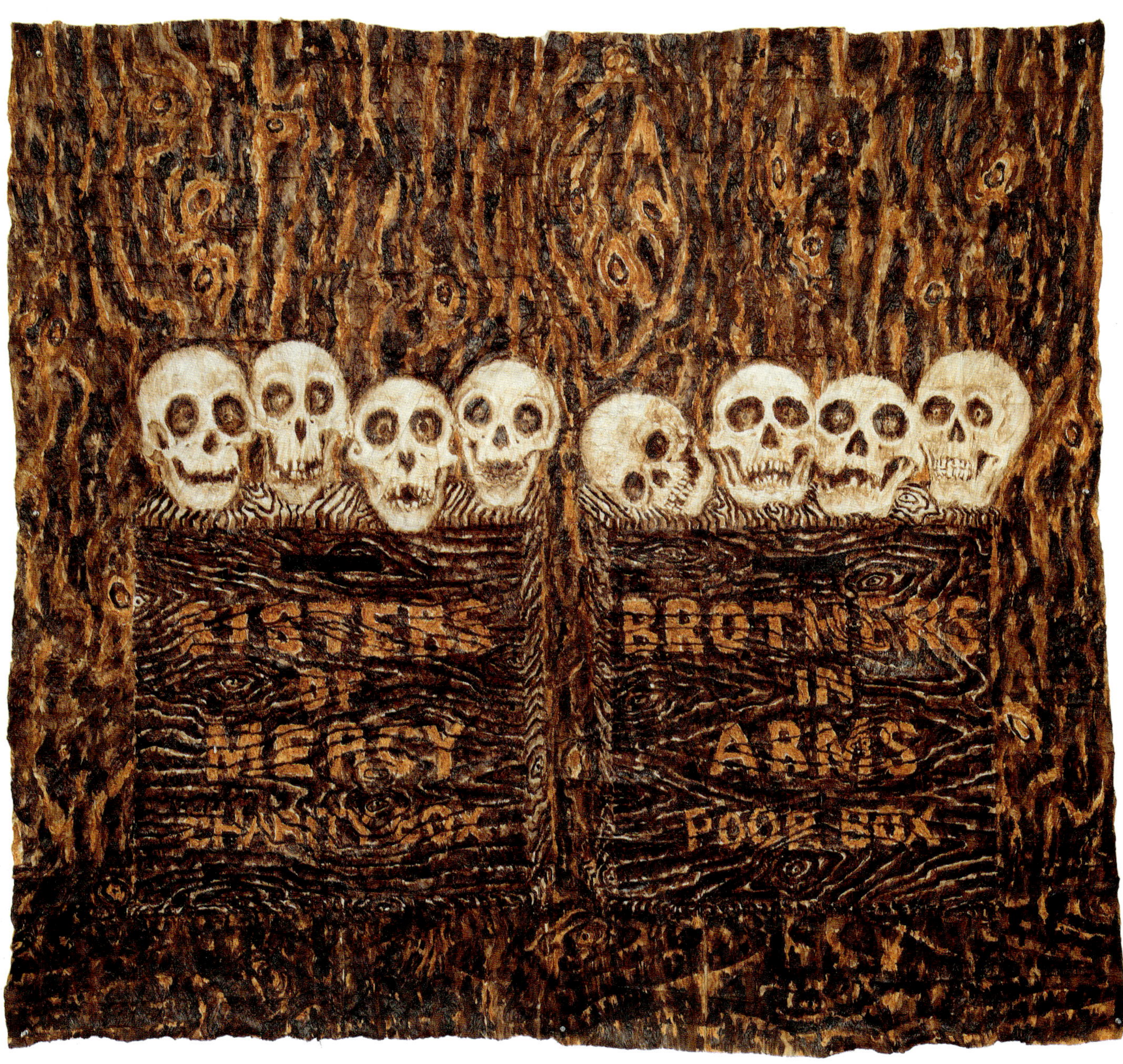

Hand Over Fist 2013
photograph: Jennifer French

Opposite
Wrong Way Time 2012–15 (detail)
photograph courtesy: Art Gallery of South Australia, Adelaide

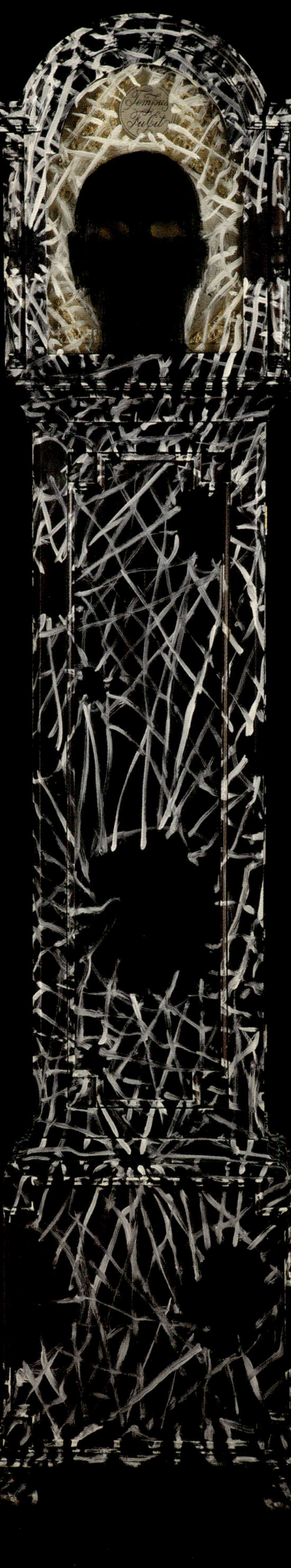
Tempus
Fugit

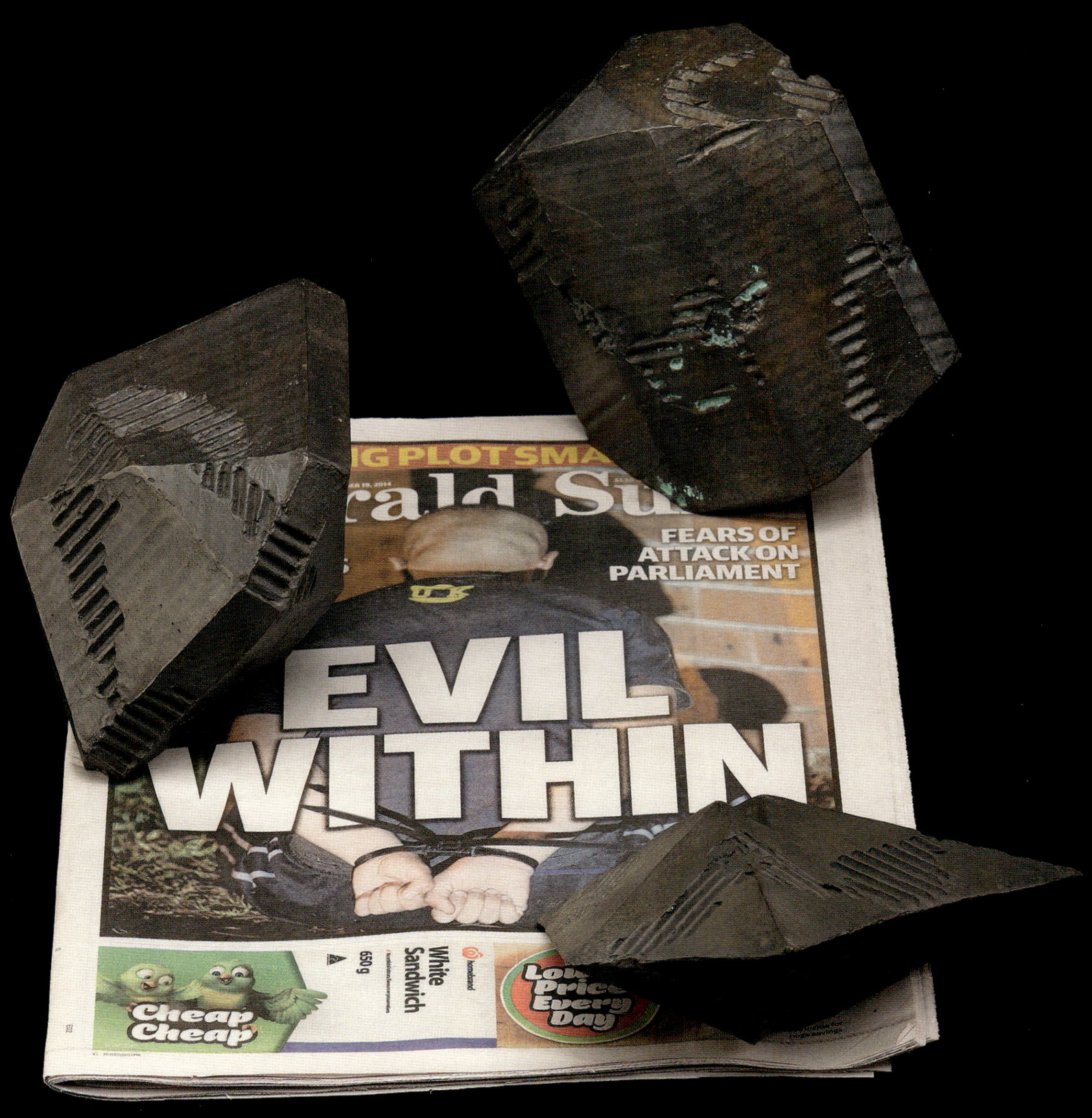

Untitled 2015

Opposite
Wrong Way Time 2012–15 (detail)

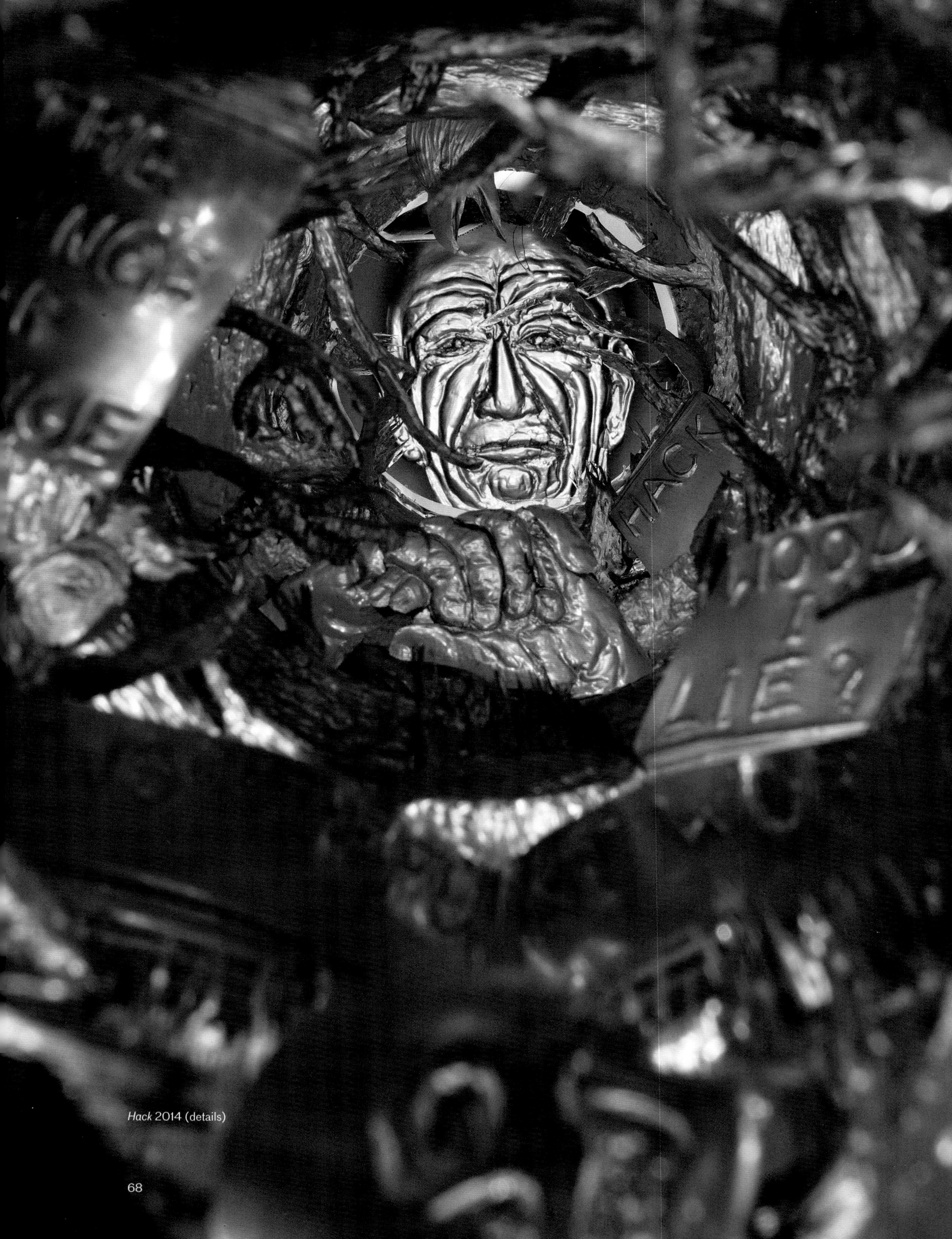

Hack 2014 (details)

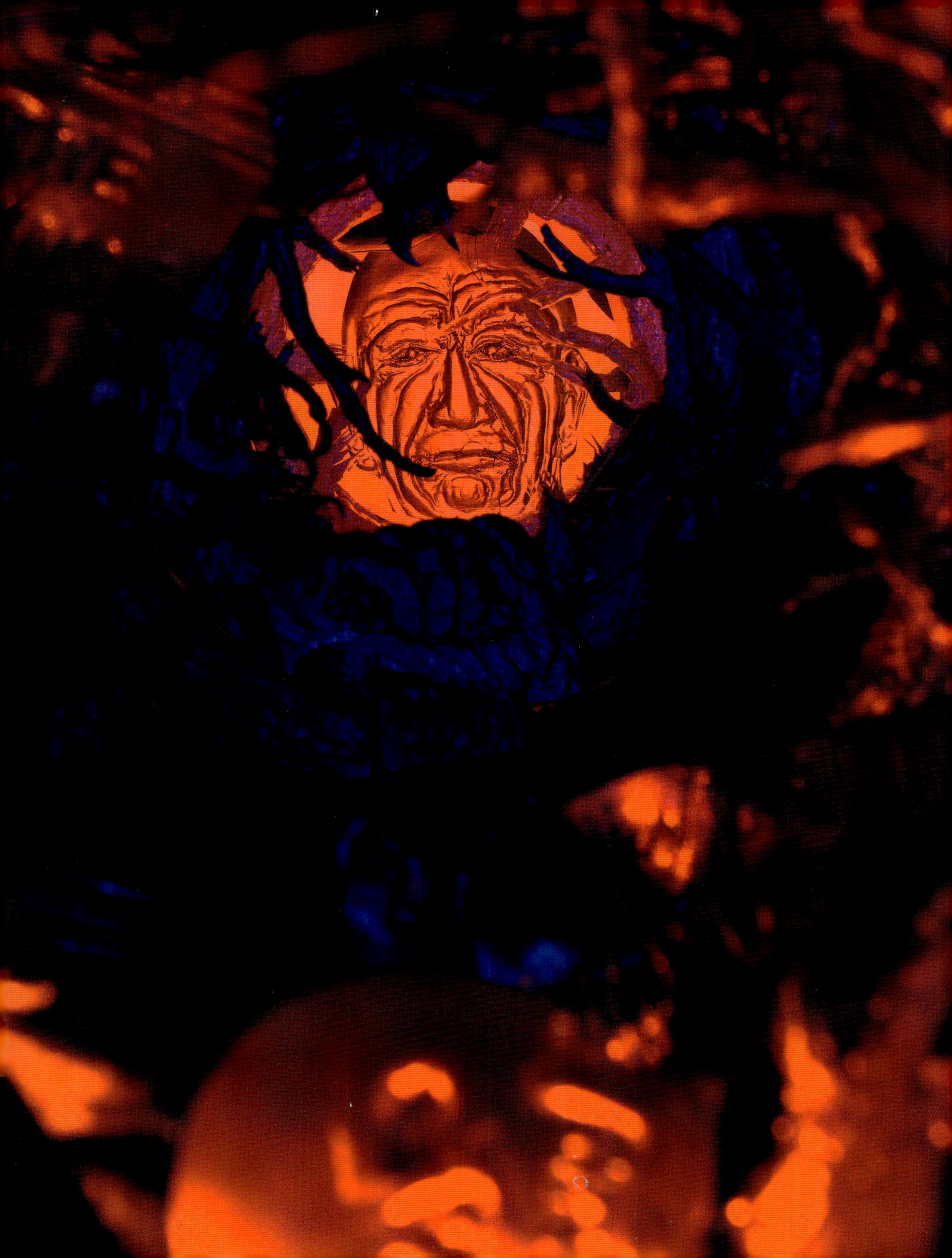

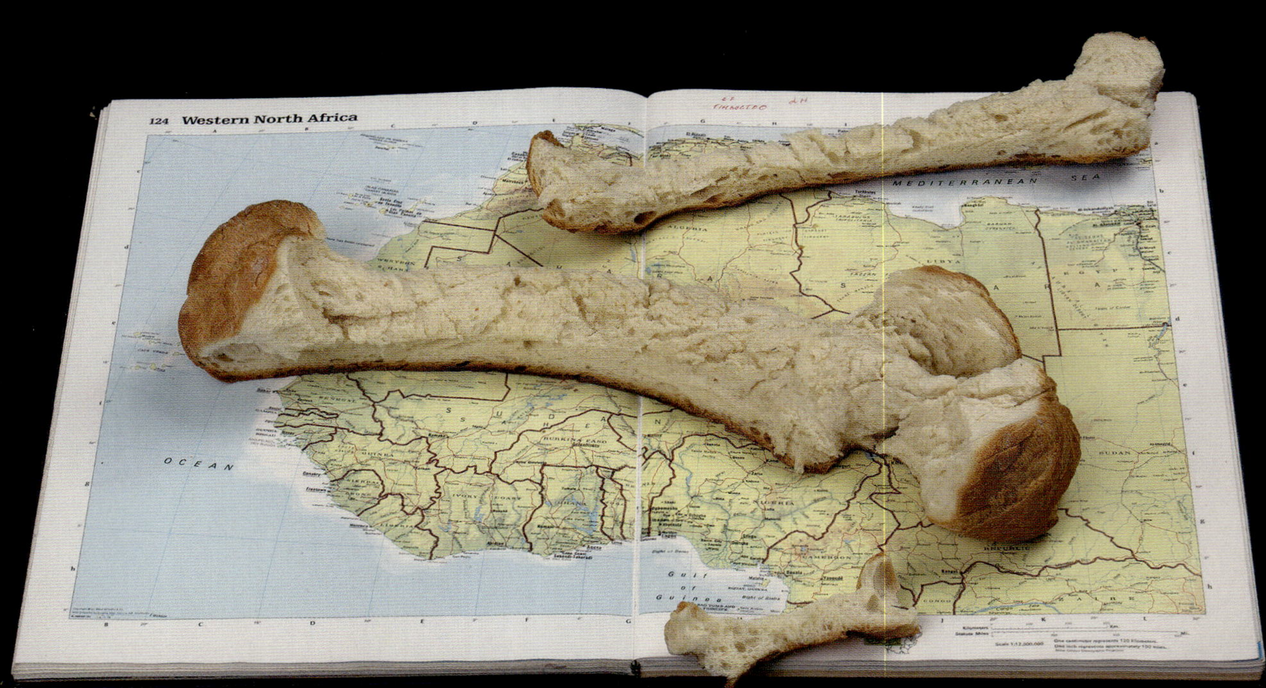

Untitled 2015 (details)

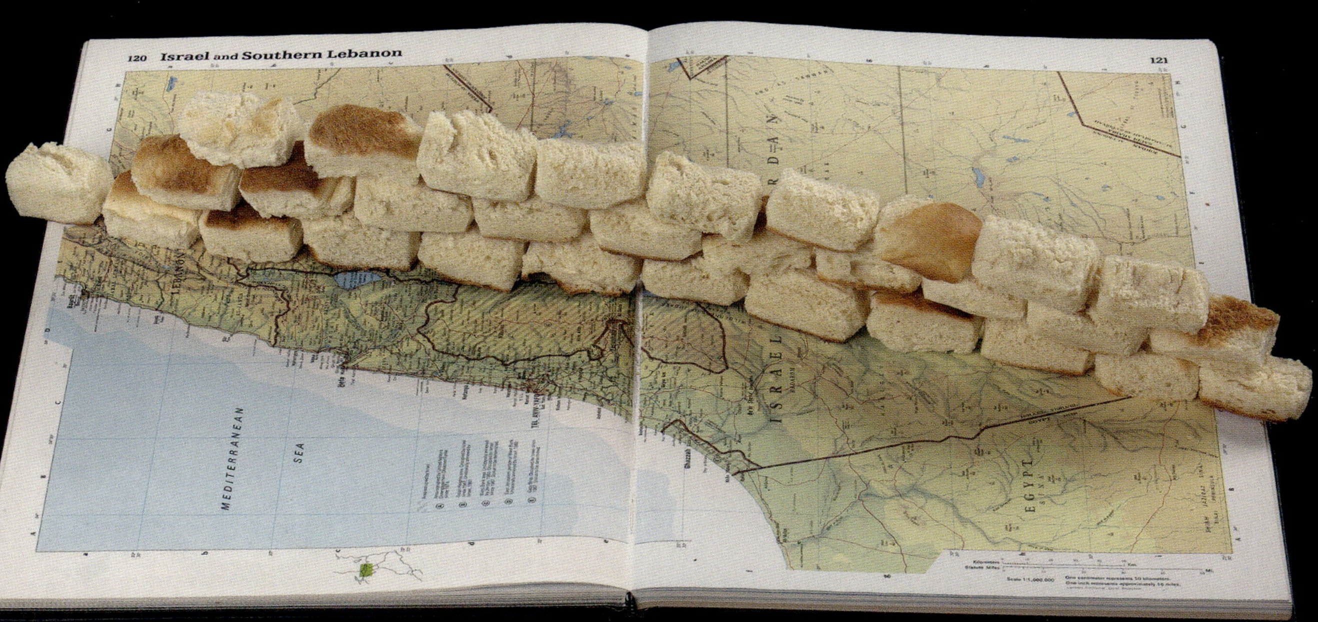
120 Israel and Southern Lebanon
121
MEDITERRANEAN
SEA
ISRAEL
EGYPT

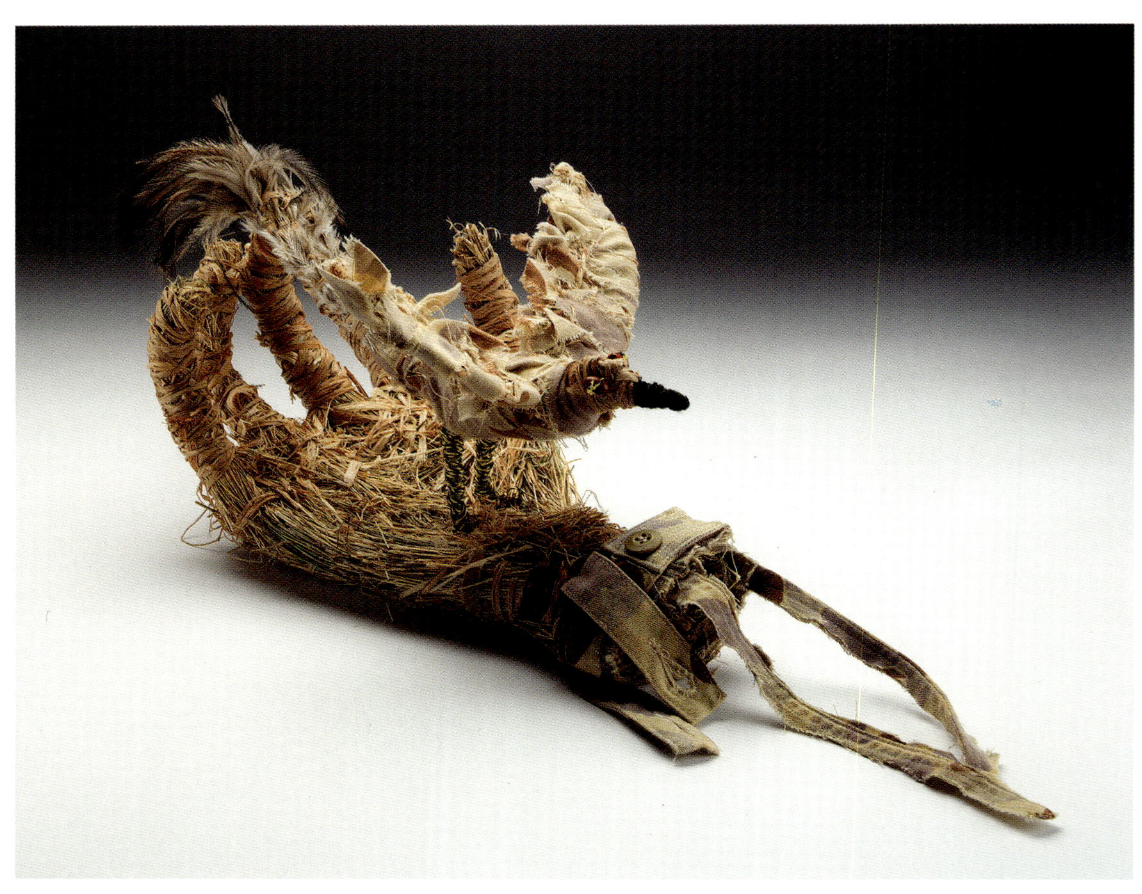

Willy Wagtail (Rhipidura leucophrys) / *Tjintir-tjintirpa maṟangka*
from *Kuka Irititja (Animals from Another Time)* 2014

Opposite
Wrong Way Time 2012–15 (detail)

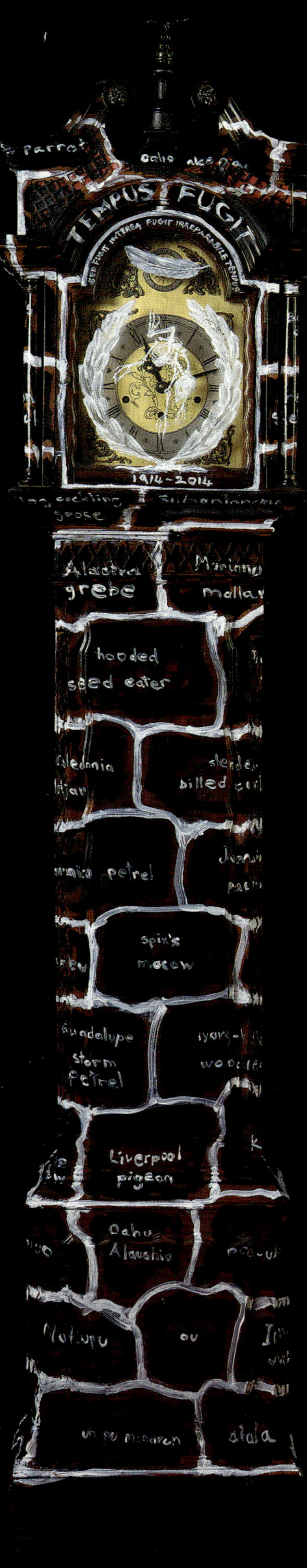

parrot
oahu akepa
TEMPUS FUGIT
SED FUGIT INTEREA FUGIT IRREPARABILE TEMPUS
1914–2014
cackling goose
Alaotra grebe
Mariana mallard
hooded seed eater
slender billed
petrel
spix's macaw
Guadalupe storm petrel
Liverpool pigeon
Oahu Alauahio
ou
alala

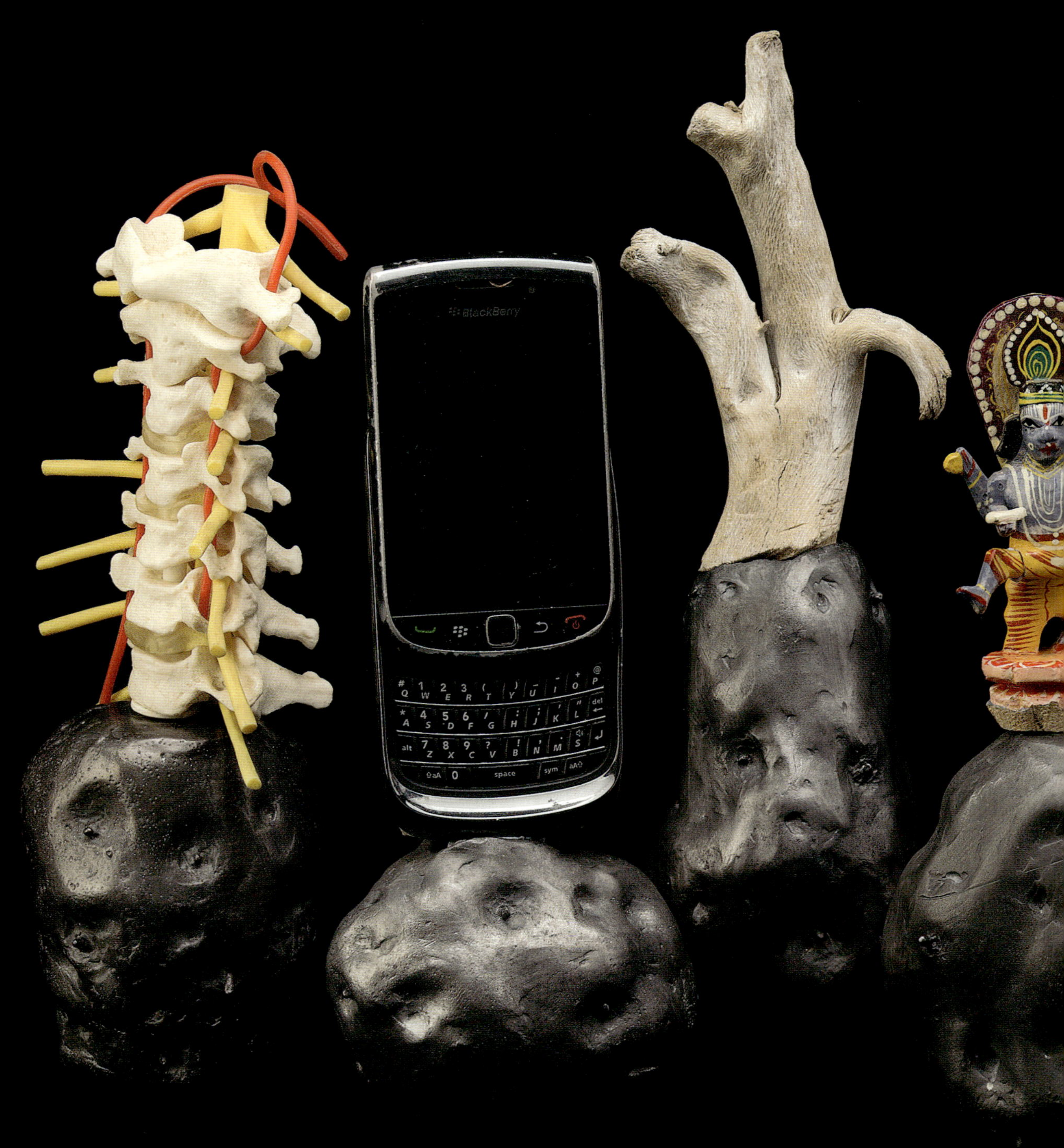

Untitled 2014

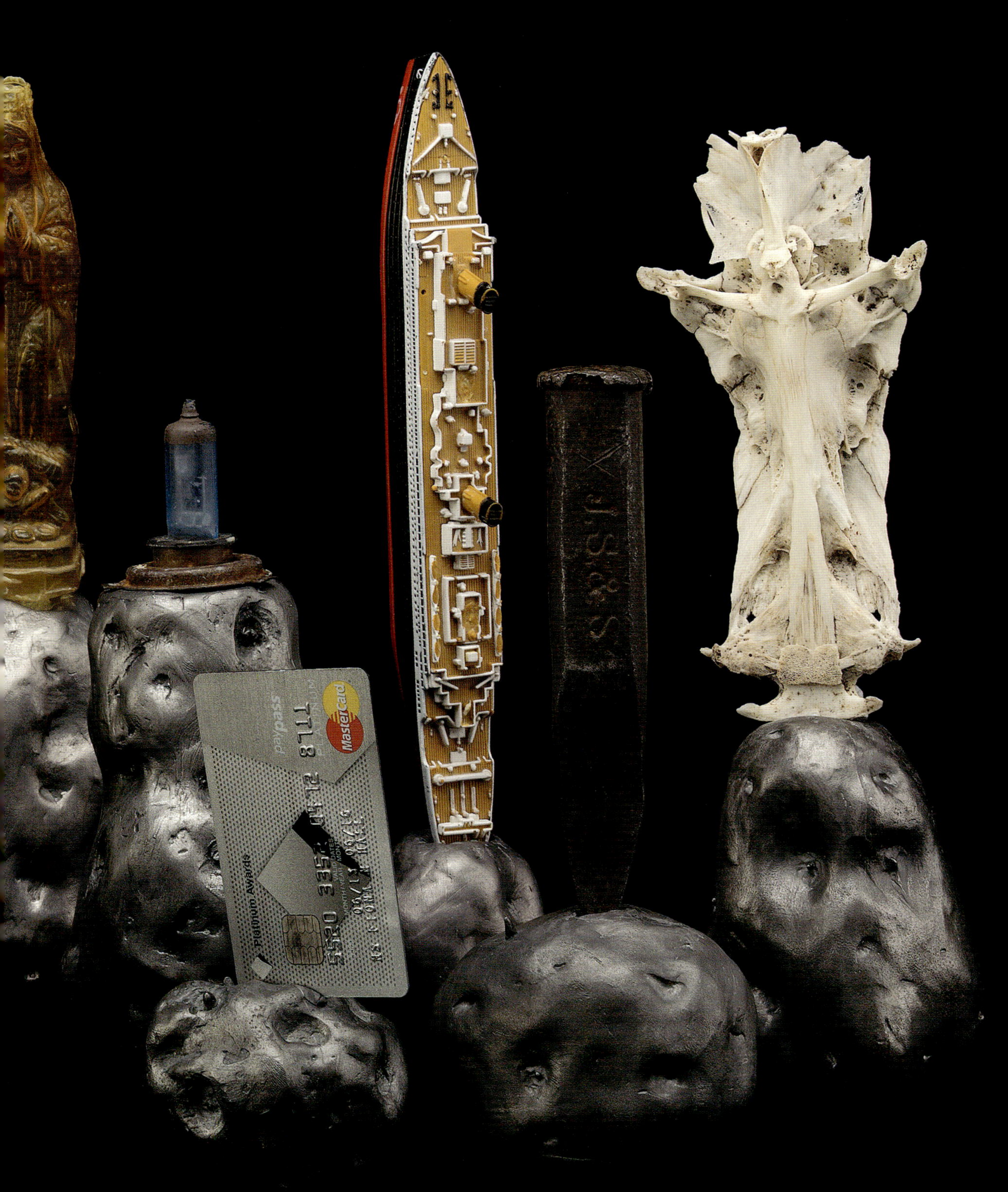
MasterCard

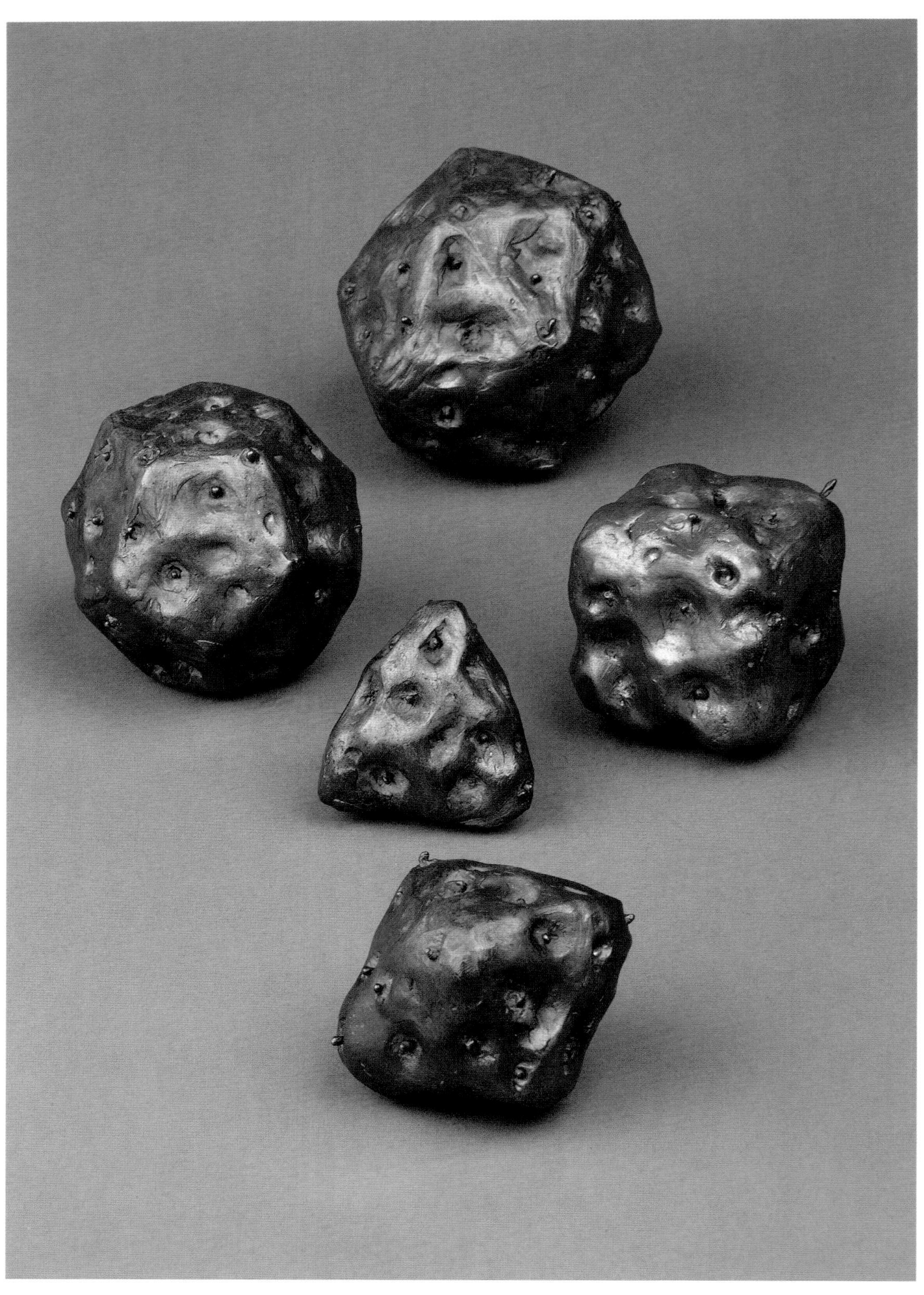

Platonic Underground 2014

Opposite
Holdfast (Macrocystis angustifolia; giant kelp*)* 2007

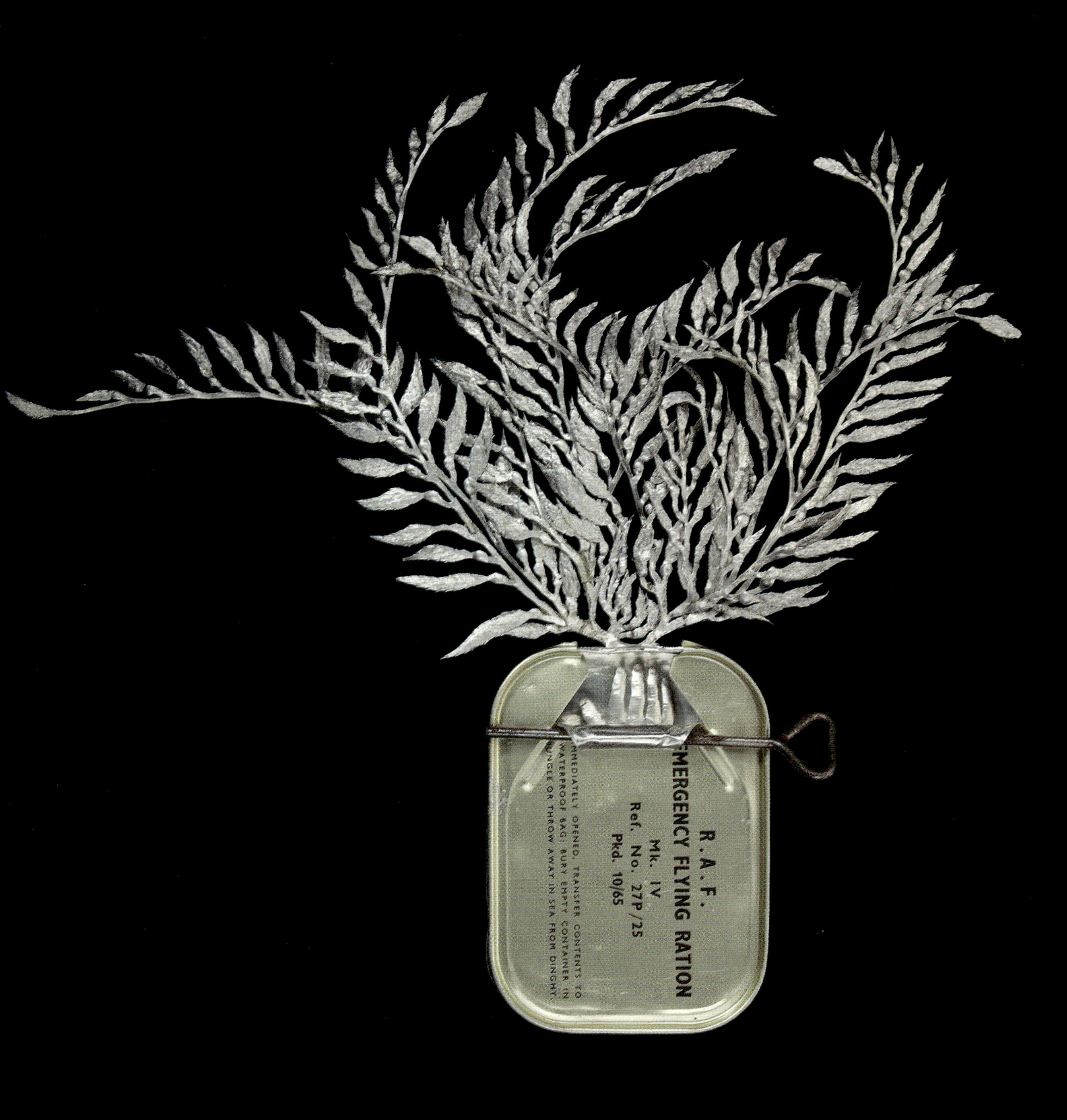
R.A.F.
EMERGENCY FLYING RATION
Mk. IV
Ref. No. 27P/25
Pkd. 10/65
IMMEDIATELY OPENED, TRANSFER CONTENTS TO
WATERPROOF BAG; BURY EMPTY CONTAINER IN
JUNGLE OR THROW AWAY IN SEA FROM DINGHY.

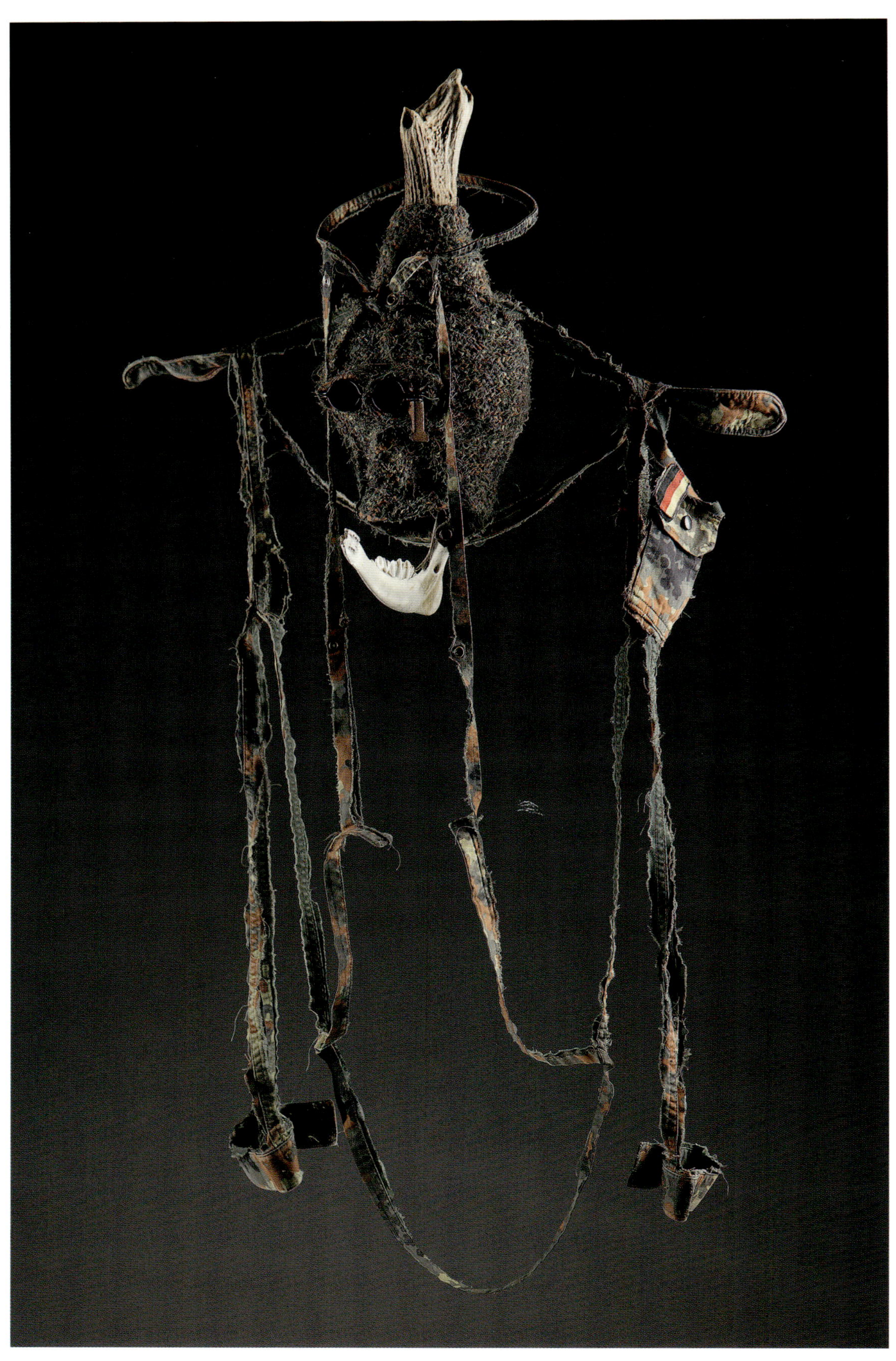

All the King's Men 2014–15 (details)

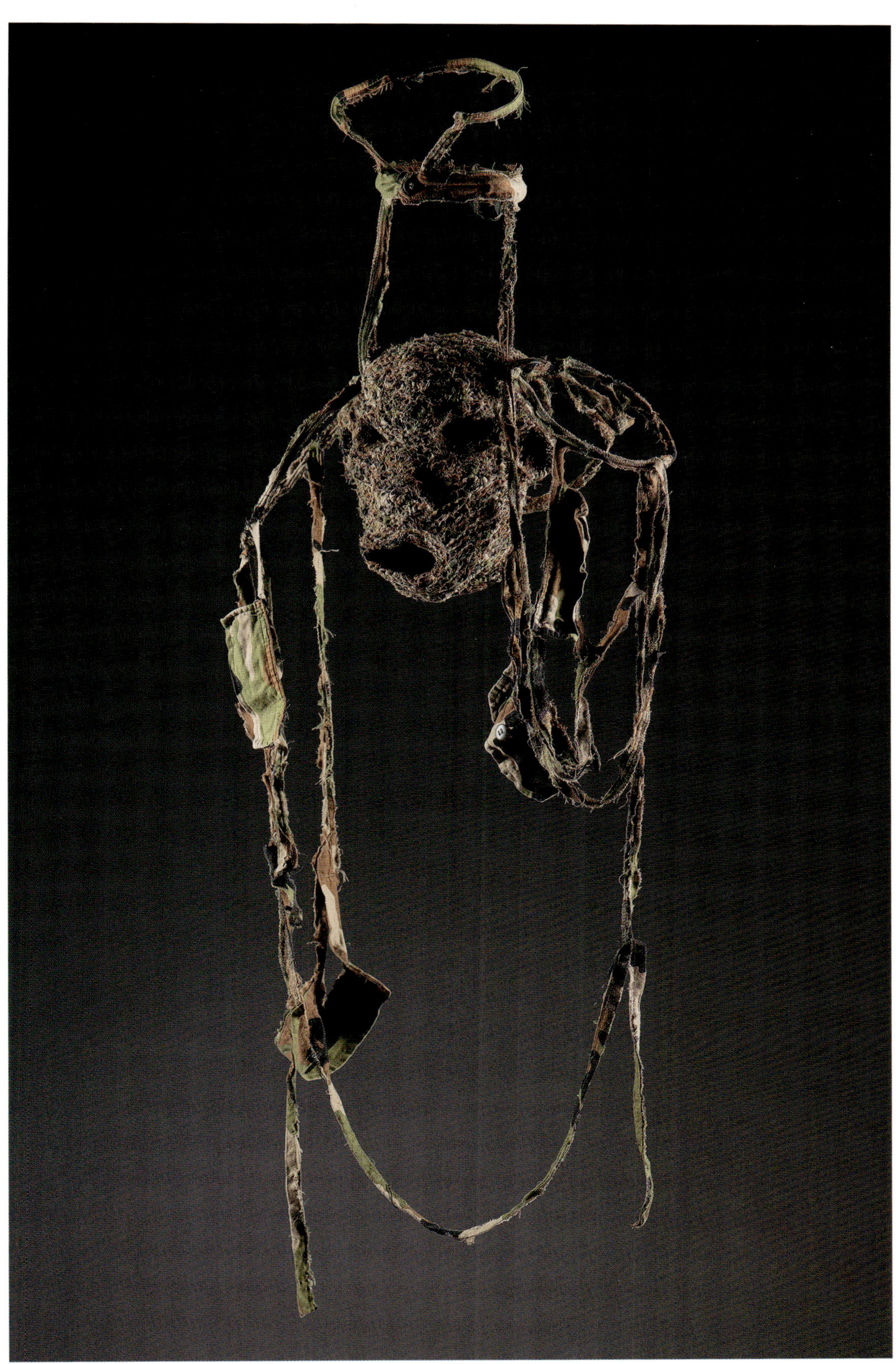

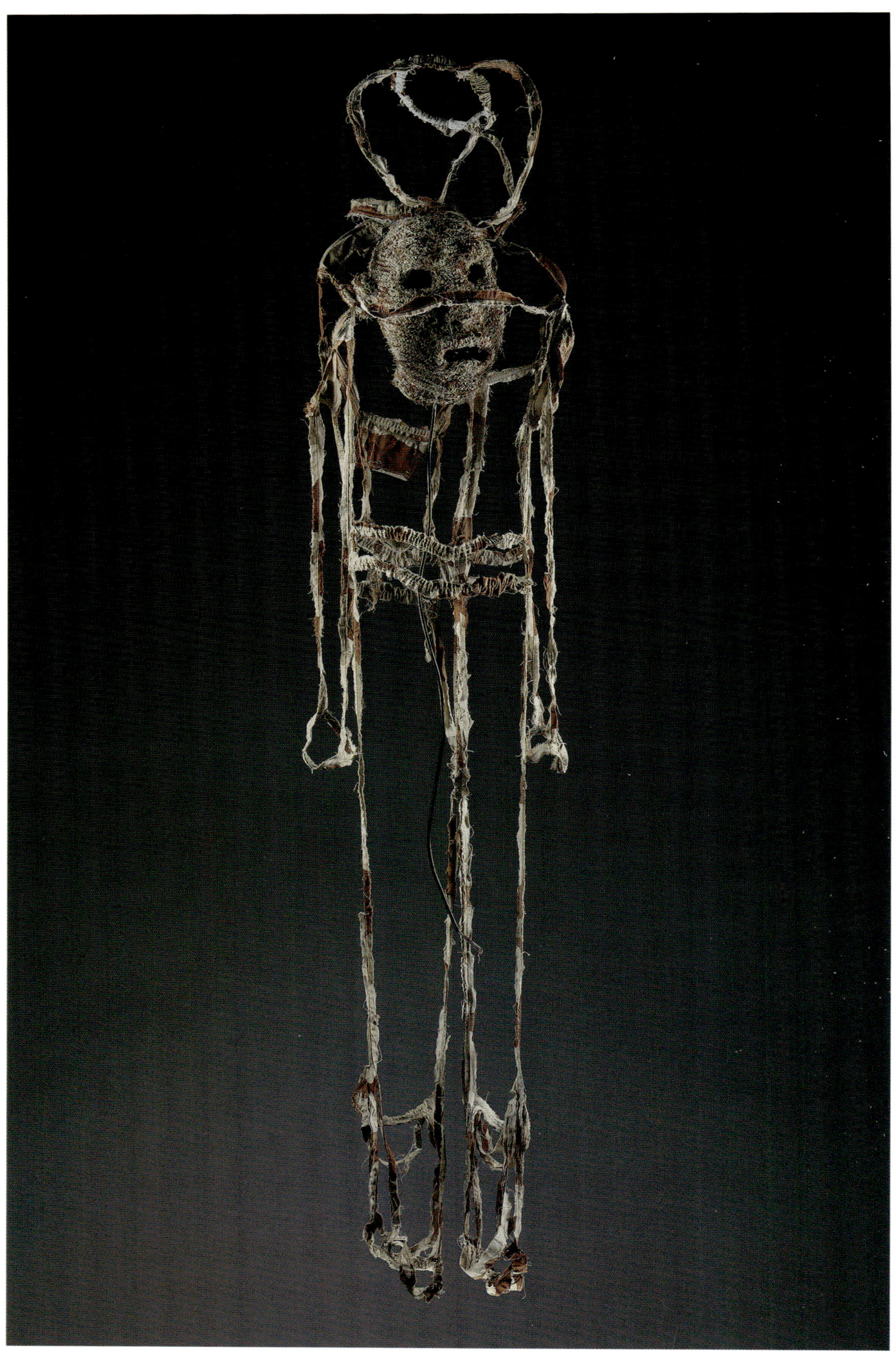

All the King's Men 2014–15 (details)

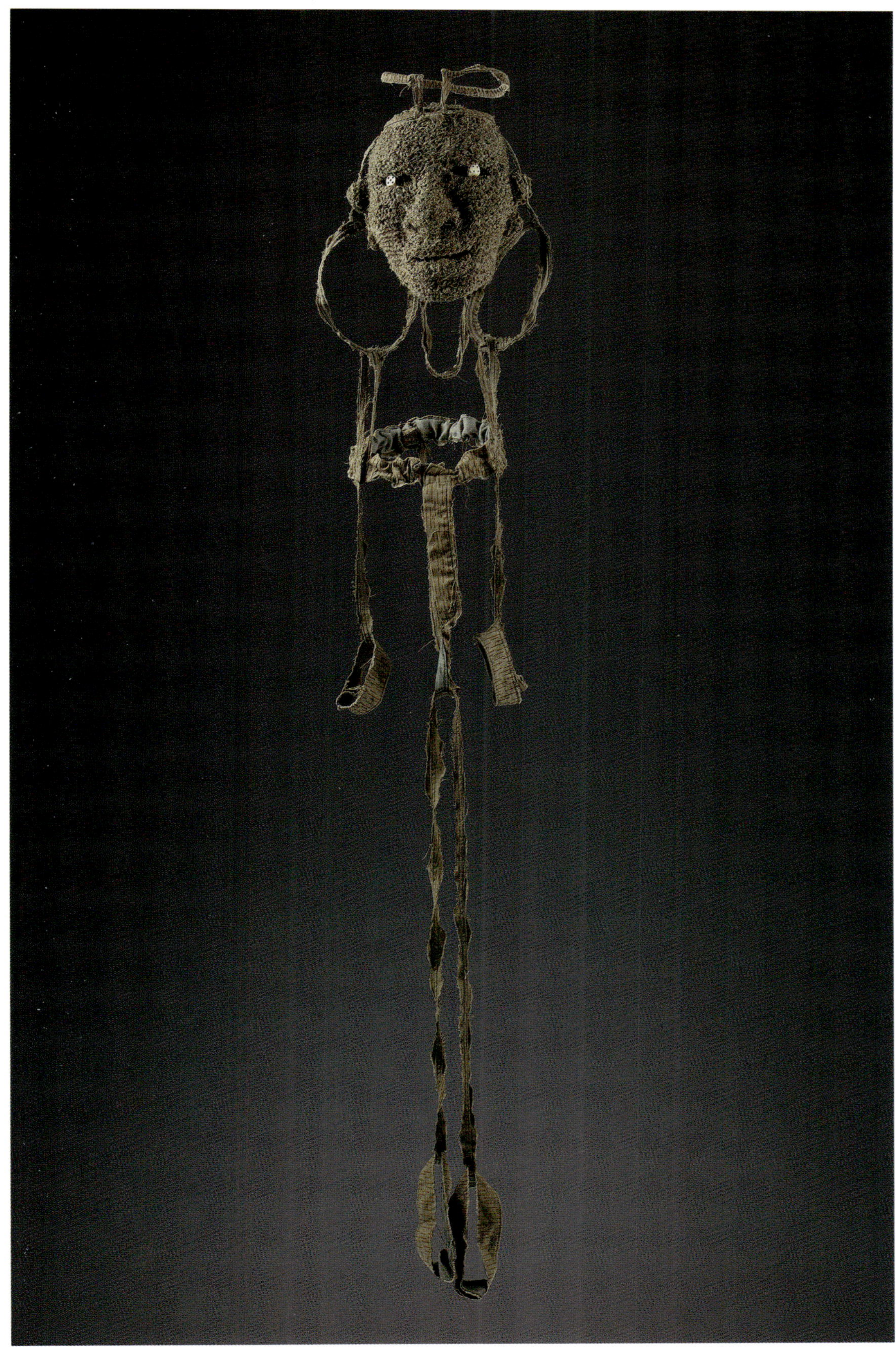

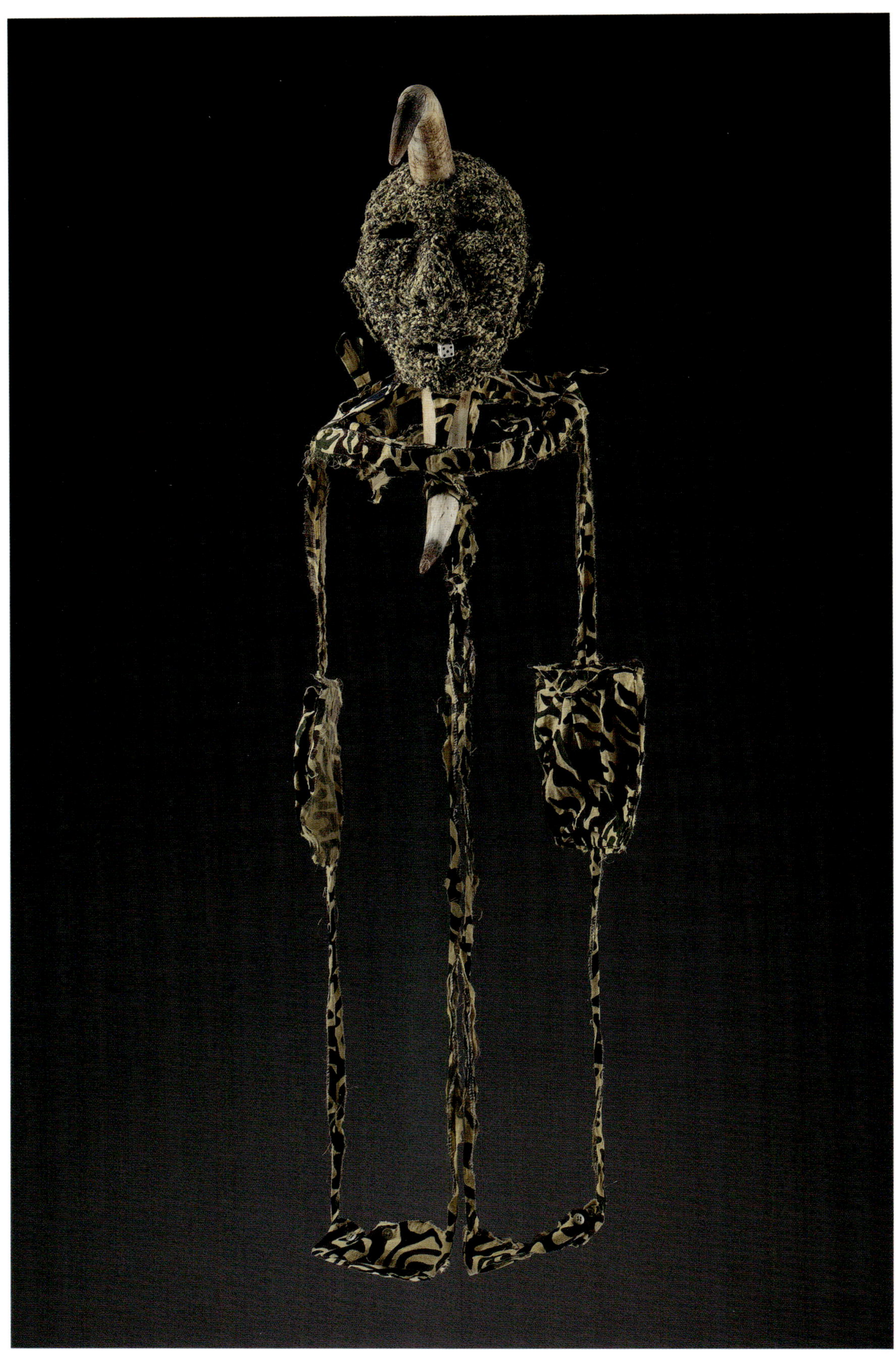

All the King's Men 2014–15 (detail)

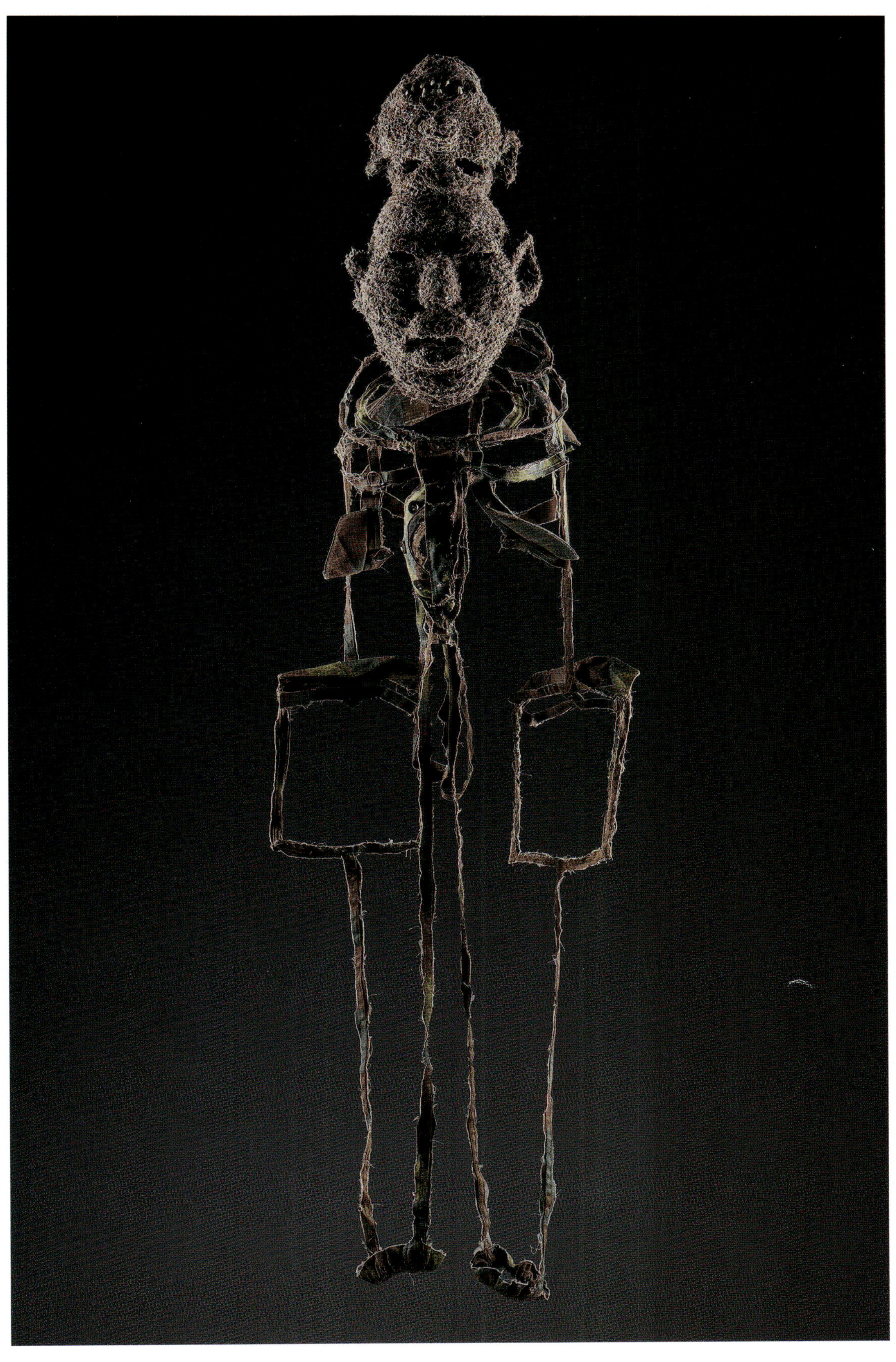

All the King's Men 2014–15 (detail)

Following pages
All the King's Men 2014 (details)

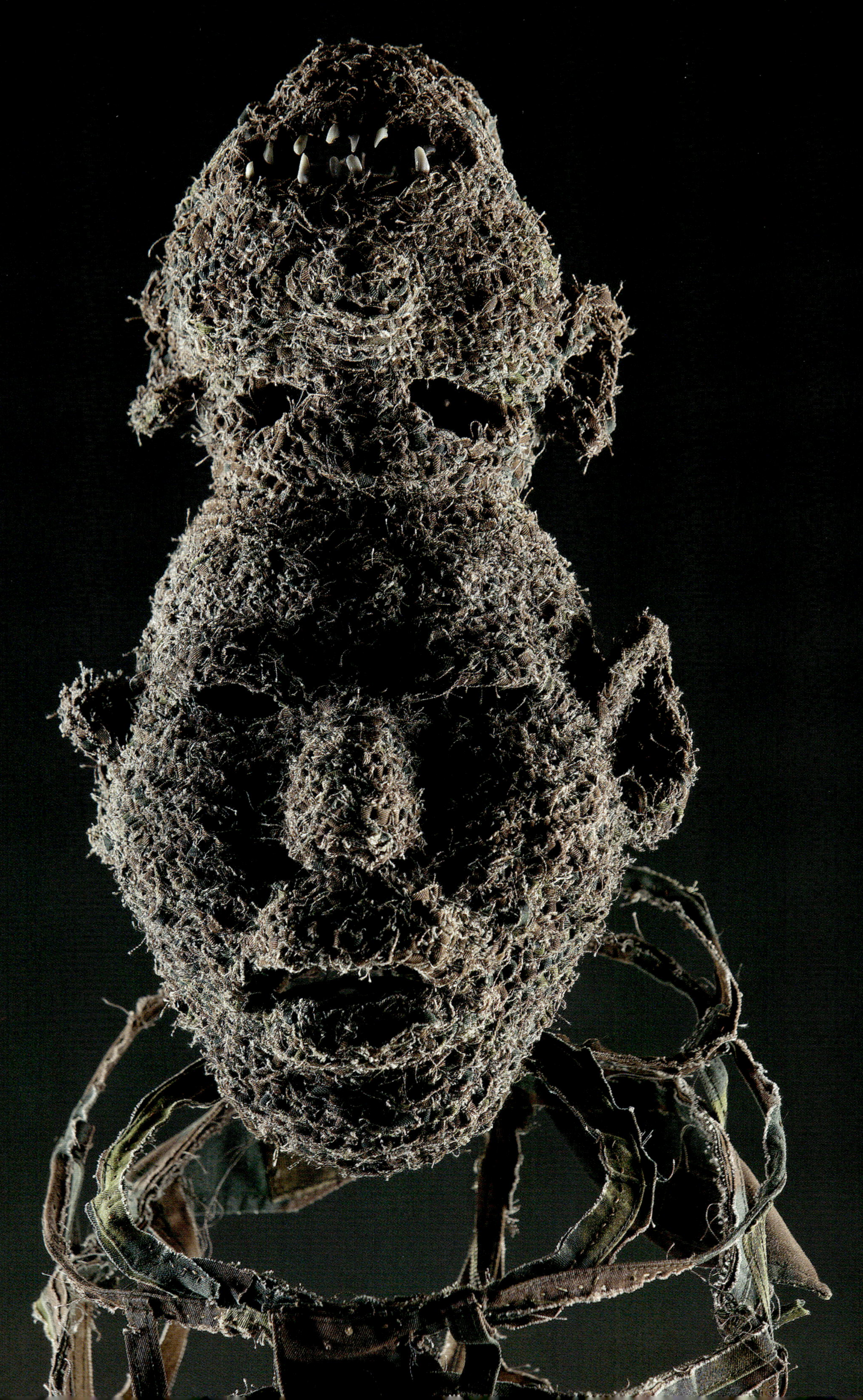

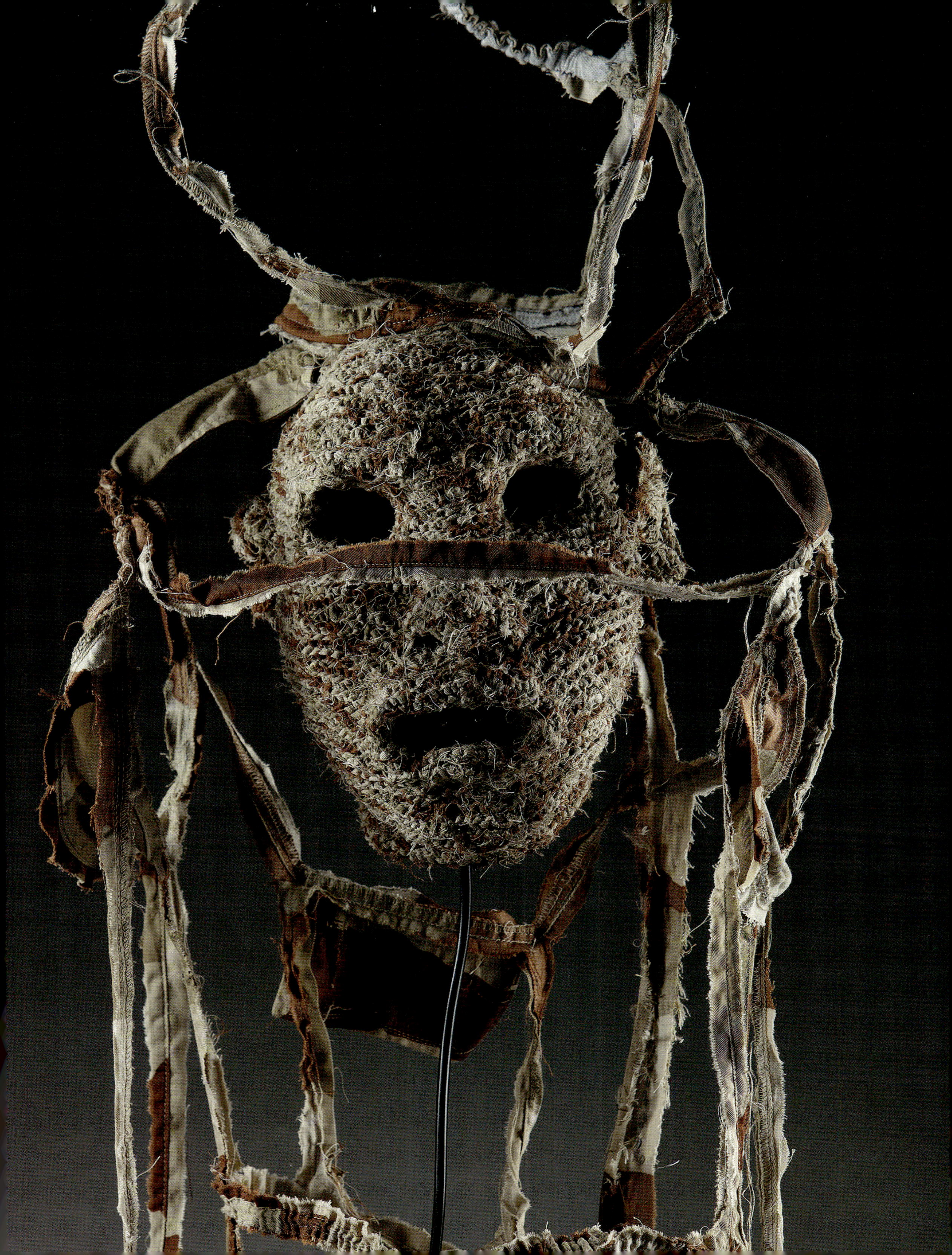

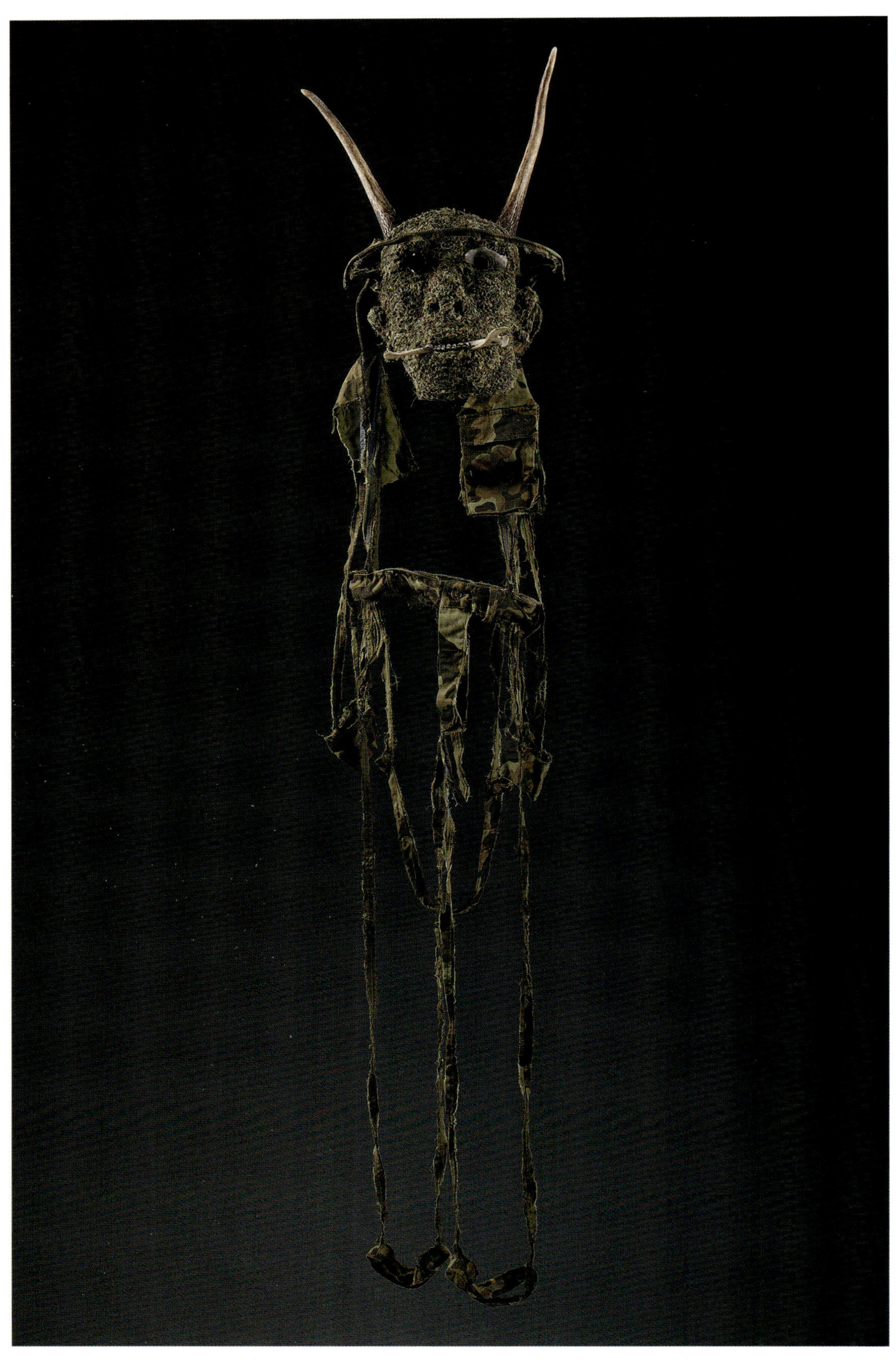

All the King's Men 2014–15 (details)

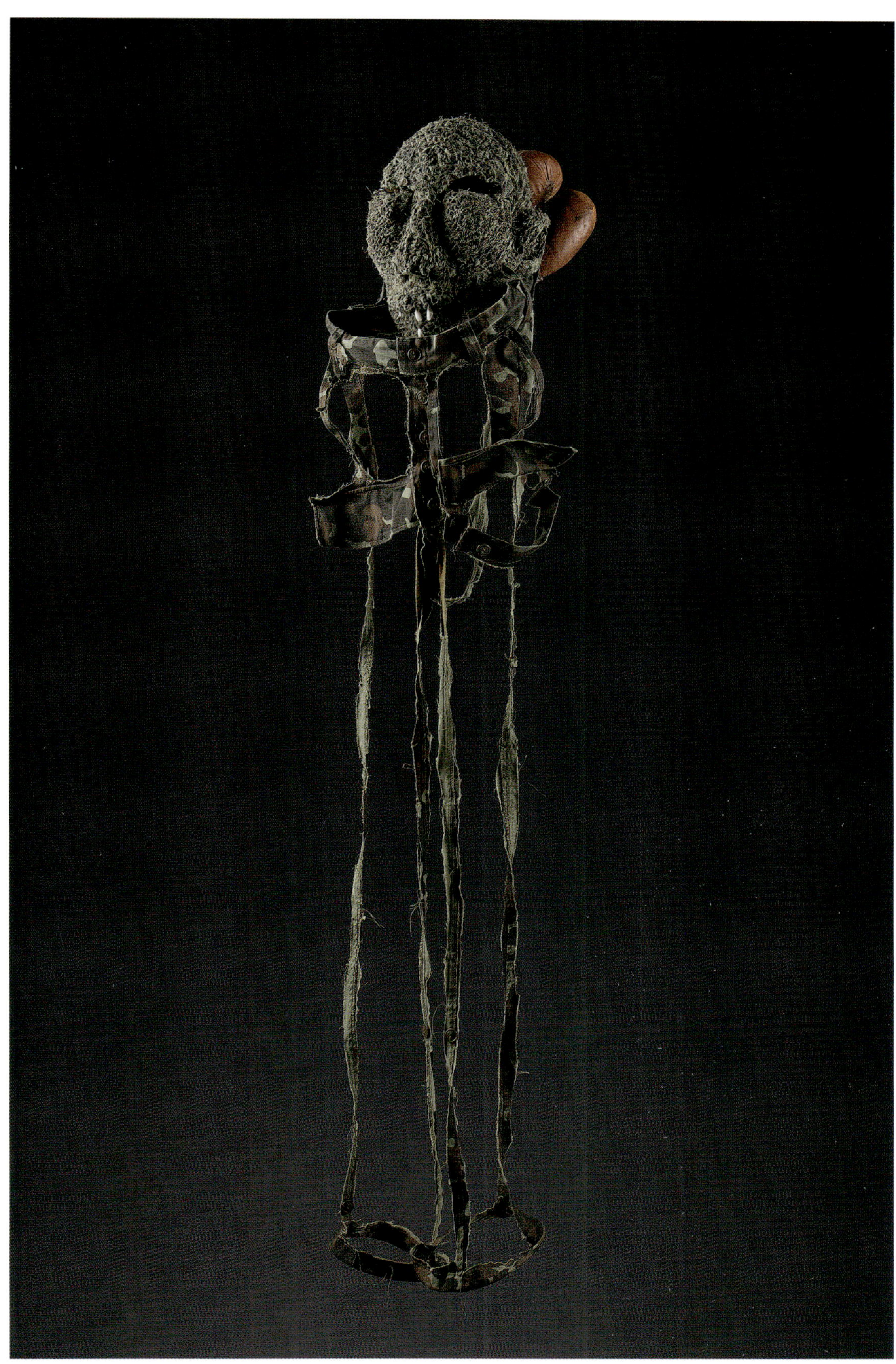

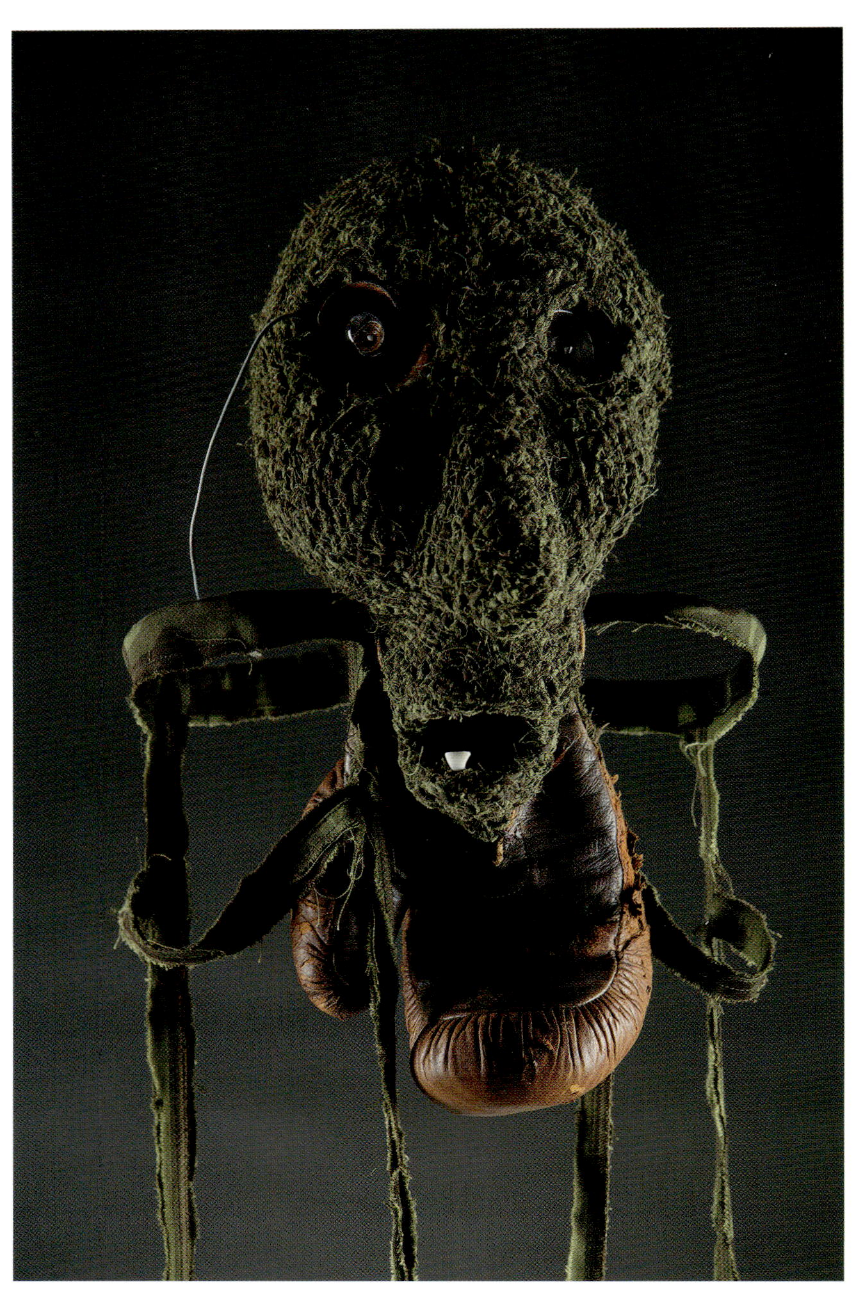

All the King's Men 2014–15 (detail)

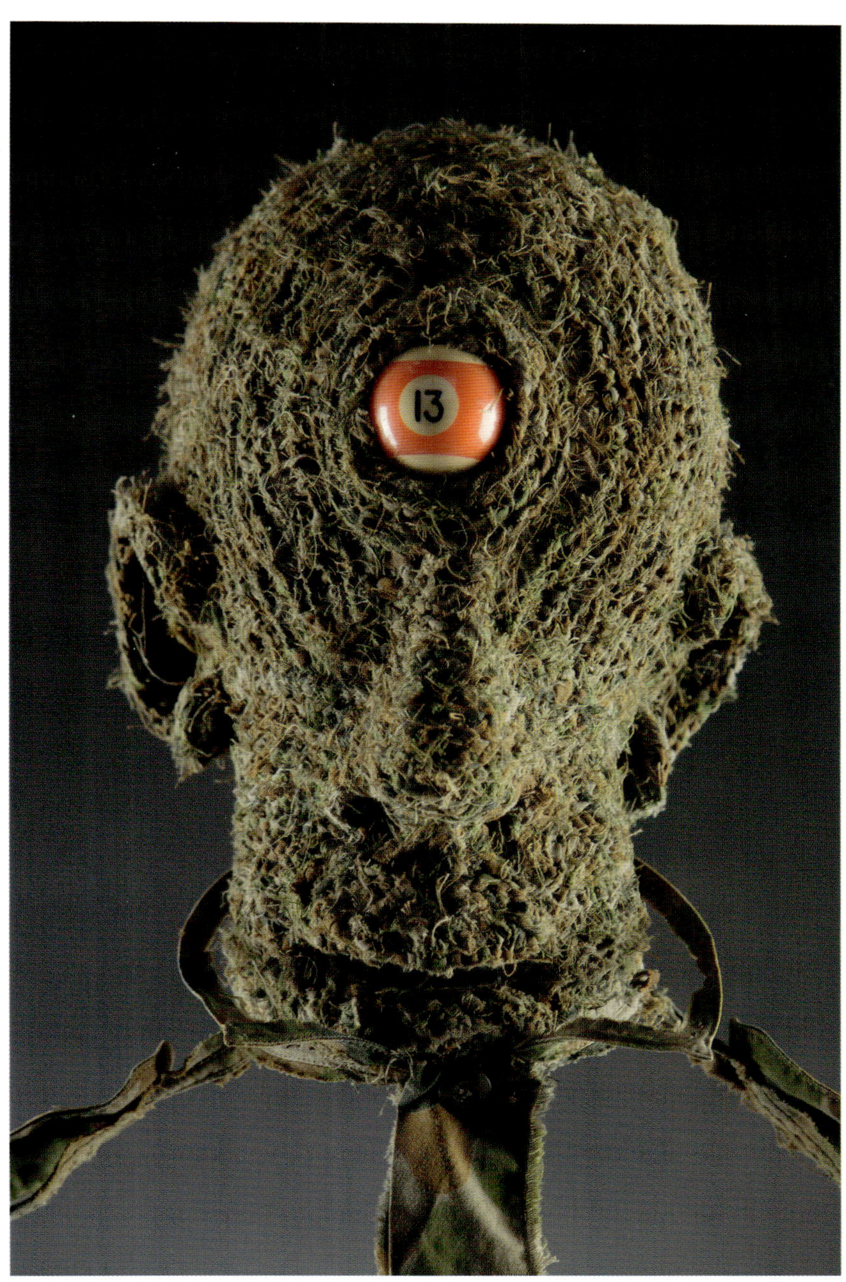

All the King's Men 2014–15 (detail)

Following page
All the King's Men 2014 (detail)

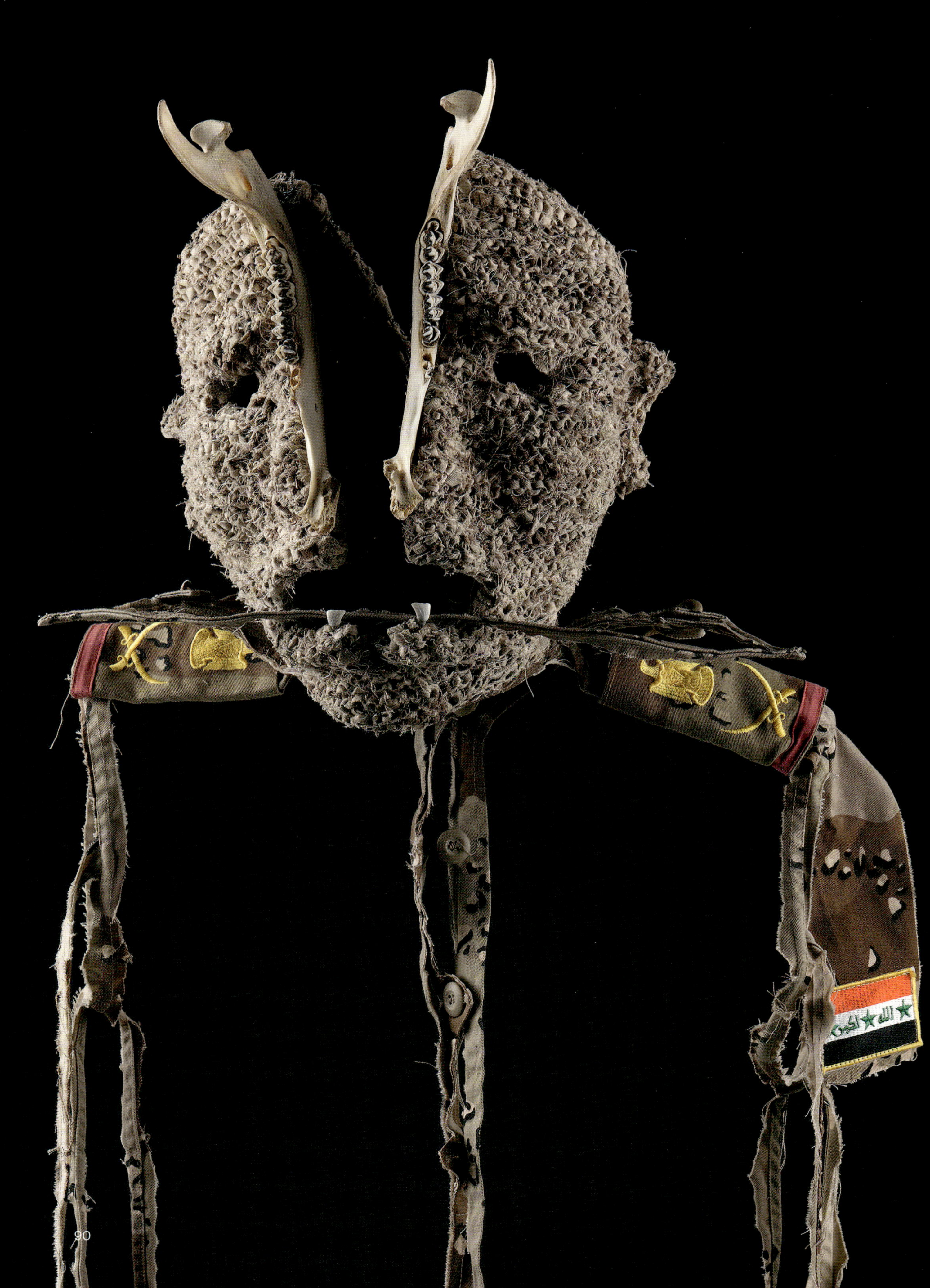

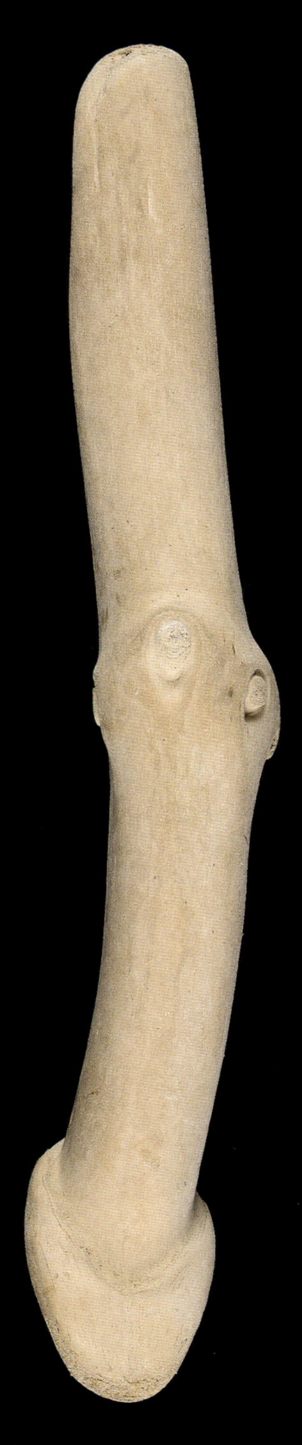

Above and following pages
Manihuri (Travellers) 2014-

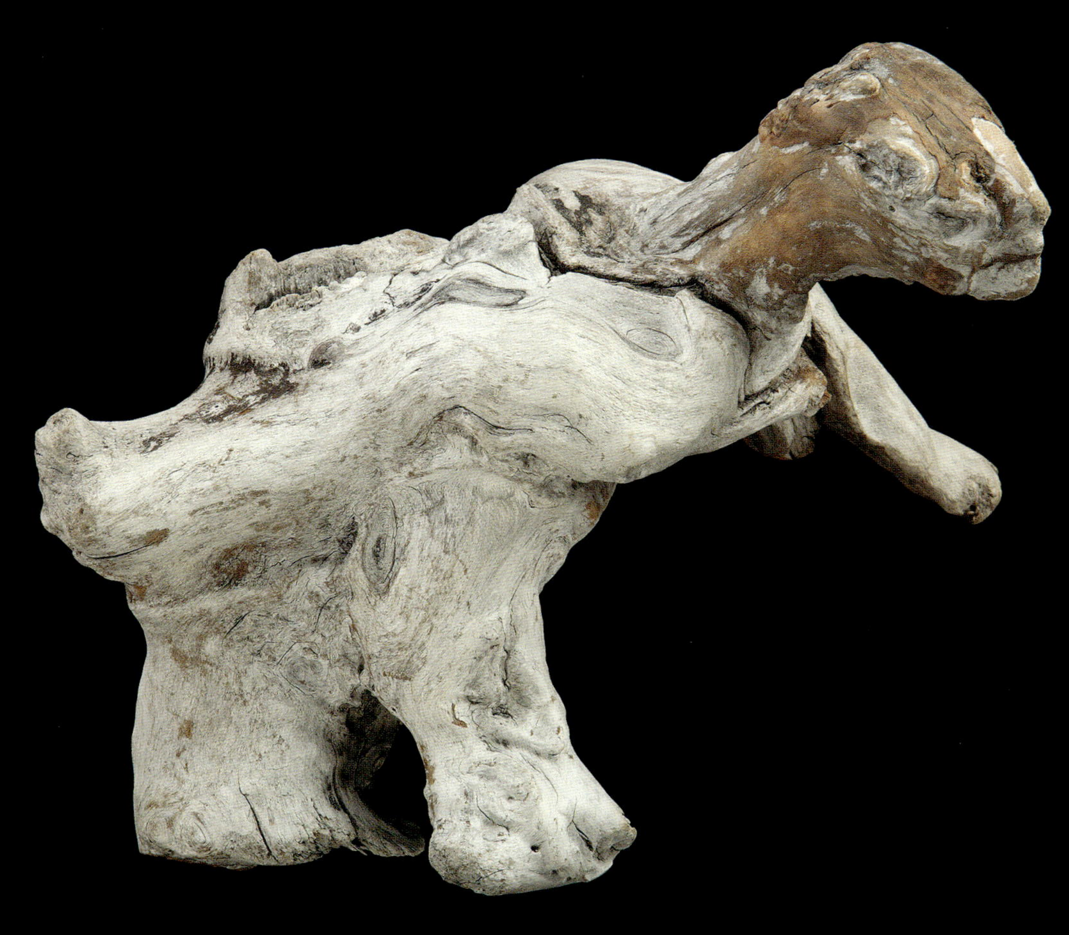

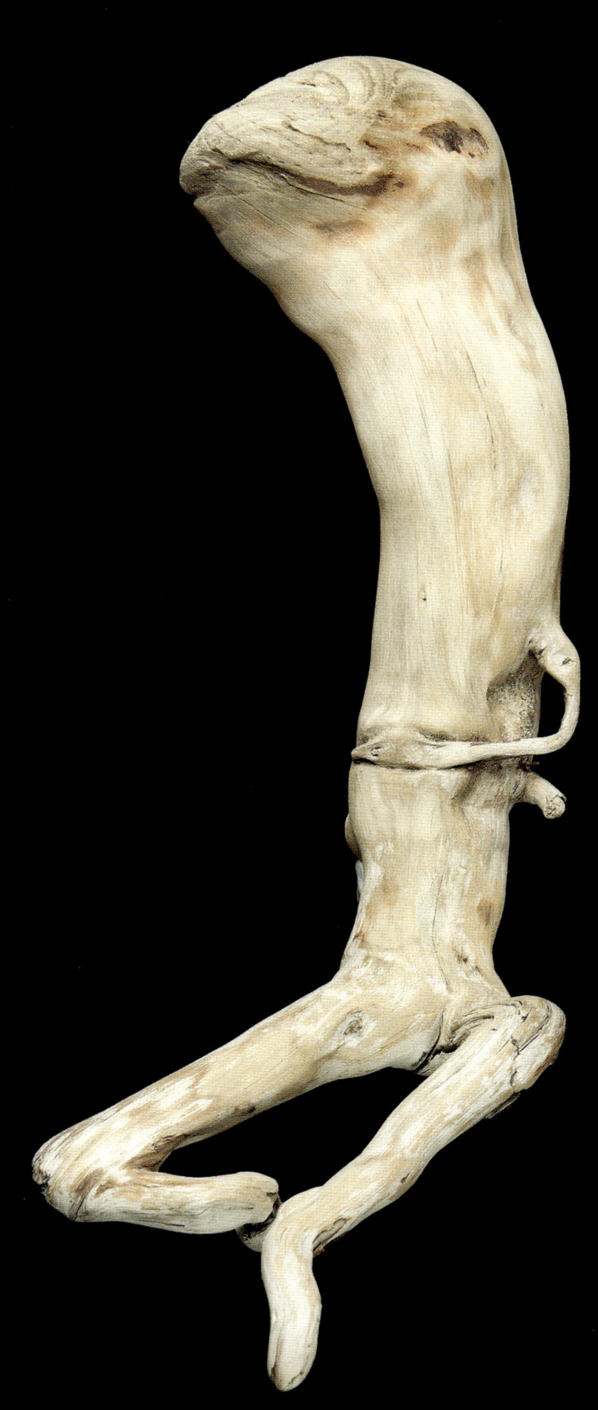

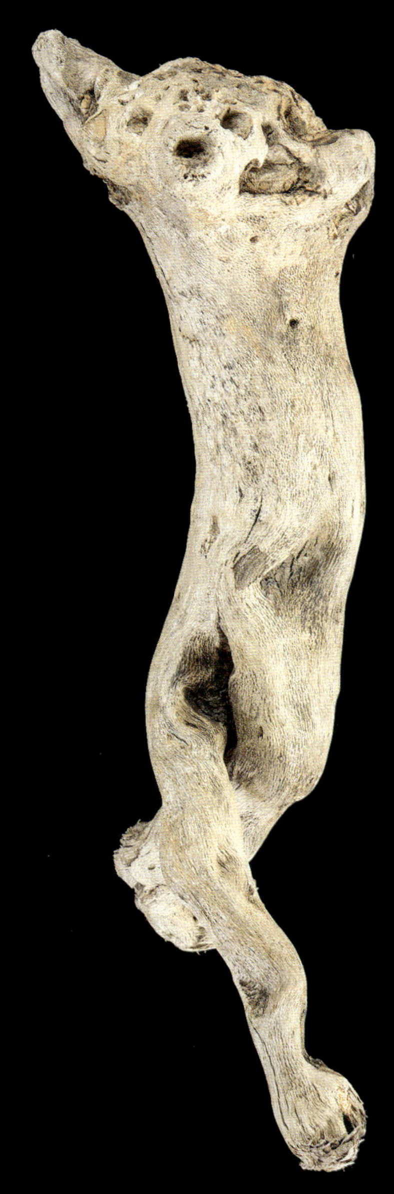

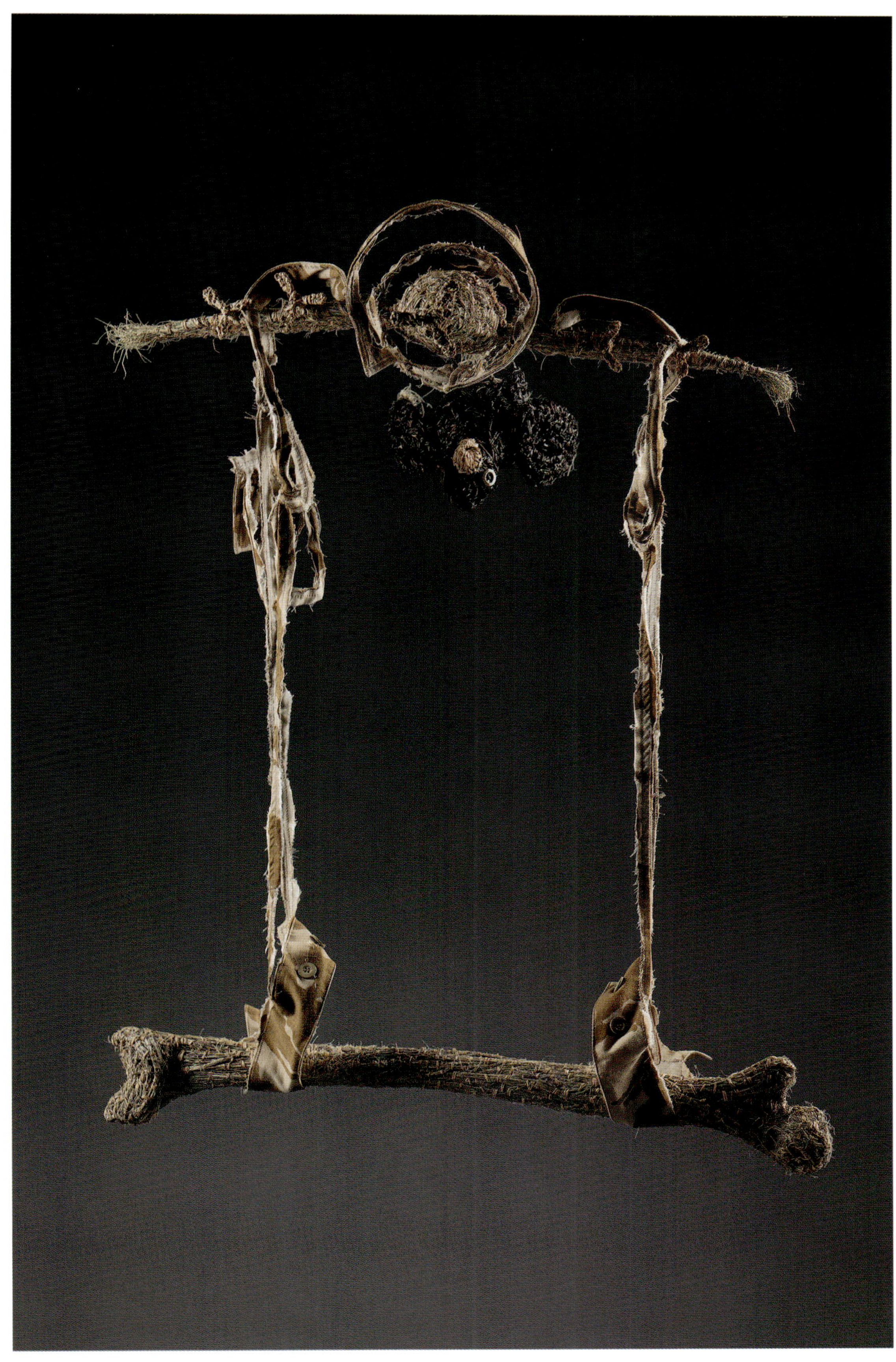

Aeroplane with Black Cockatoo and Bone / Iṟupuḻaina, kaki maṟu munu tarka
from *Kuka Irititja (Animals from Another Time)* 2014

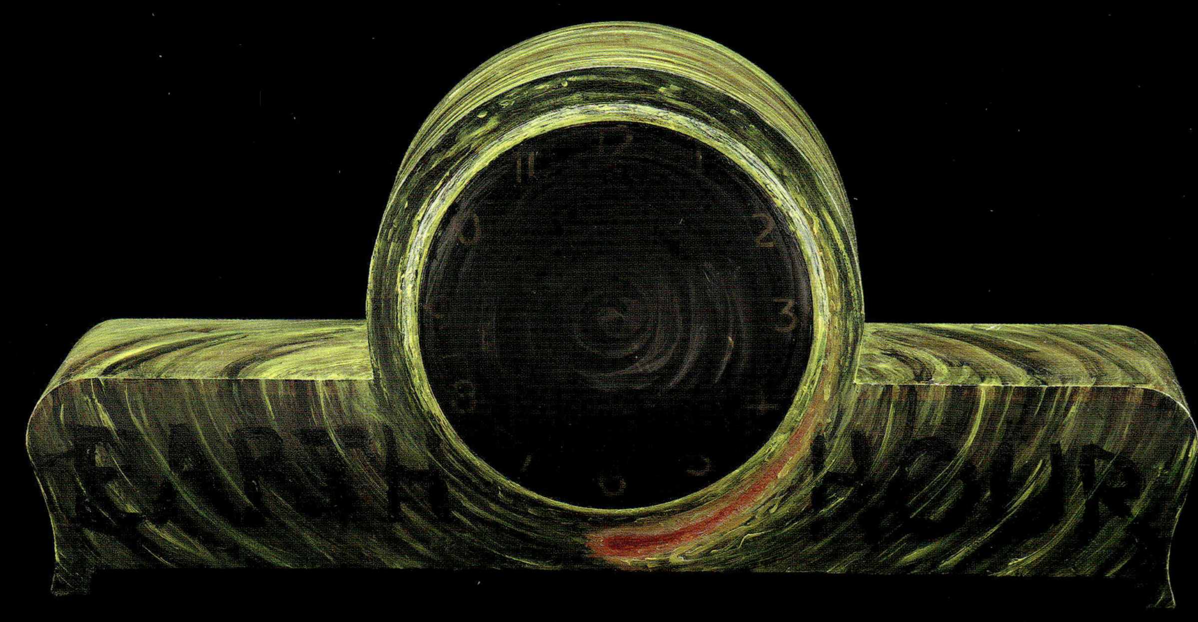

Untitled 2014

Opposite
Mamu and Frog / Mamu munu ngaa̲nngi
from *Kuka Irititja (Animals from Another Time)* 2014

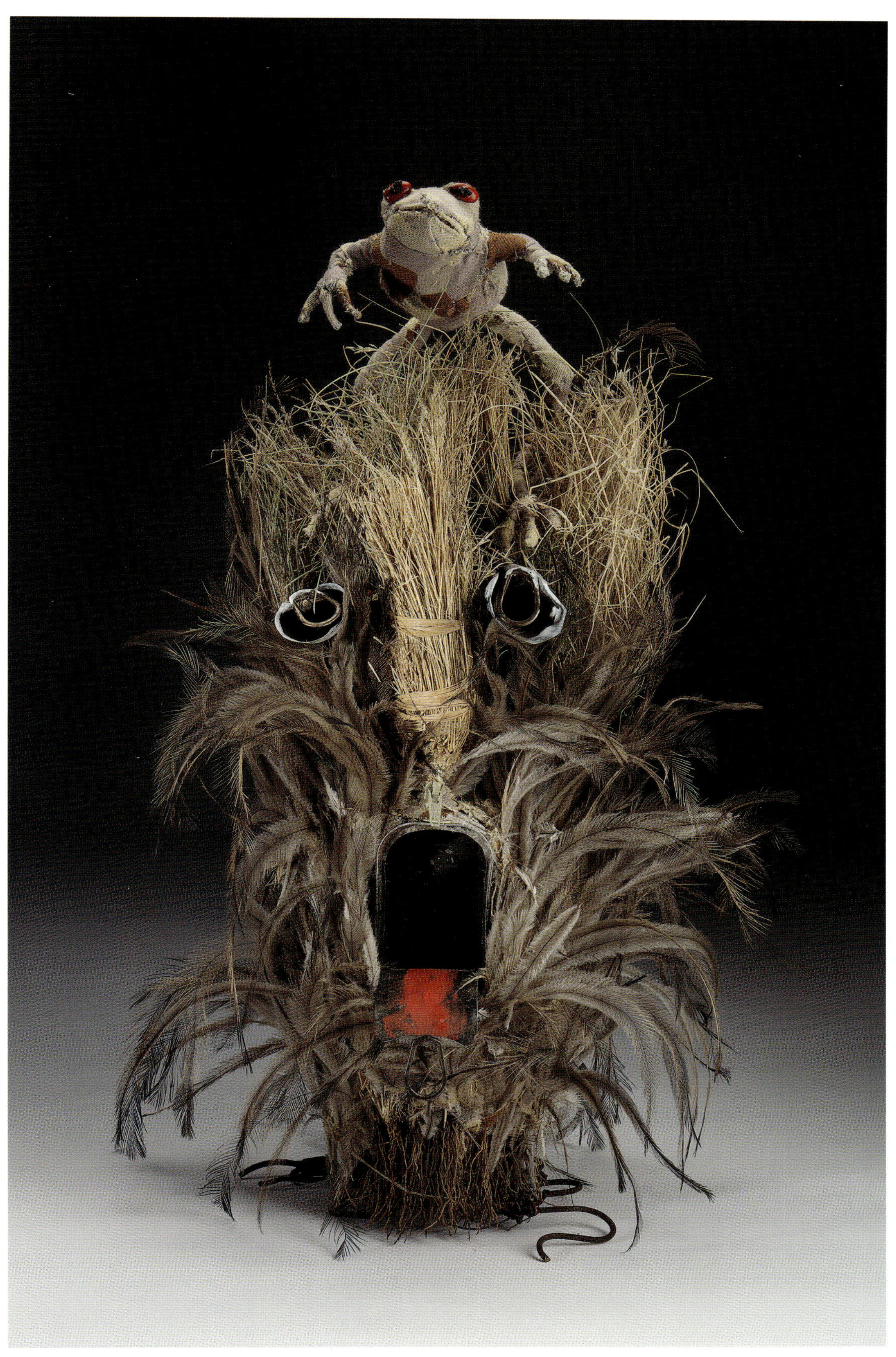

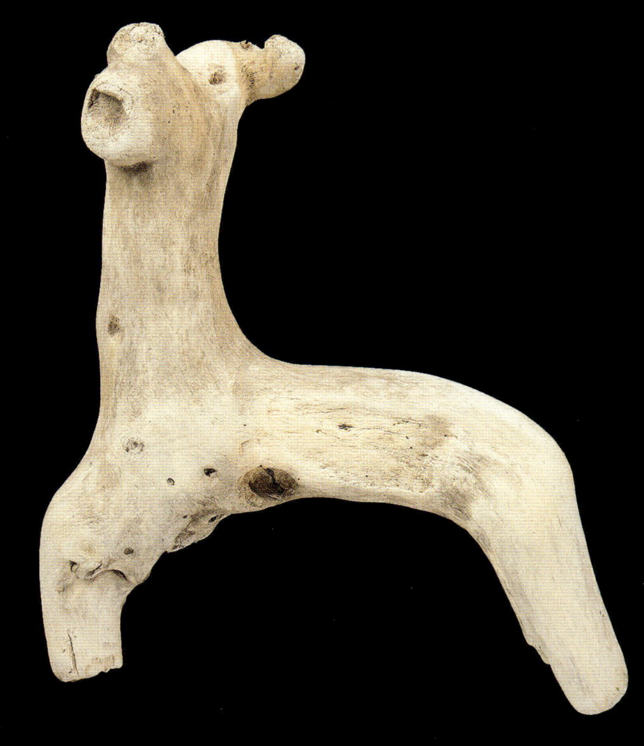

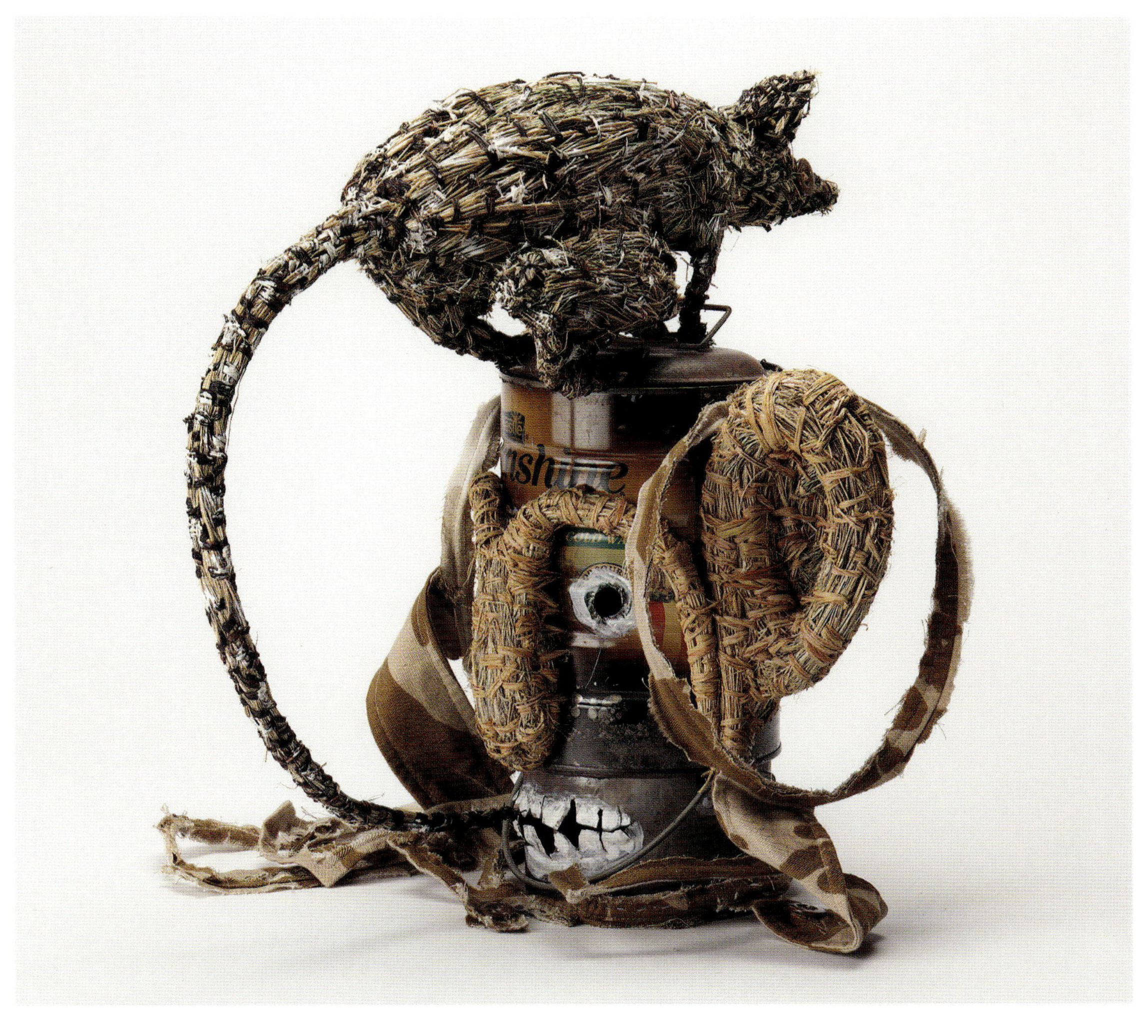

Mamu and Western Quoll (Dasyurus geoffroii*) /*
Mamu munu Partjaṯa
from *Kuka Irititja (Animals from Another Time)* 2014

Opposite
Manihuri (Travellers) 2014–15 (detail)

Following pages
Kuka Irititja (Animals from Another Time) 2014

From left to right:

Angkaliya Nelson
Ngaya (Feral Cat; Felis catus*)*

Molly Miller
Tjuwaḻpi (Lesser Stick-nest Rat; Leporillus apicalis*)*
Mitika (Burrowing Bettong; Bettongia lesueur*)*
Piiwi (Tawny Frogmouth; Podargus strigoides*)*, on billy can

Tjawina Roberts
Yirtarrutju (Marsupial Mole; Notoryctes typhlops*)*

Niningka Lewis
Mala (Rufous Hare-wallaby; Lagorchestes hirsutus*)*, on billy can
Ngaya (Feral Cat; Felis catus*)*

Nyanu Watson
Mala (Rufous Hare-wallaby; Lagorchestes hirsutus*)*
photograph: Christian Capurro

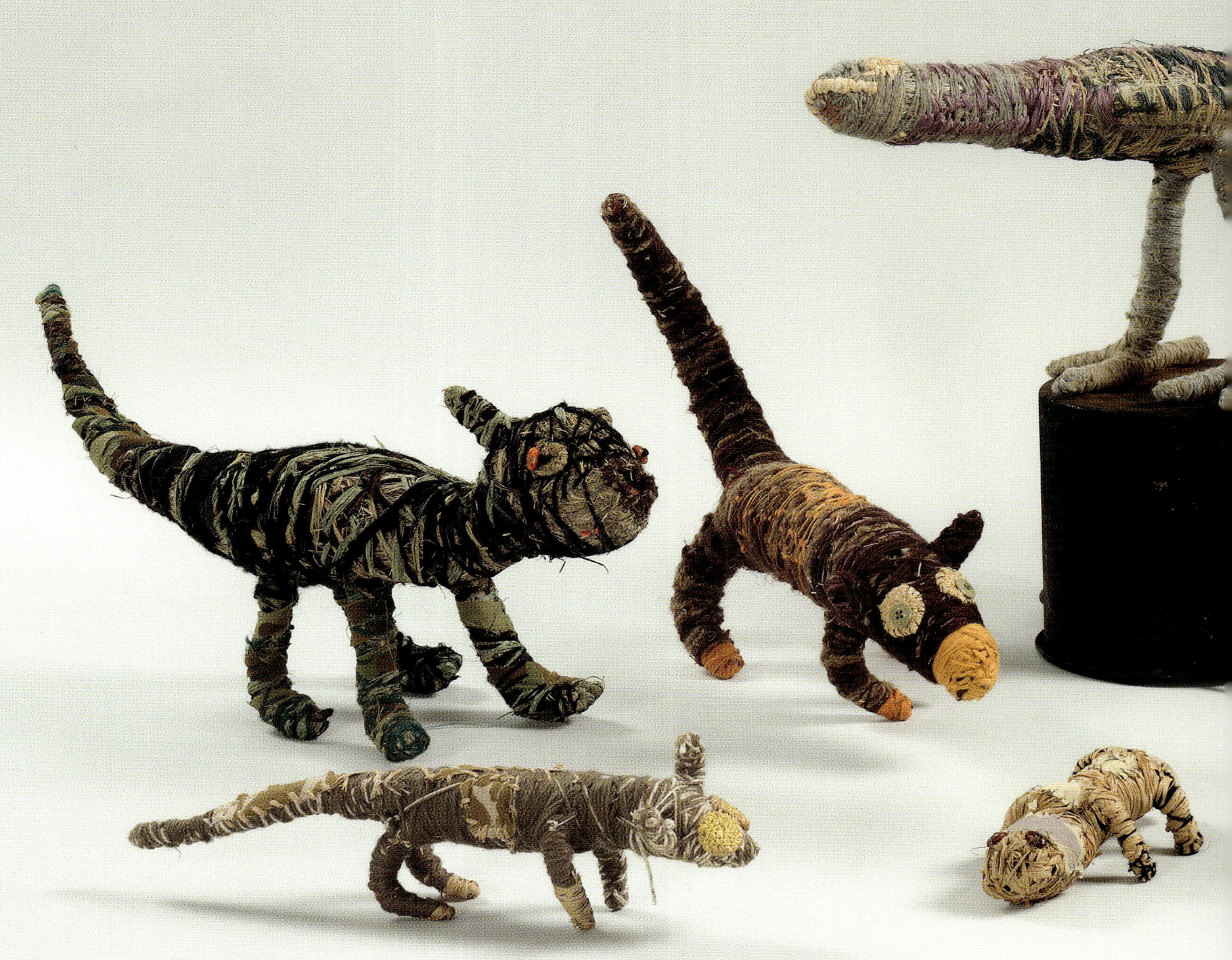

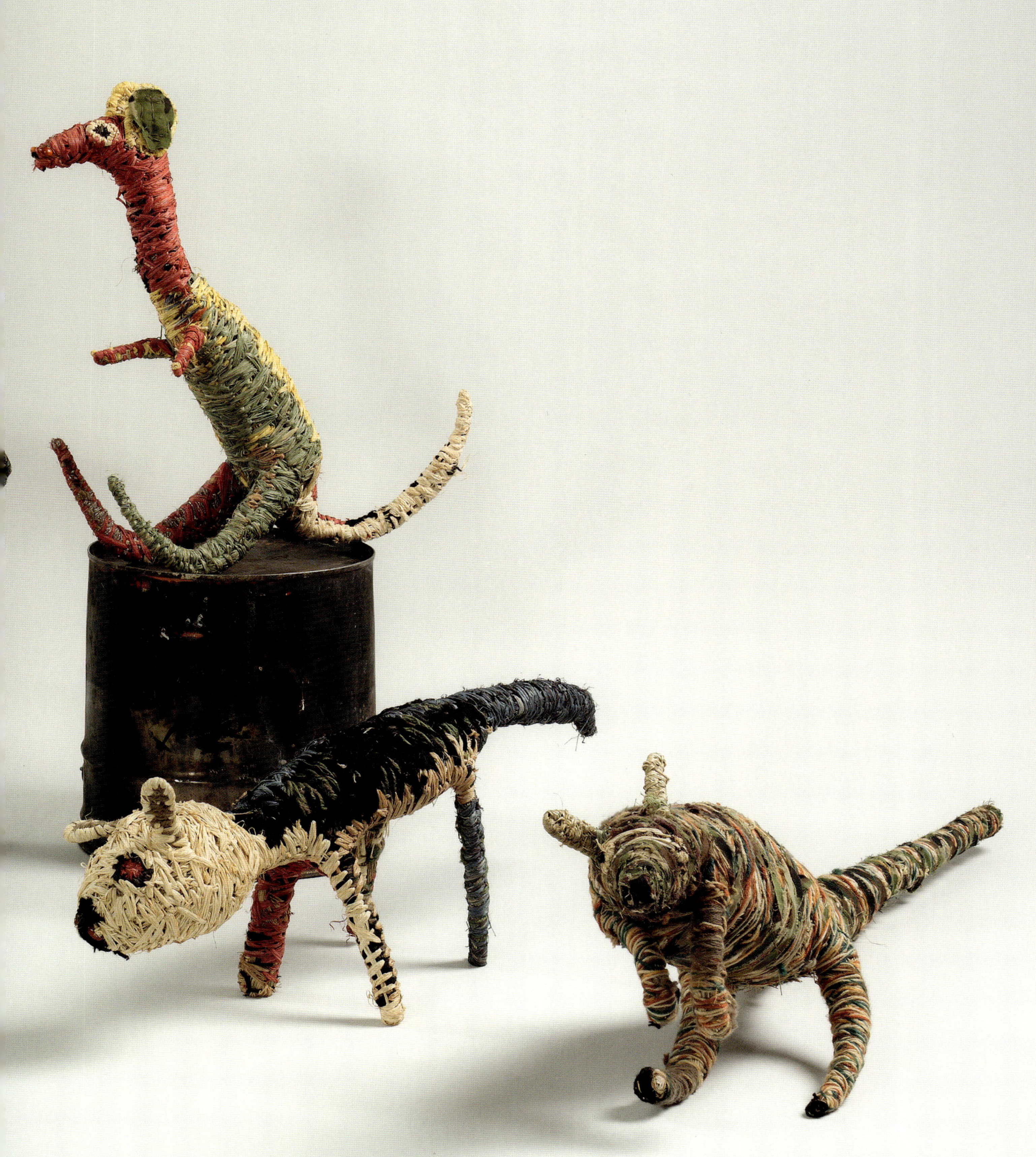

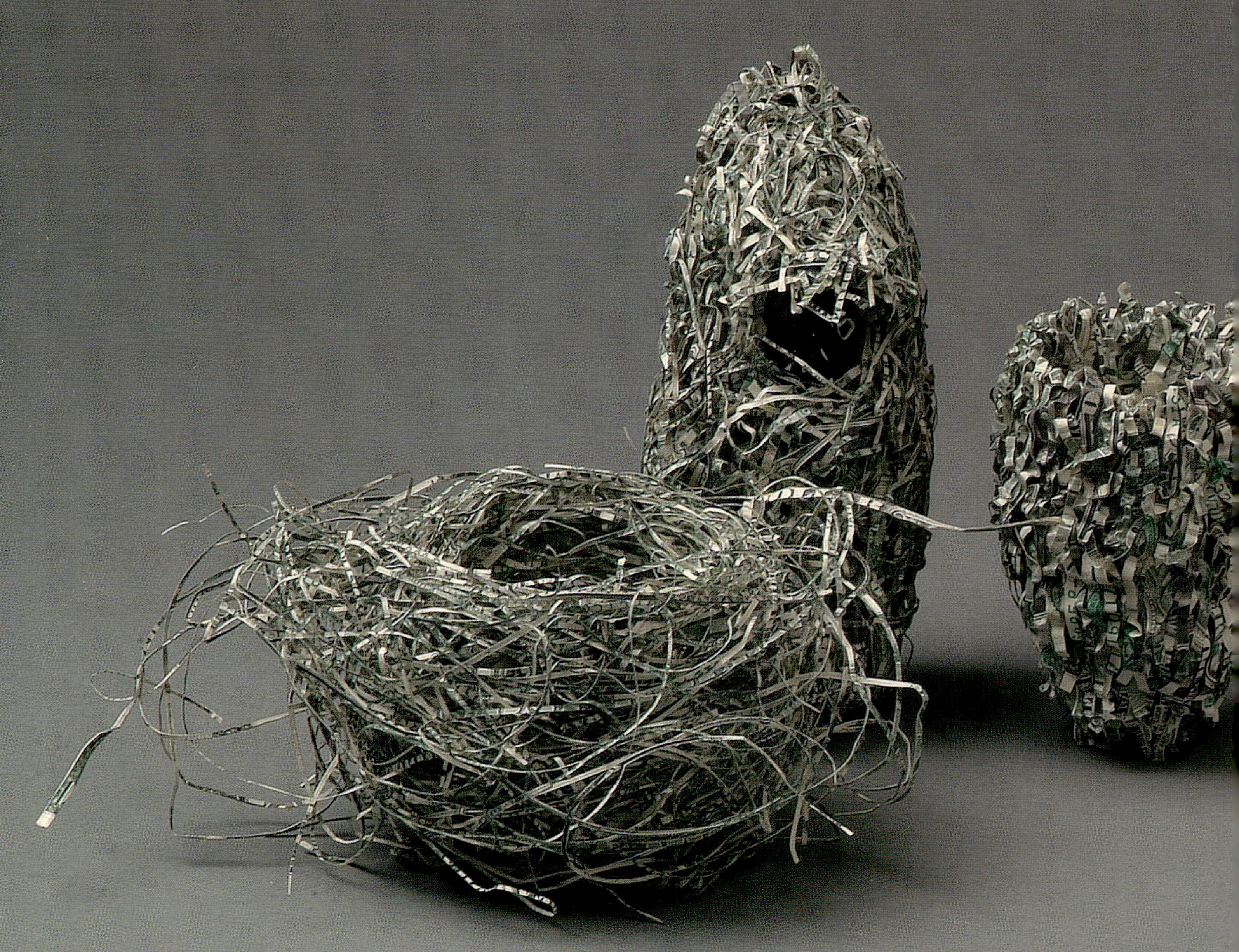

Tender 2003–06 (details)

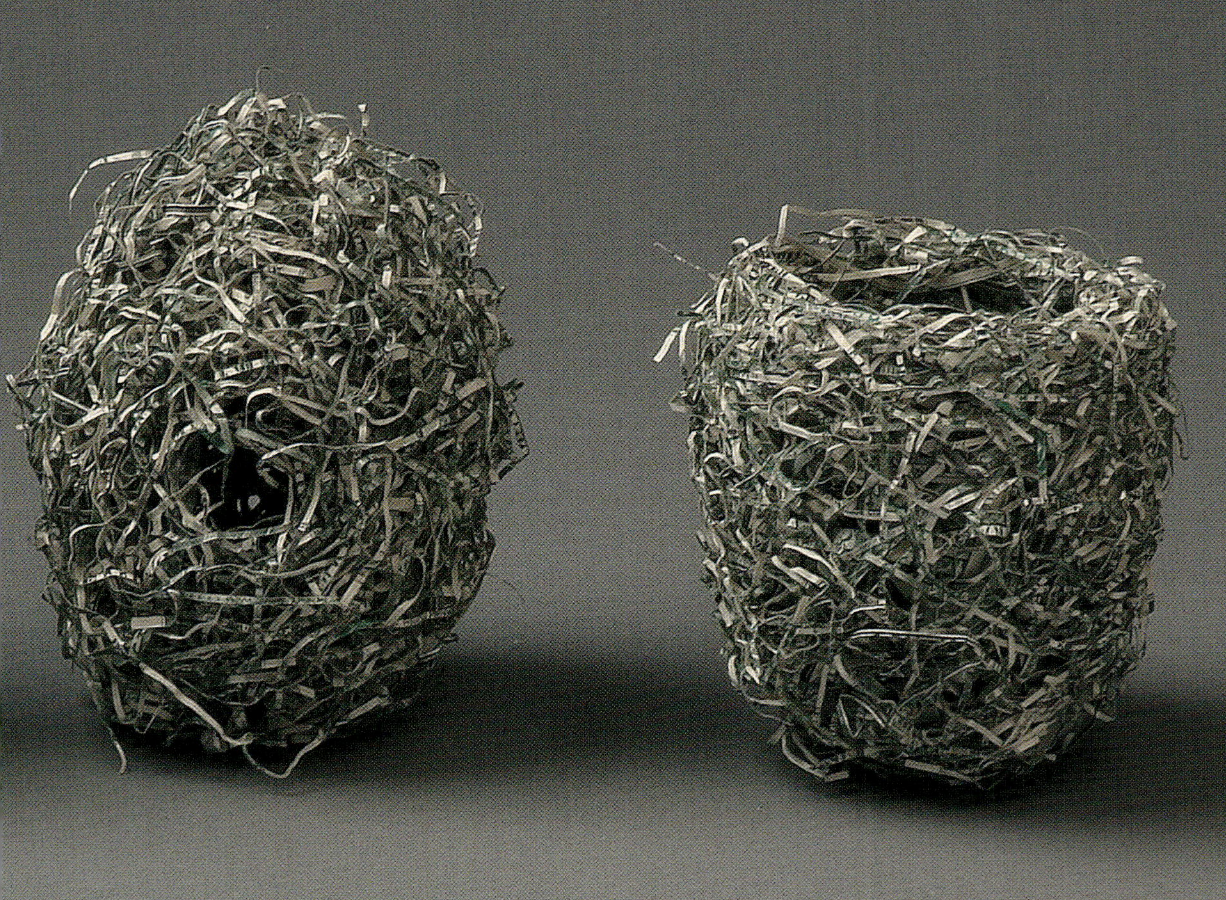

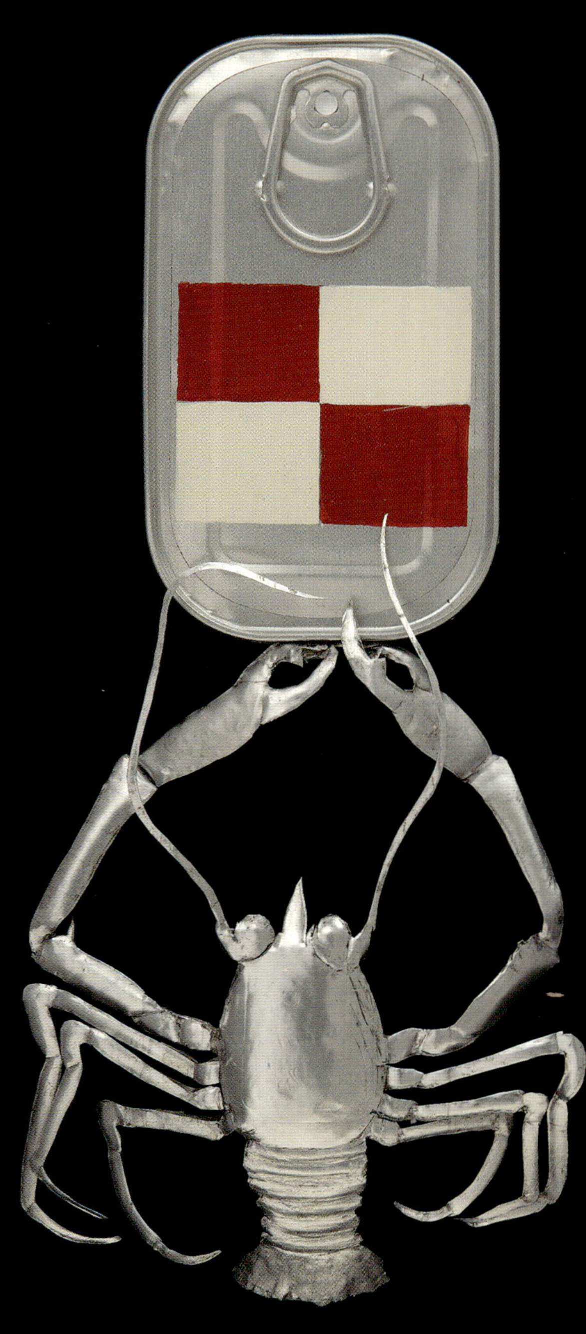

Uroptychus sp.; squat lobster
Flag U (Uniform): 'You are running into danger.'
from *Fleet* 2012

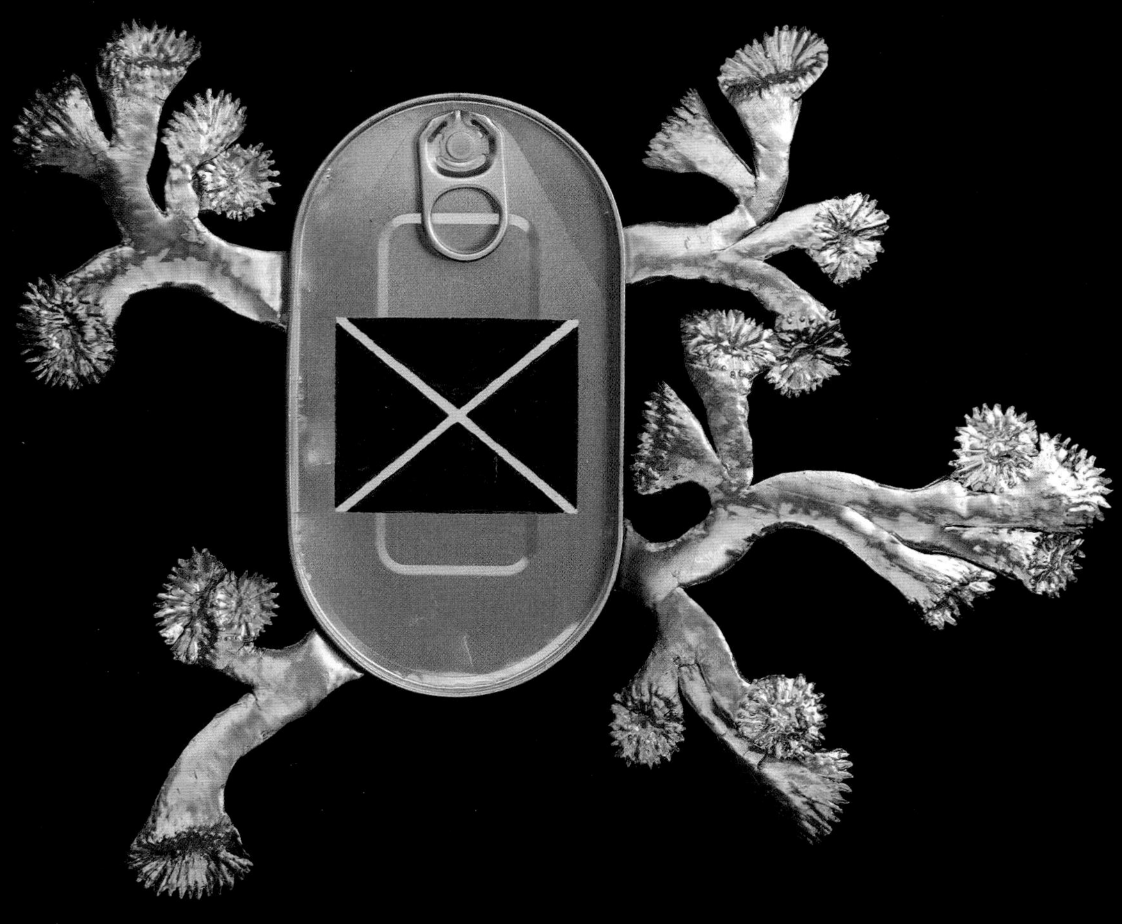

Solenosmillia variabilis; branching stony coral
Flag M (Mike): 'My vessel is stopped and making no way through the water.'
from *Fleet* 2012

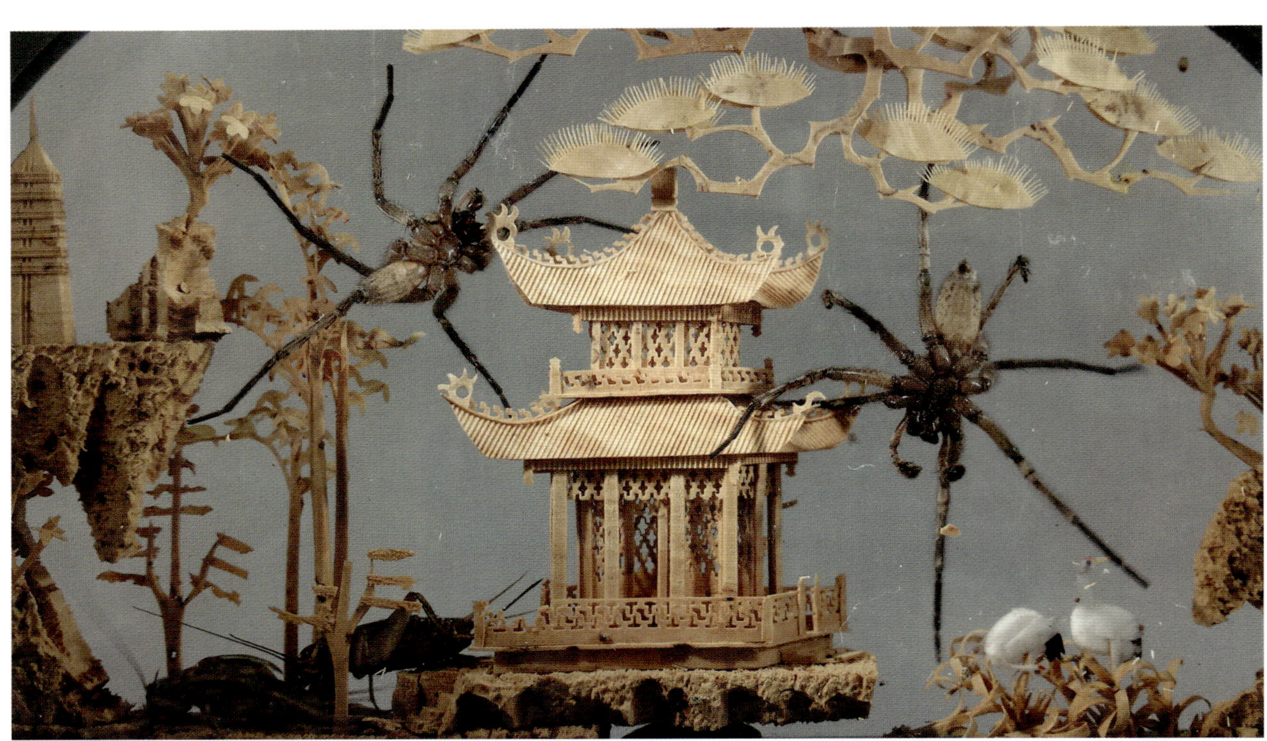

Untitled 2014 (detail)

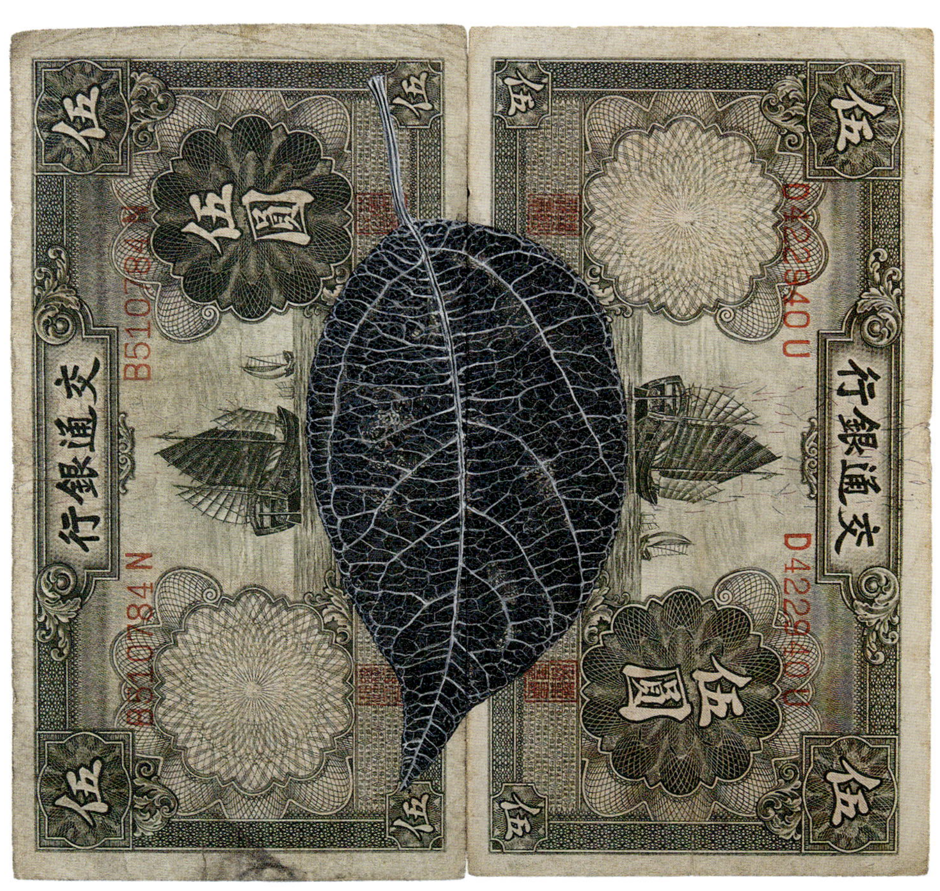

Cinnamomum camphora; camphor
from *When My Boat Comes In* 2003–

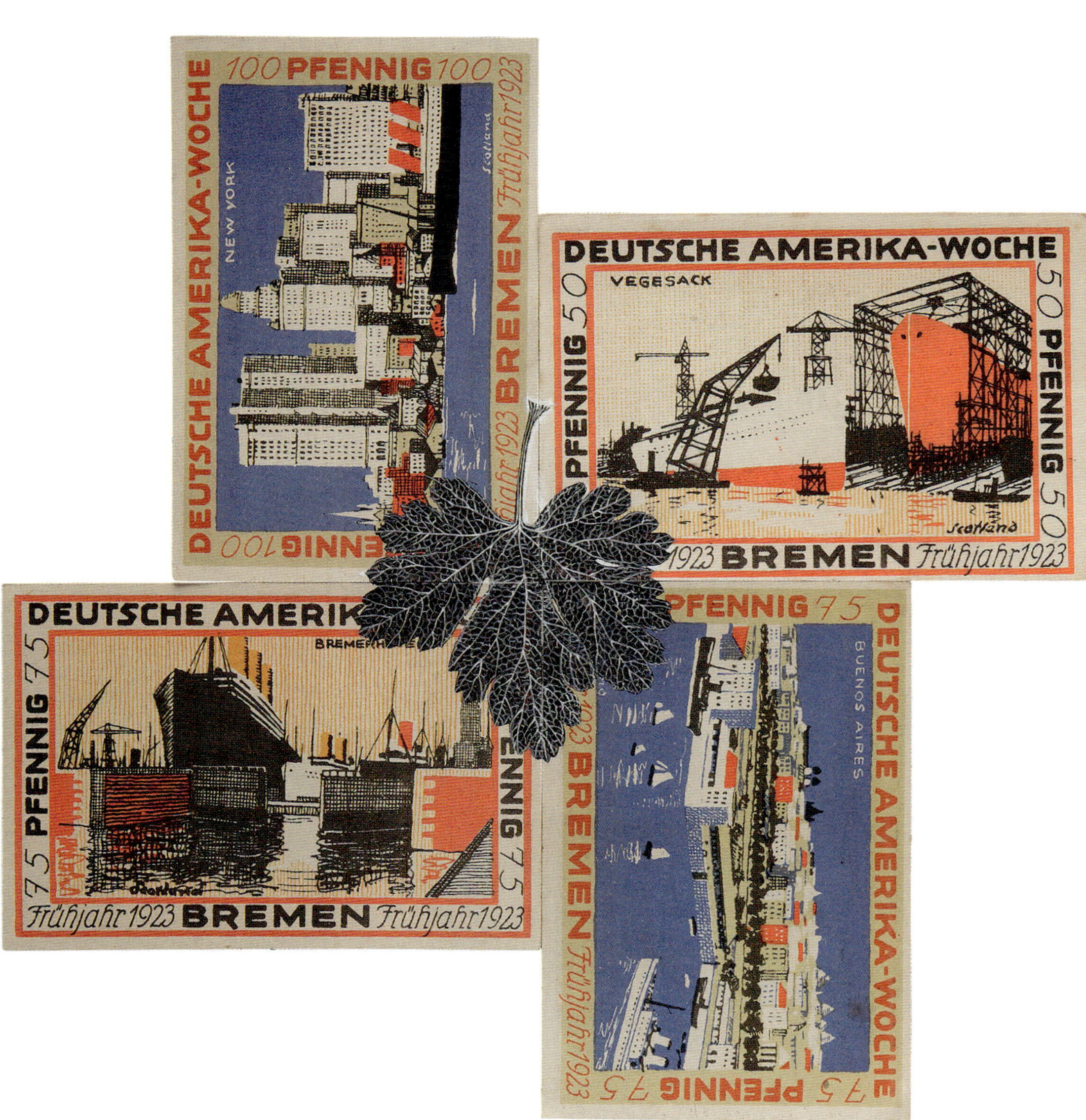

Ribes grossularia; gooseberry
from *When My Boat Comes In* 2003–

Opposite
Pinus radiata; radiata pine
from *When My Boat Comes In* 2003–

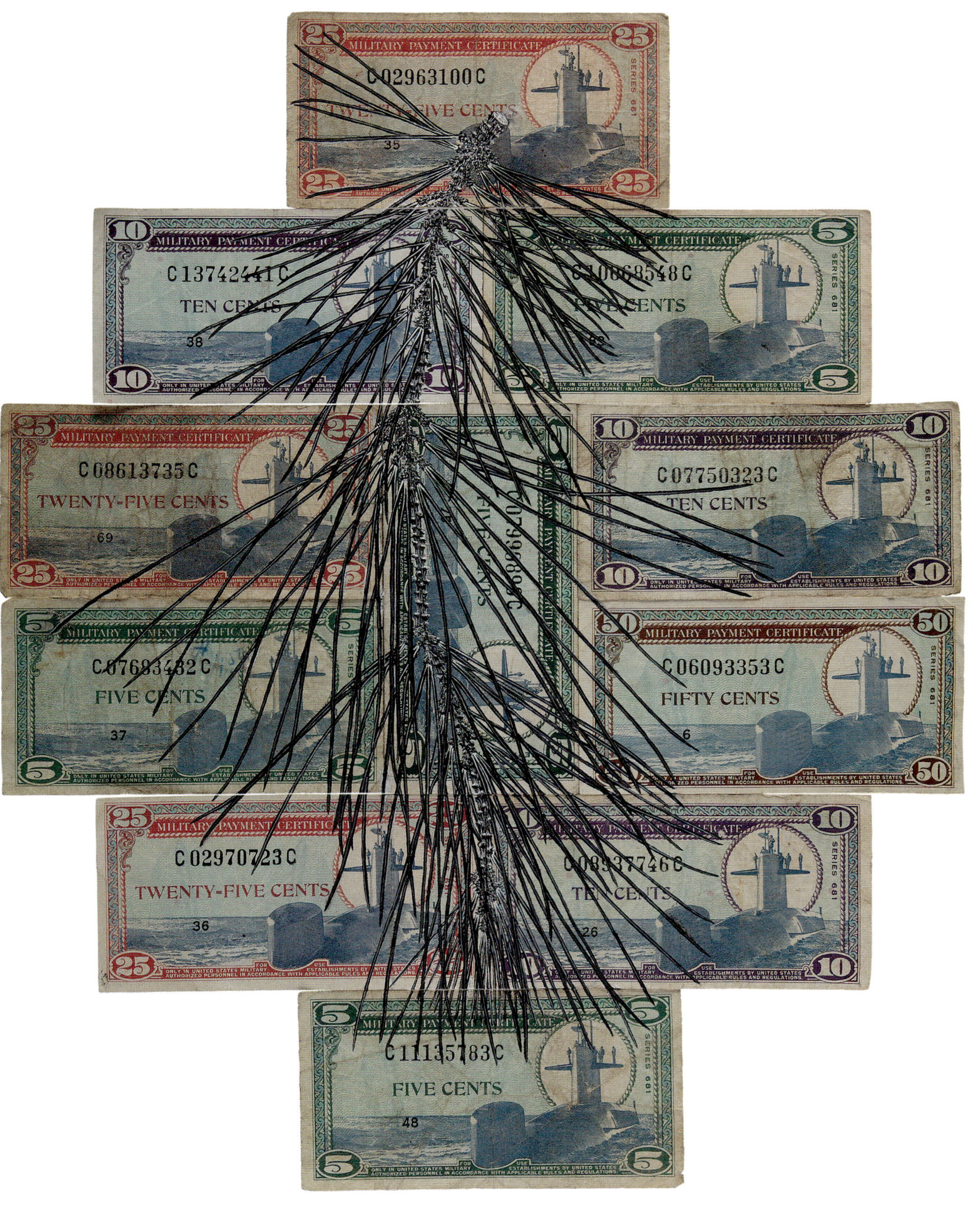

MILITARY PAYMENT CERTIFICATE
C02963100C
C13742441C
TEN CENTS
C08613735C
TWENTY-FIVE CENTS
C07750323C
TEN CENTS
FIVE CENTS
C06093353C
FIFTY CENTS
C02970723C
TWENTY-FIVE CENTS
FIVE CENTS

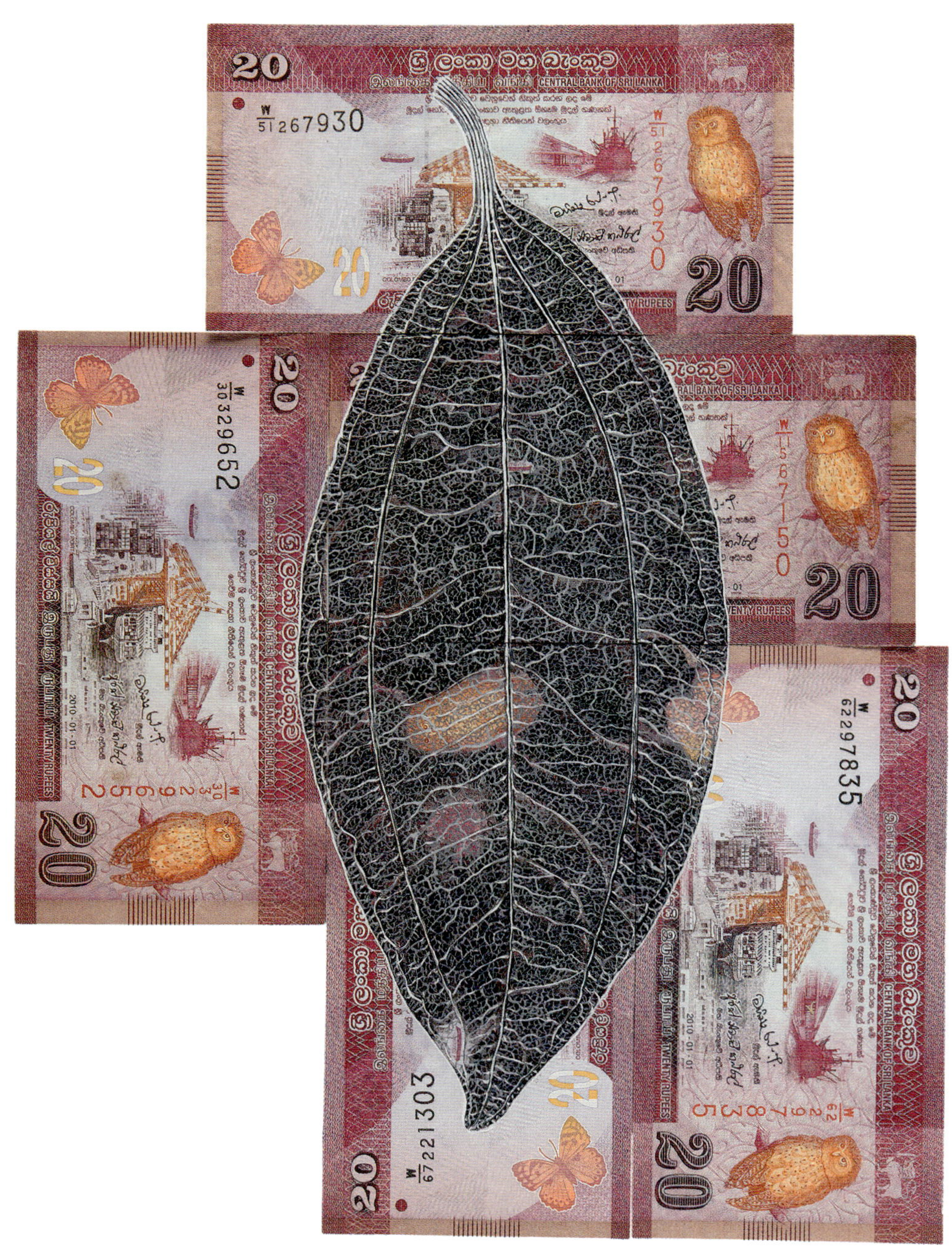

Cinnamomum camphora; camphor
from *When My Boat Comes In* 2003–

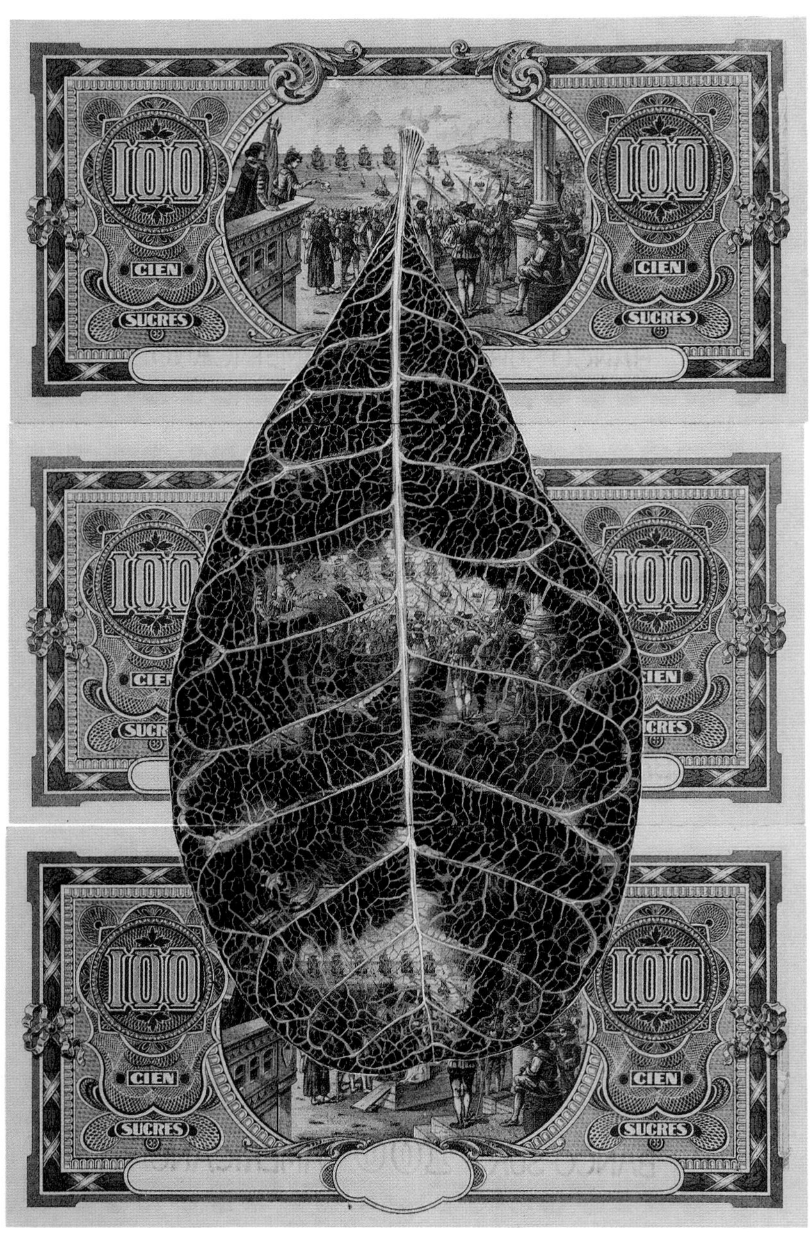

Anacardium occidentale; cashew nut
from *When My Boat Comes In* 2003–

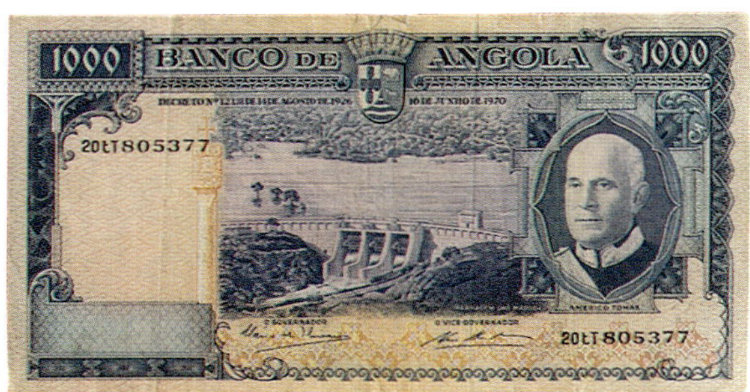

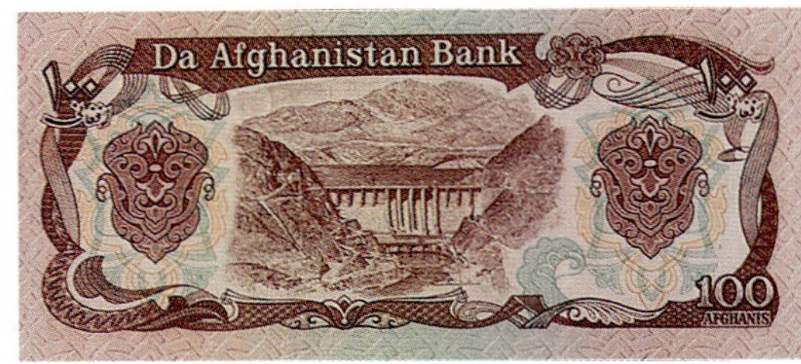

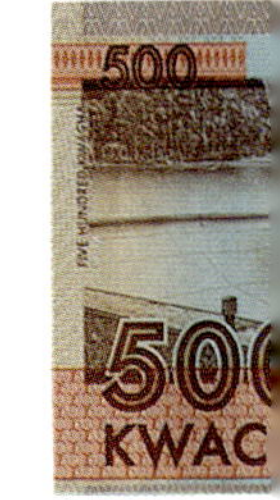

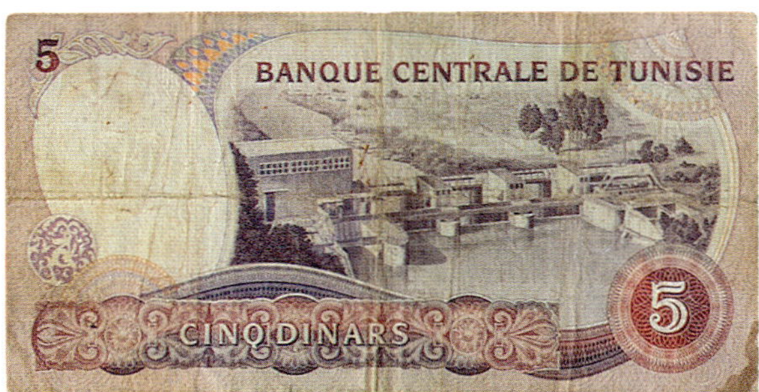

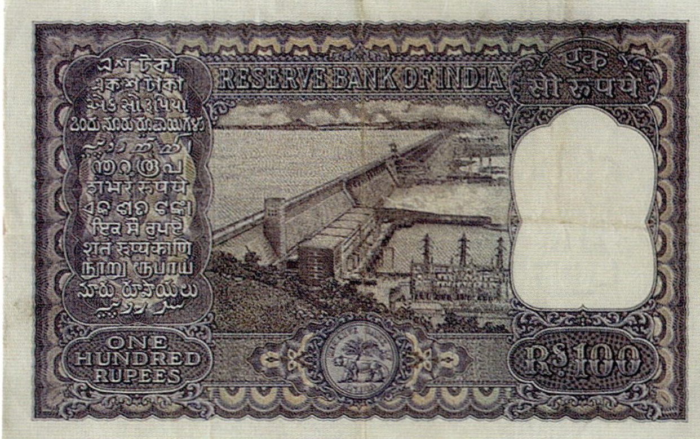

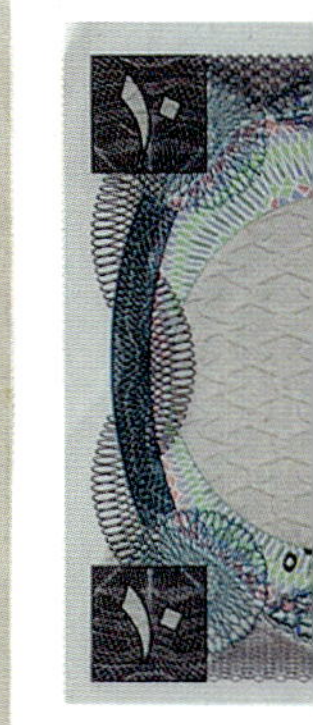

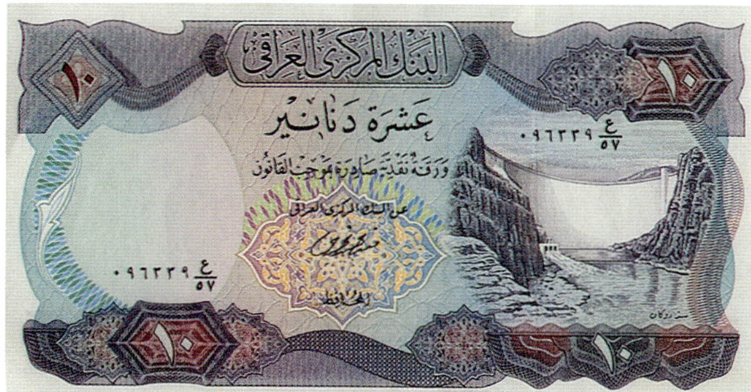

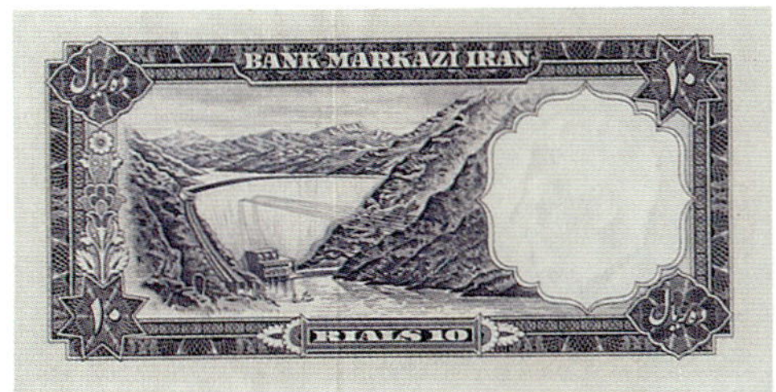

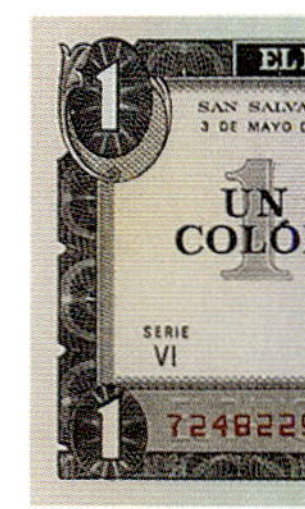

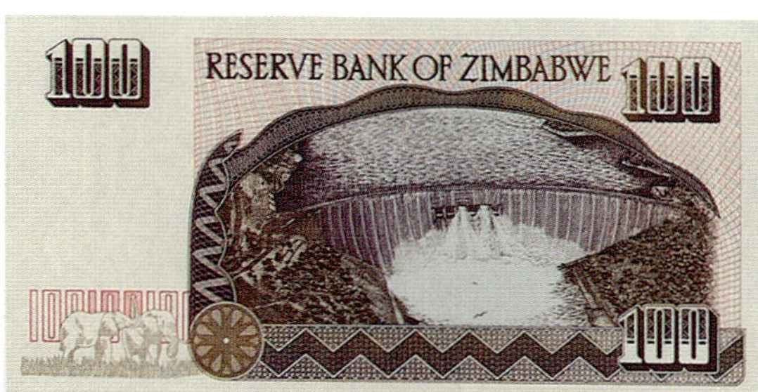

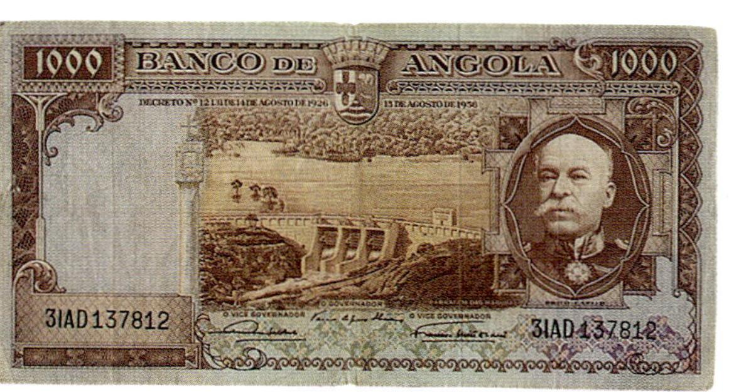

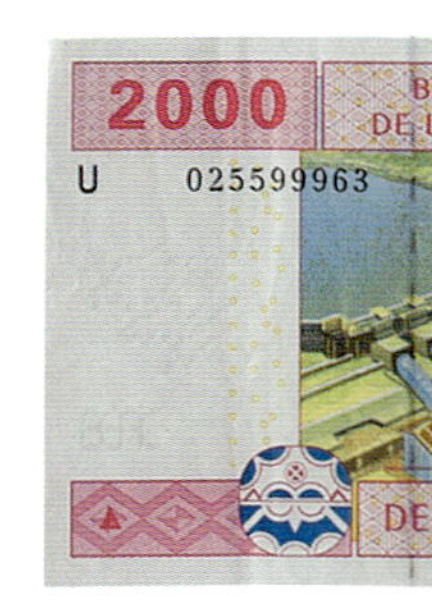

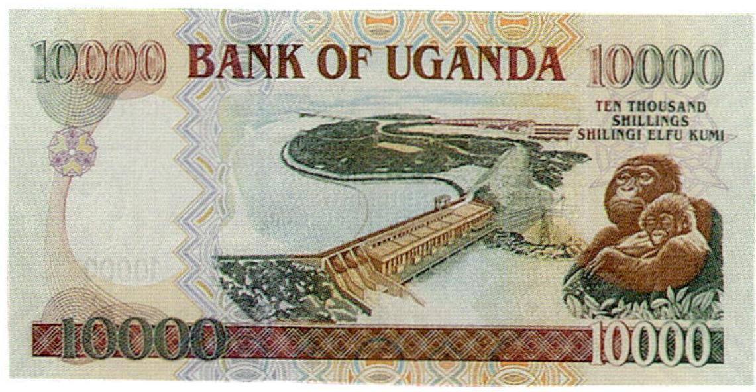

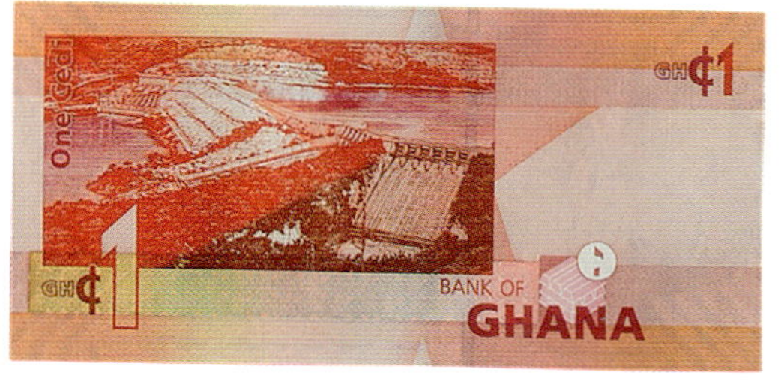

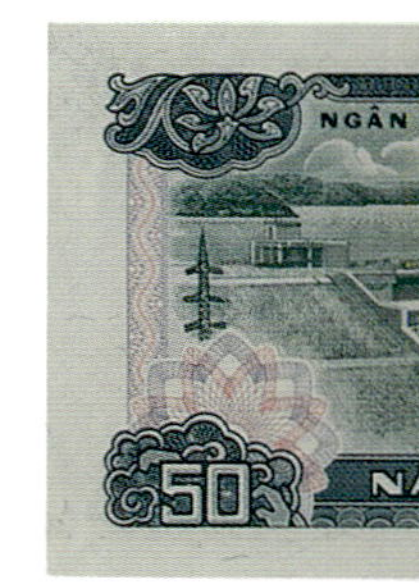

Triumph of the Damned 2015 (detail)

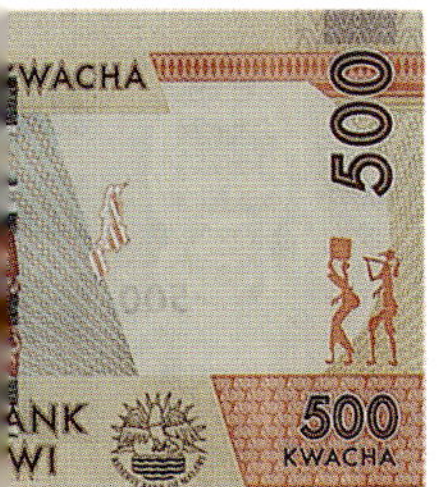
500
500
KWACHA

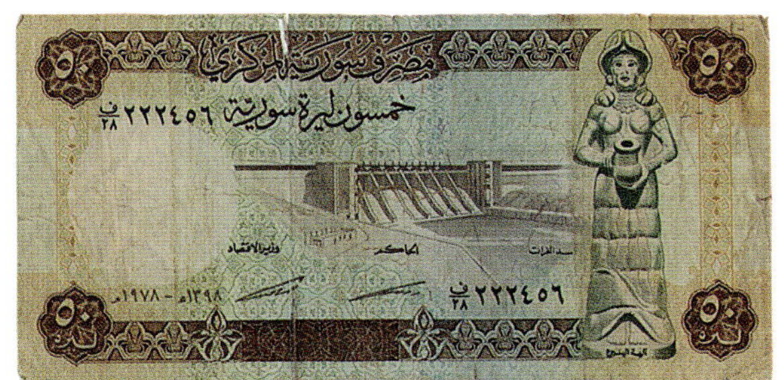
مصرف سورية المركزي
خمسون ليرة سورية

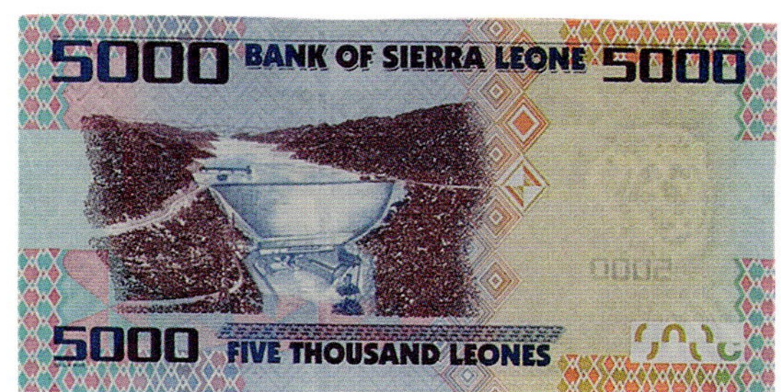
5000 BANK OF SIERRA LEONE 5000
5000 FIVE THOUSAND LEONES

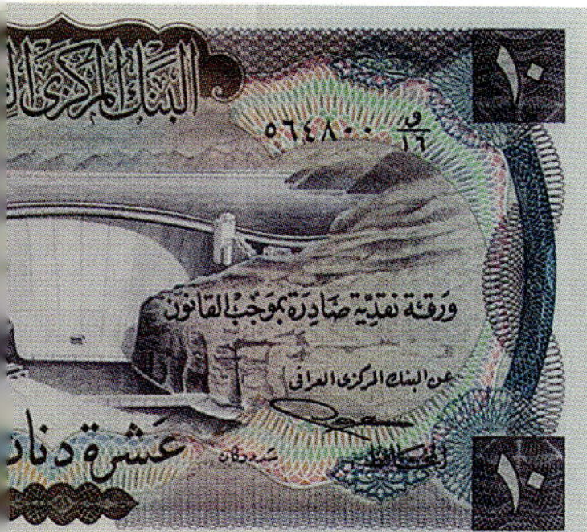
ورقة نقدية صادرة بموجب القانون
عن البنك المركزي العراقي

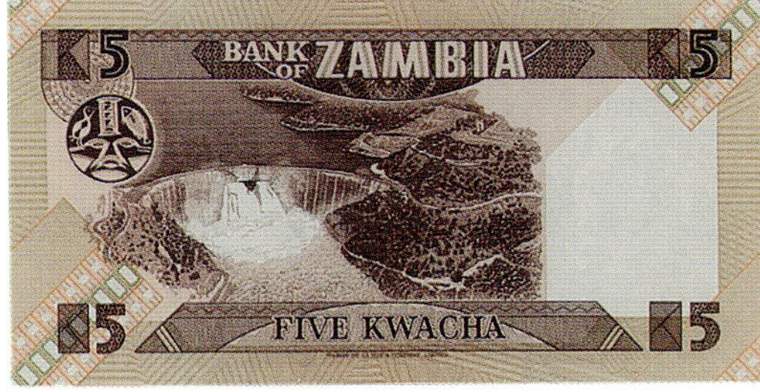
5
BANK OF ZAMBIA
5
5
FIVE KWACHA
5

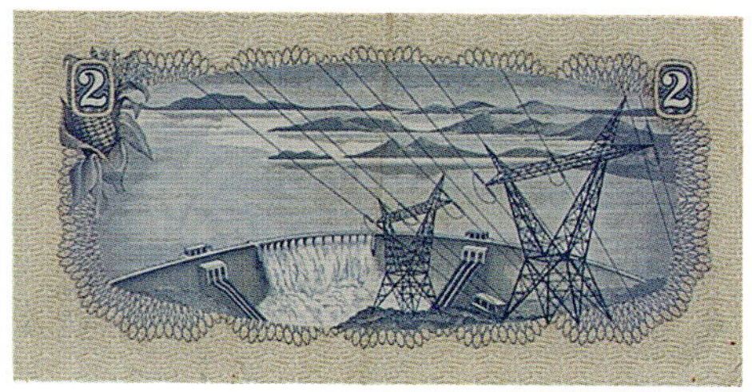
2
2

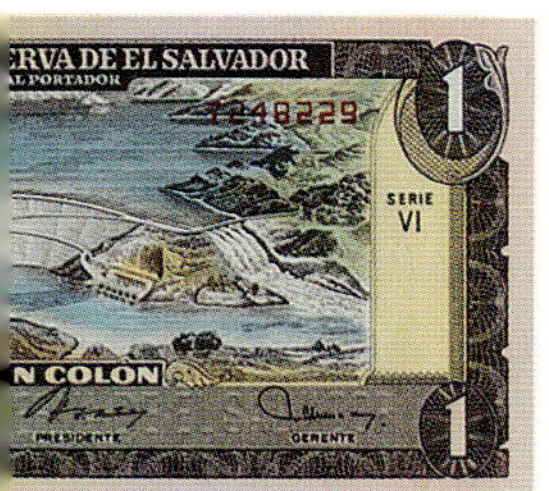
1
SERIE
VI
1

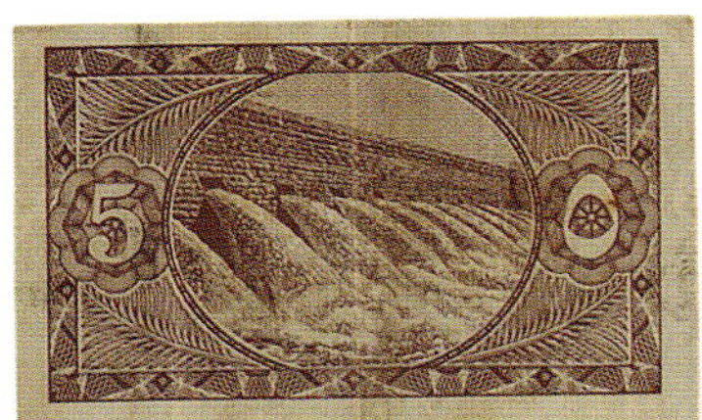
5

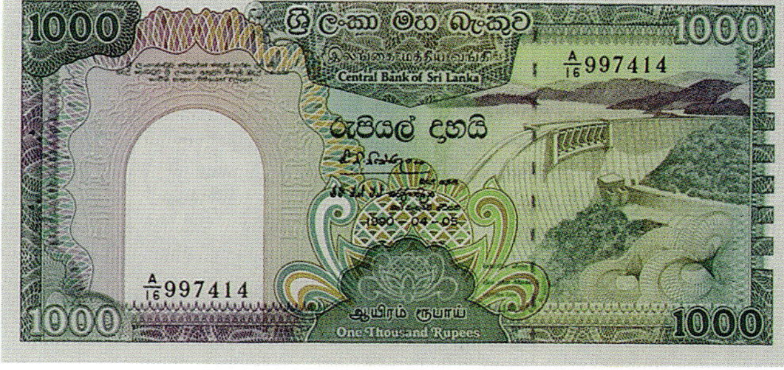
1000
1000
Central Bank of Sri Lanka
A/16 997414
A/16 997414
One Thousand Rupees
1000
1000

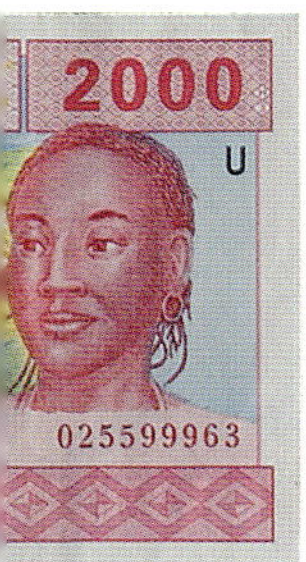
2000
U
025599963

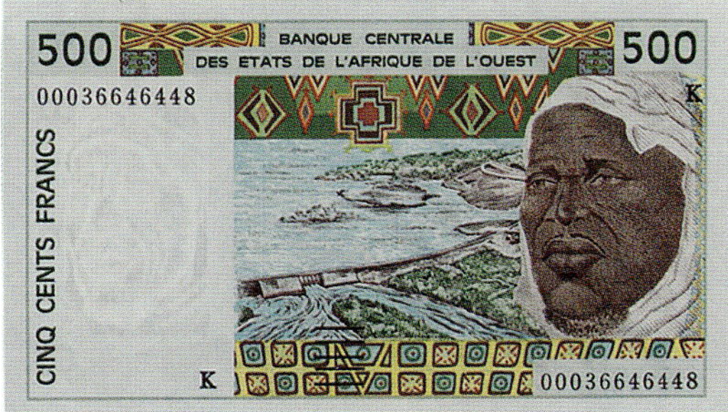
500
BANQUE CENTRALE
DES ETATS DE L'AFRIQUE DE L'OUEST
500
00036646448
K
CINQ CENTS FRANCS
K
00036646448

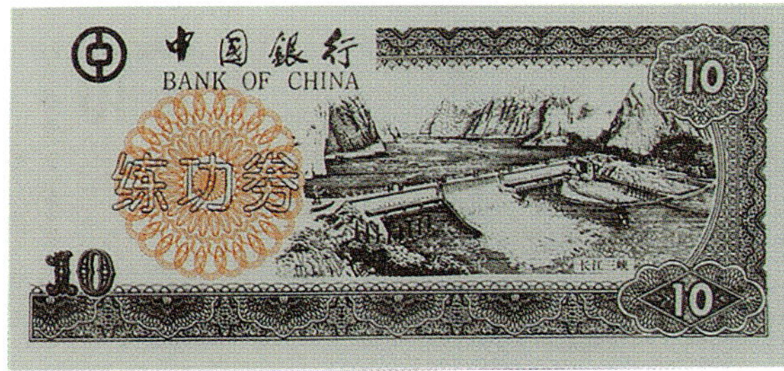
中國銀行
BANK OF CHINA
10
练功券
10
10

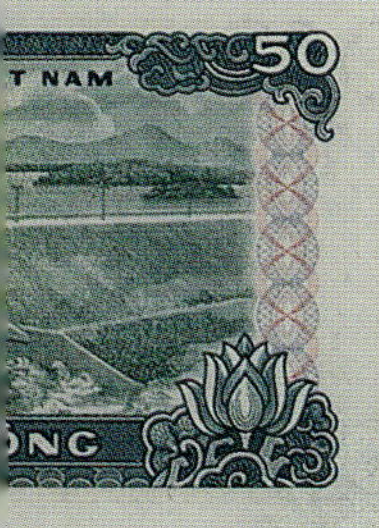
50

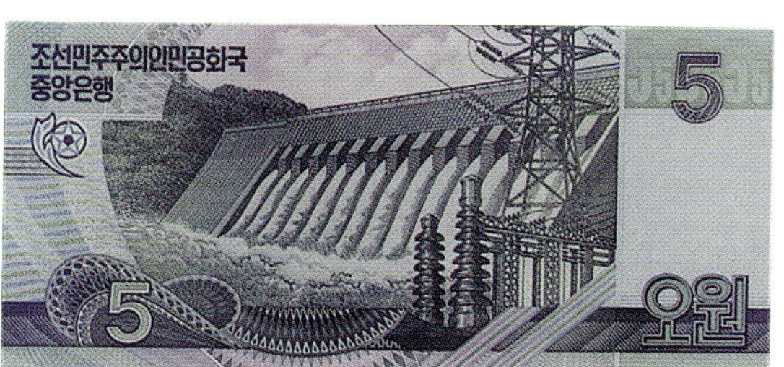
조선민주주의인민공화국
중앙은행
5
5
오원

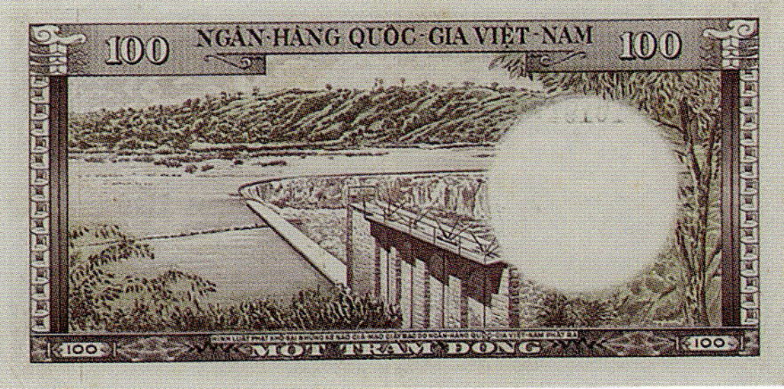
100
NGÂN-HÀNG QUỐC-GIA VIỆT-NAM
100
MỘT TRĂM ĐỒNG

1000
भारतीय रिज़र्व बैंक
1000 एक हज़ार रुपये
ONE THOUSAND RUPEES
2007

9426529444
ÉTATS DE L'AFRIQUE CENTRALE
P
5000 CINQ MILLE
9426529444

50

WE SEEK GOD'S ASSISTANCE
CENTRAL BANK of KUWAIT
FIVE DINARS
5

拾
C392560

DIX
10
TEN
BANK OF CANADA - BANQUE DU CANADA

₦500
Central Bank
Of Nigeria
Five
Hundred Naira
500

5000

Central Bank of Syria
10
1988
Ten Syrian Pounds

البنك المركزي العراقي
دينار واحد

DIX
10
TEN
BANK OF CANADA - BANQUE DU CANADA

1000
RÉPUBLIQUE GABONAISE
008644479
1000
44479
MILLE FRANCS
M.4

100
BOLIVIANOS

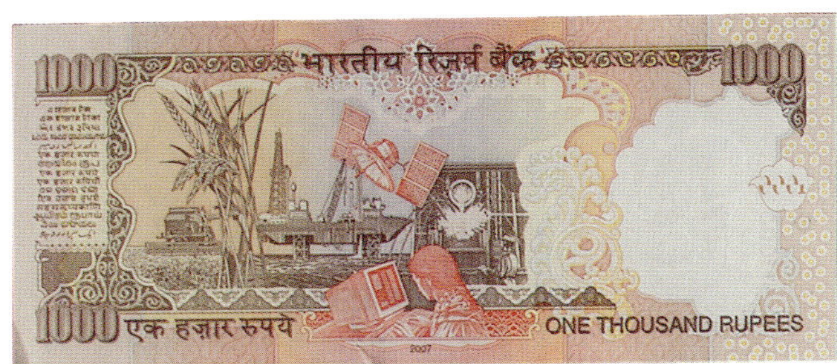

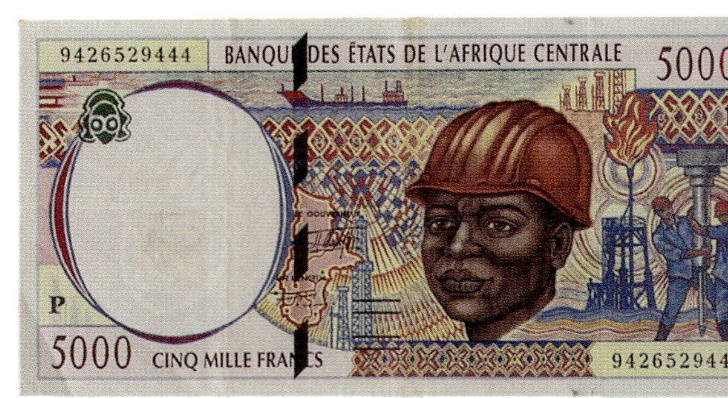

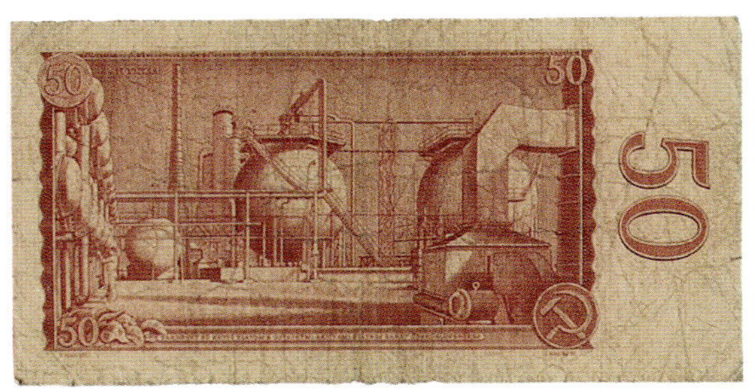

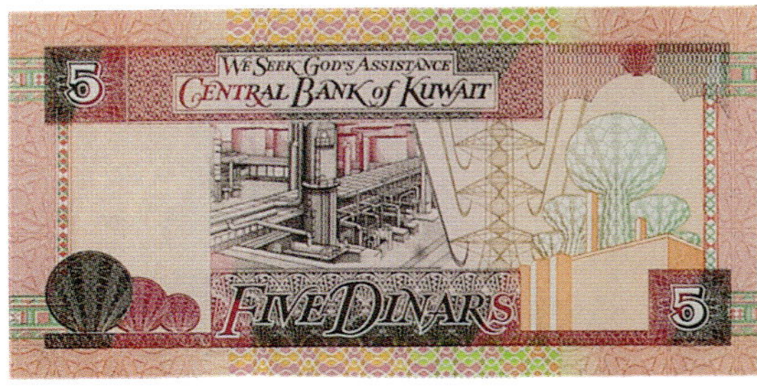

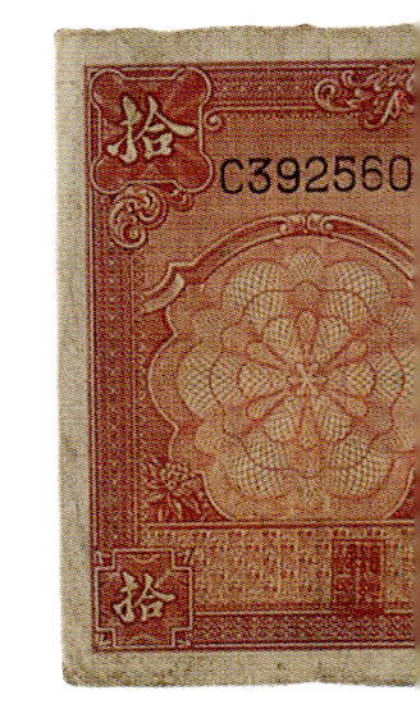

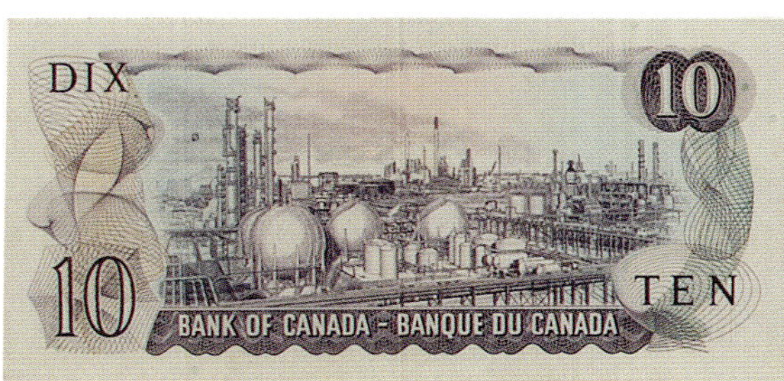

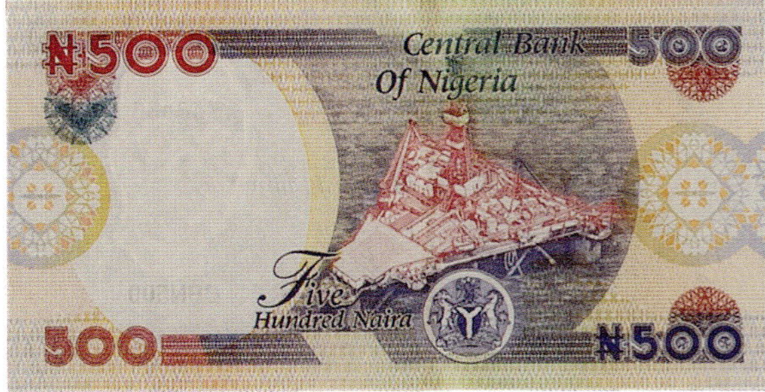

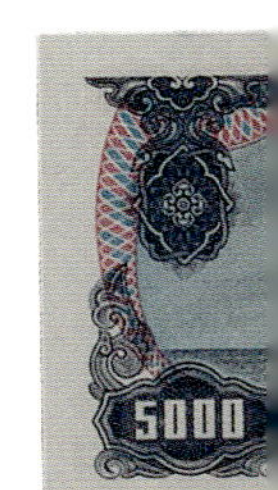

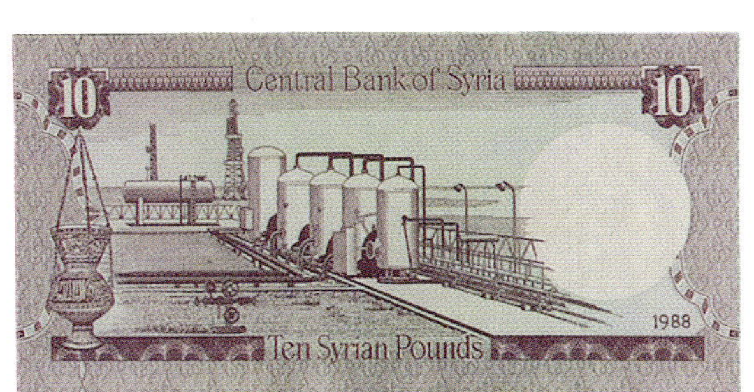

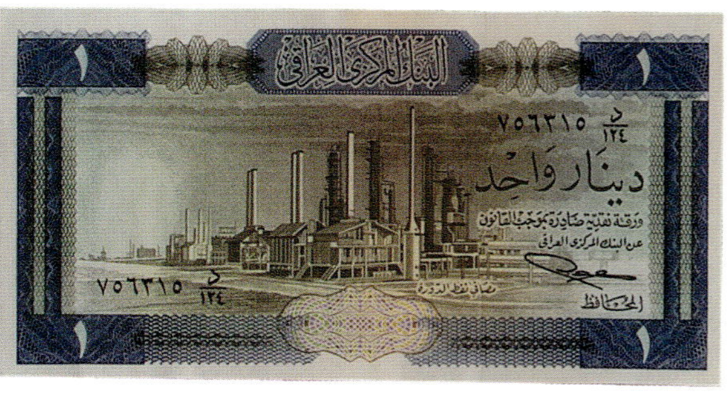

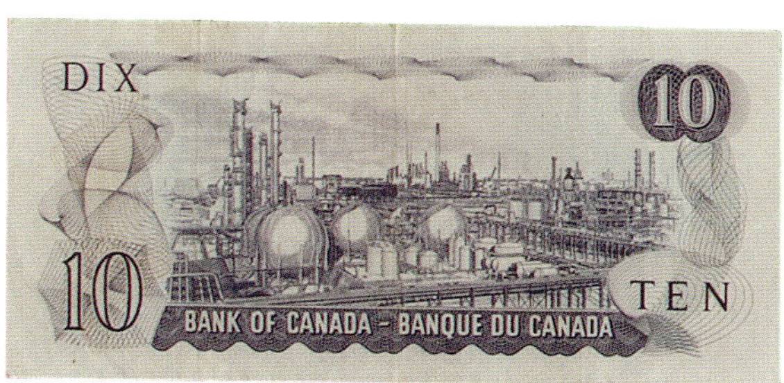

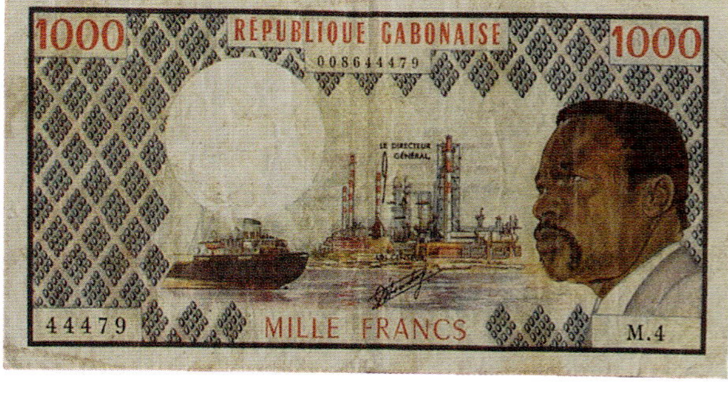

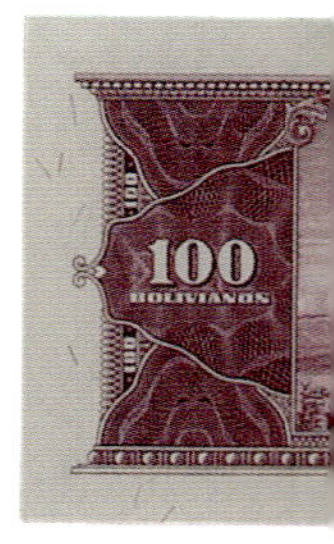

Spill 2015

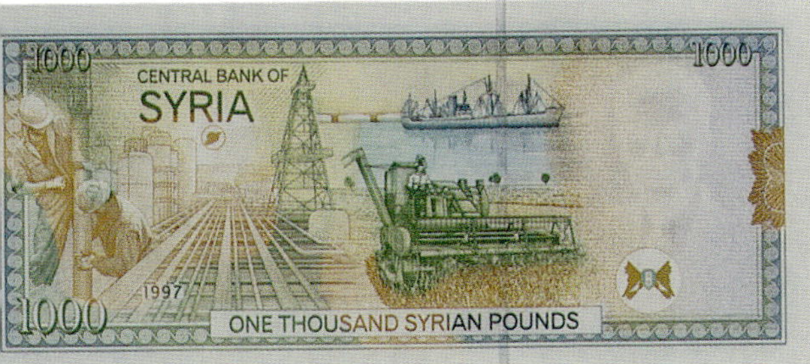
1000
CENTRAL BANK OF
SYRIA
1997
ONE THOUSAND SYRIAN POUNDS

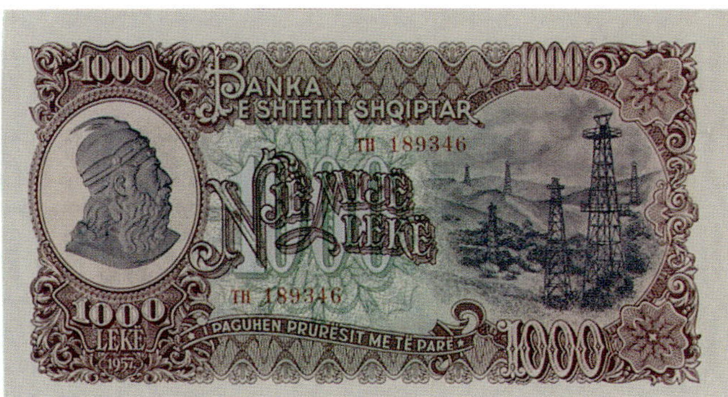
1000
BANKA
E SHTETIT SHQIPTAR
TH 189346
1000 LEKË
1957

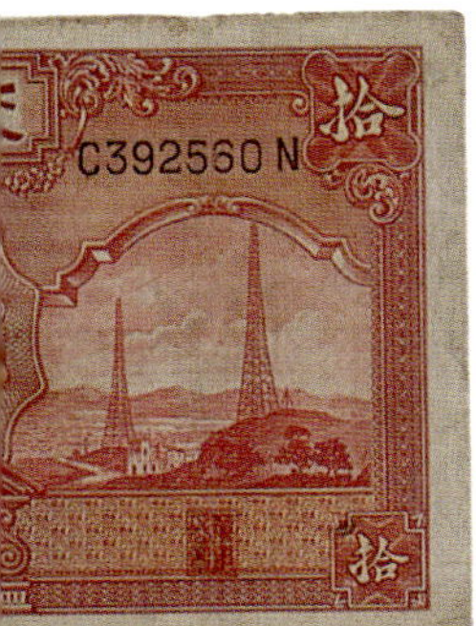
拾
C392560 N

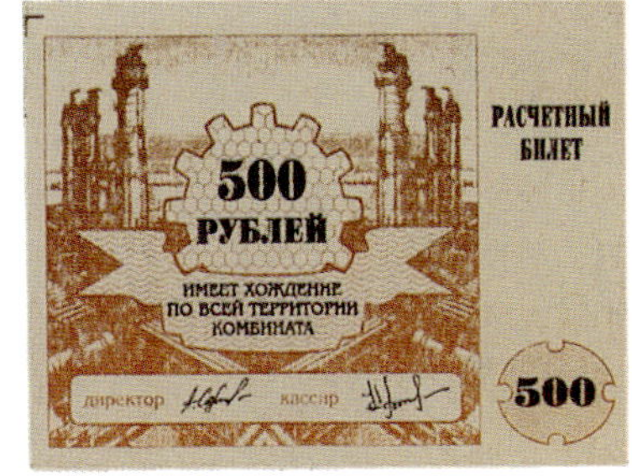
500
РУБЛЕЙ
РАСЧЕТНЫЙ
БИЛЕТ
ИМЕЕТ ХОЖДЕНИЕ
ПО ВСЕЙ ТЕРРИТОРИИ
КОМБИНАТА
директор
кассир
500

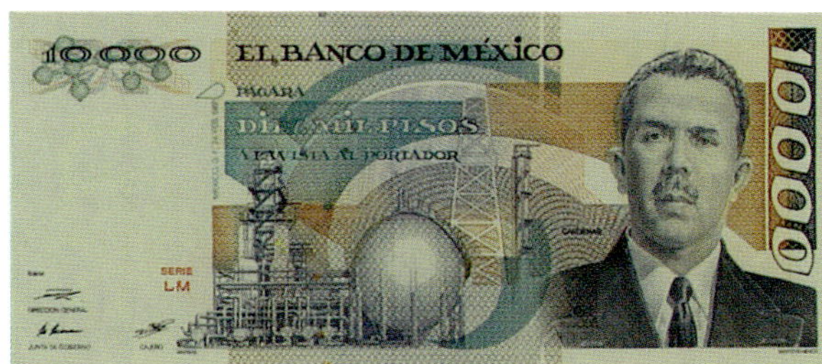
10000
EL BANCO DE MÉXICO
SERIE
LM

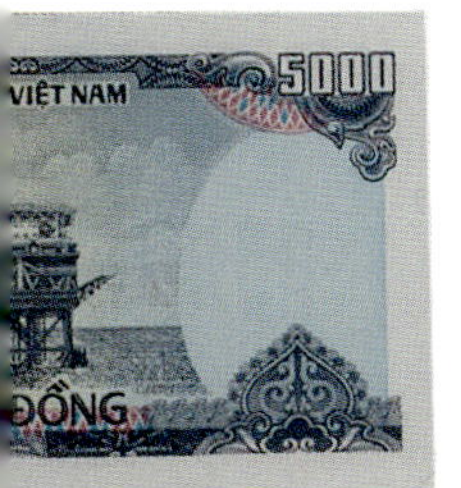
VIỆT NAM
5000
ĐỒNG

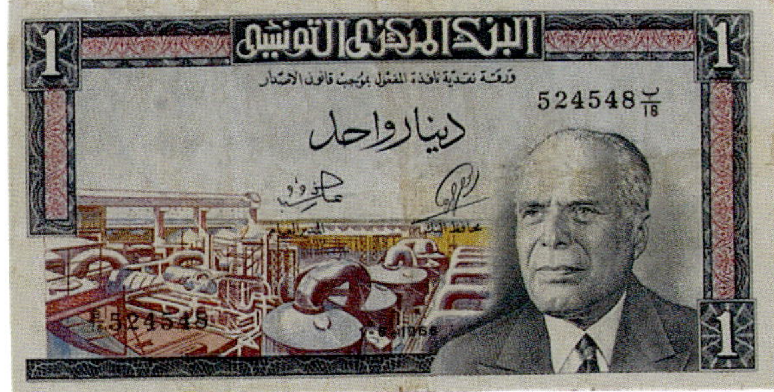
البنك المركزي التونسي
1
524548
دينار واحد

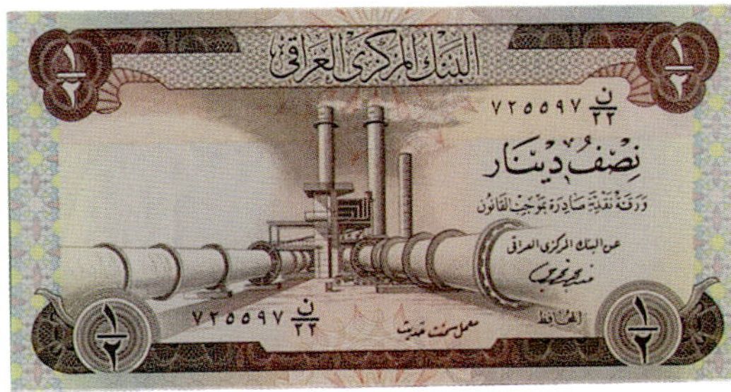
البنك المركزي العراقي
نصف دينار

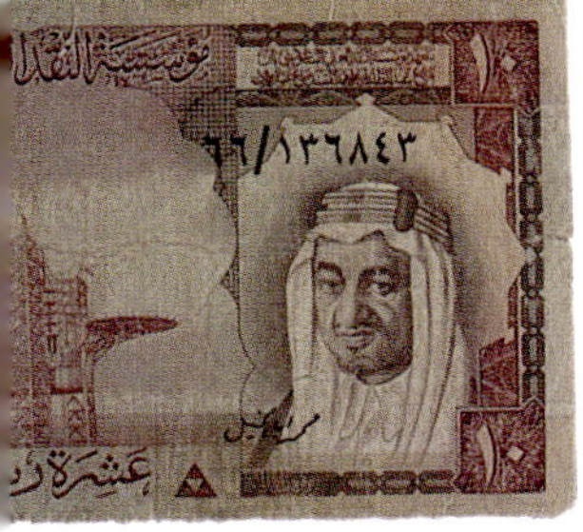

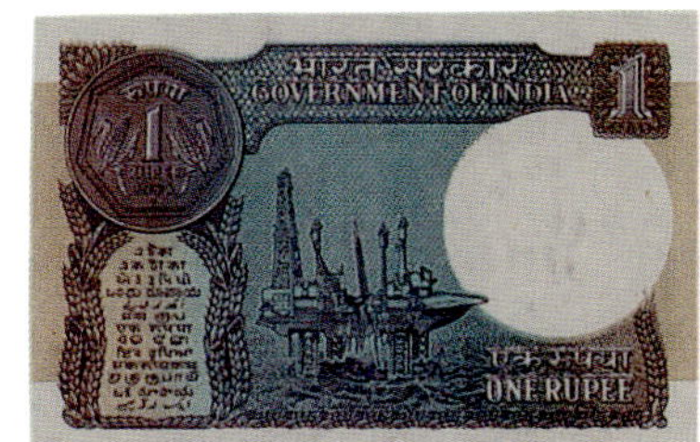
GOVERNMENT OF INDIA
1
ONE RUPEE

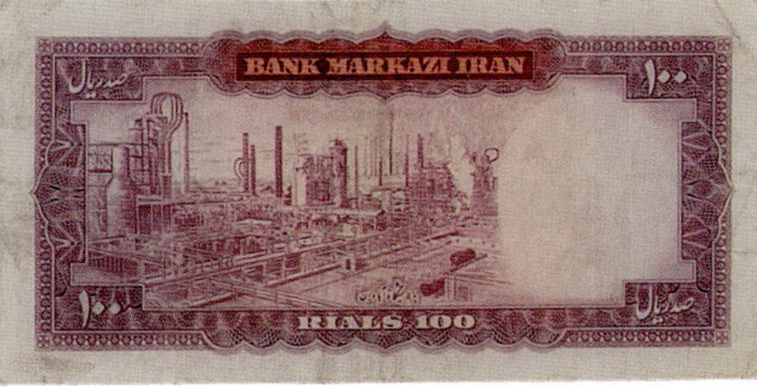
BANK MARKAZI IRAN
RIALS 100

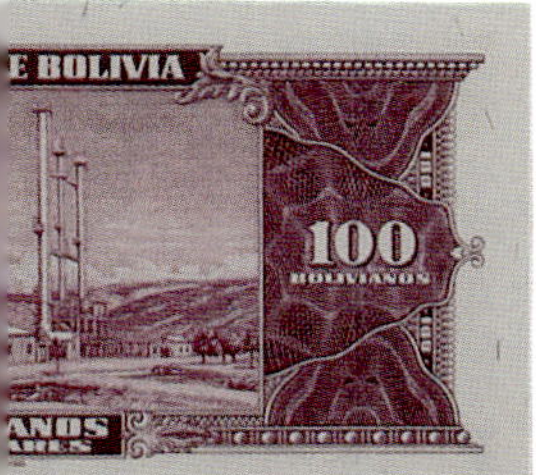
BOLIVIA
100
BOLIVIANOS

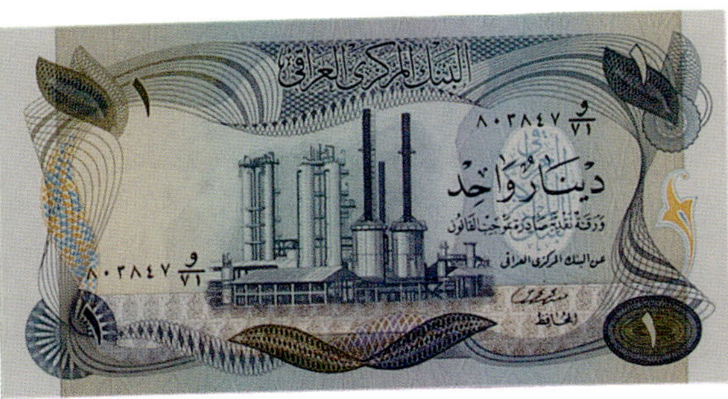
البنك المركزي العراقي
دينار واحد

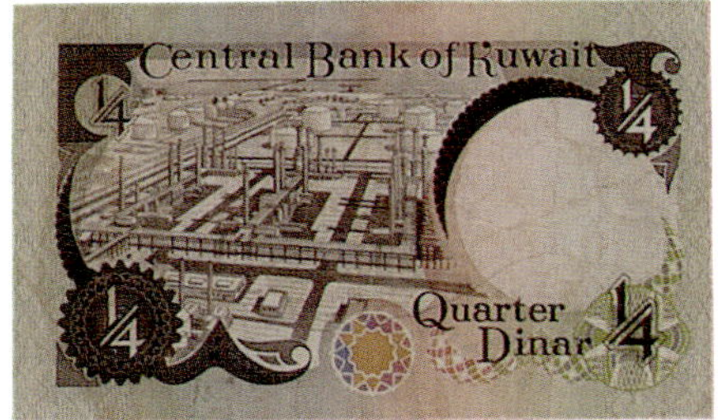
Central Bank of Kuwait
1/4
Quarter
Dinar

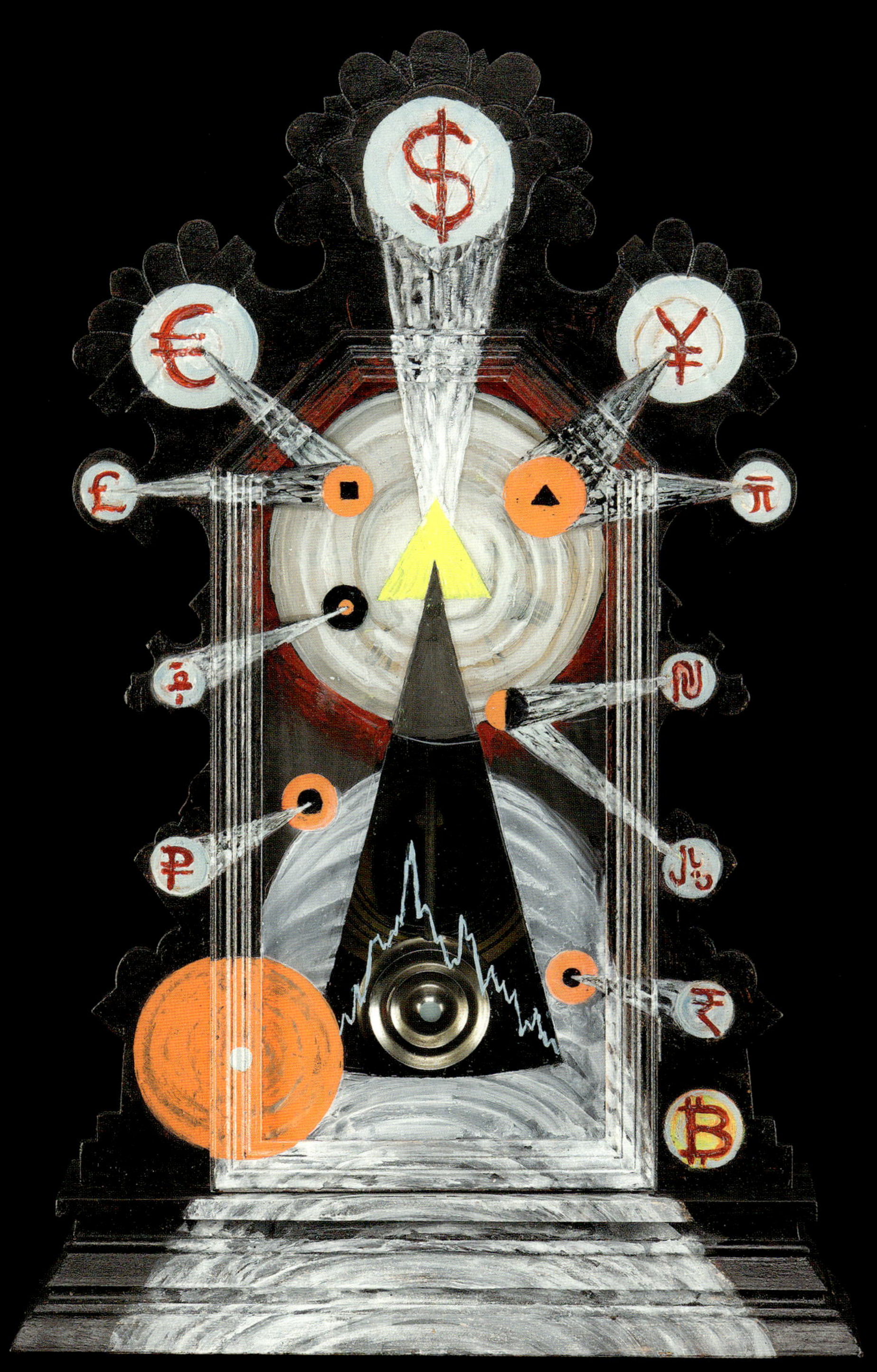

Wrong Way Time 2012–15 (details)

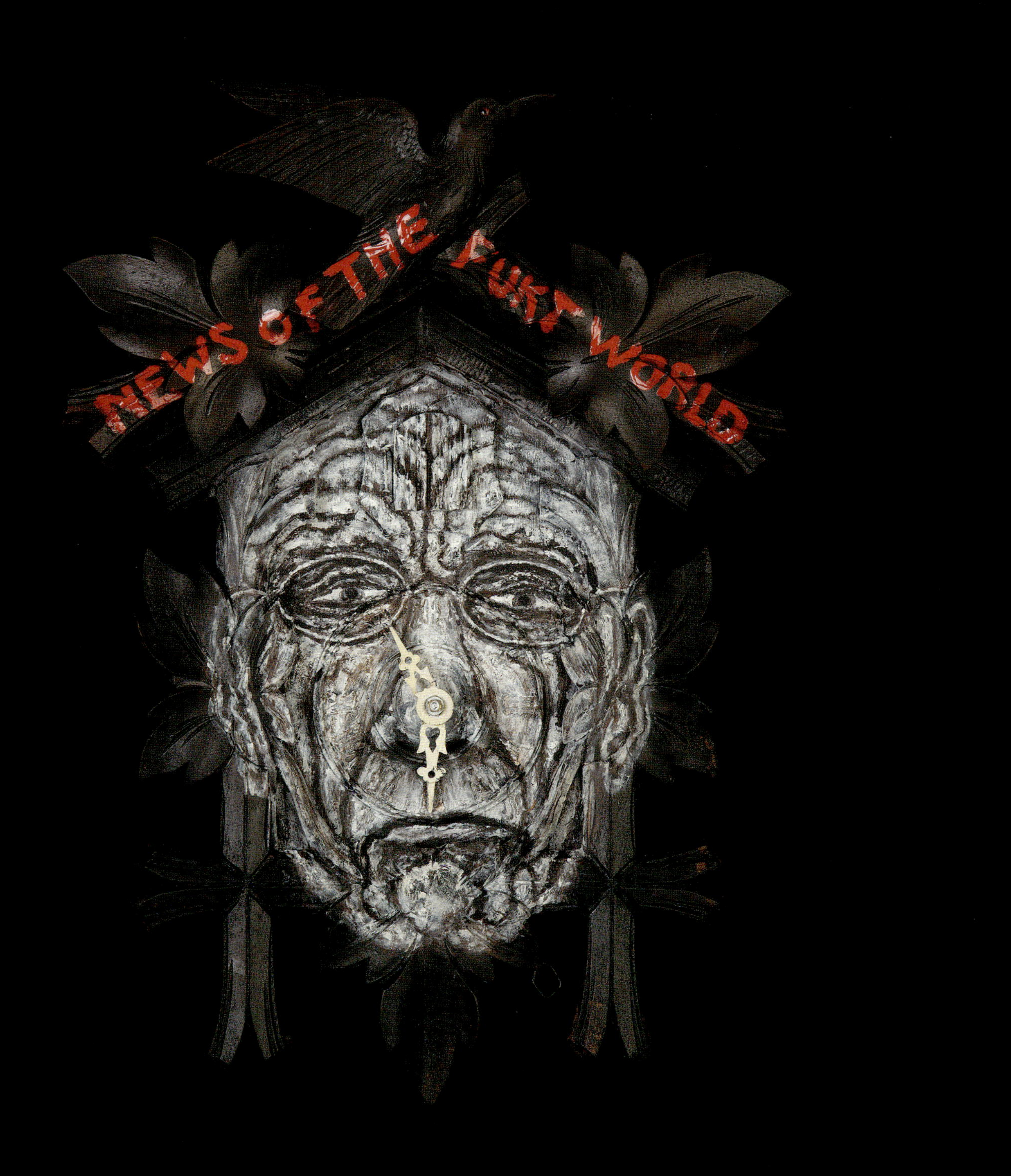
NEWS OF THE FUKT WORLD

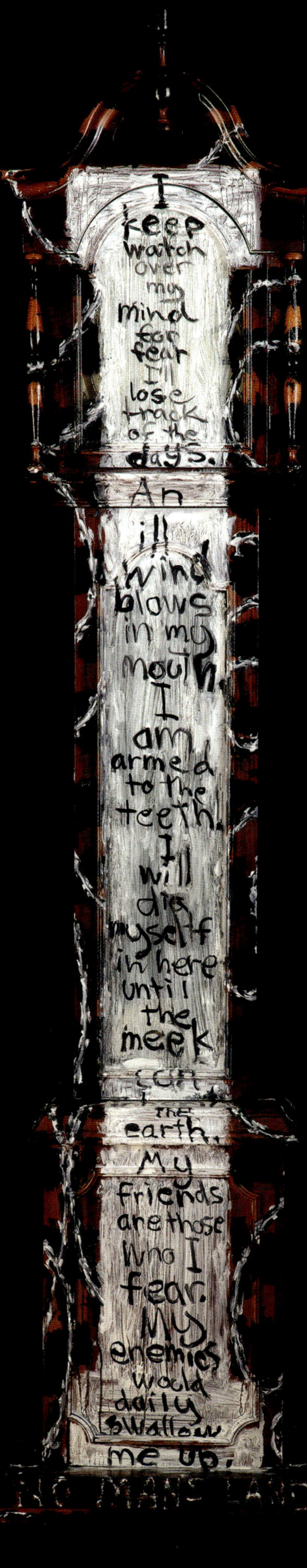

I
keep
watch
over
my
mind
for
fear
I'll
lose
track
of the
days.
An
ill
wind
blows
in my
mouth.
I
am
armed
to the
teeth.
I'll
will
dig
myself
in here
until
the
meek
can
[illegible] the
earth.
My
friends
are those
who I
fear.
My
enemies
would
daily
swallow
me up.

NO MAN'S LAND

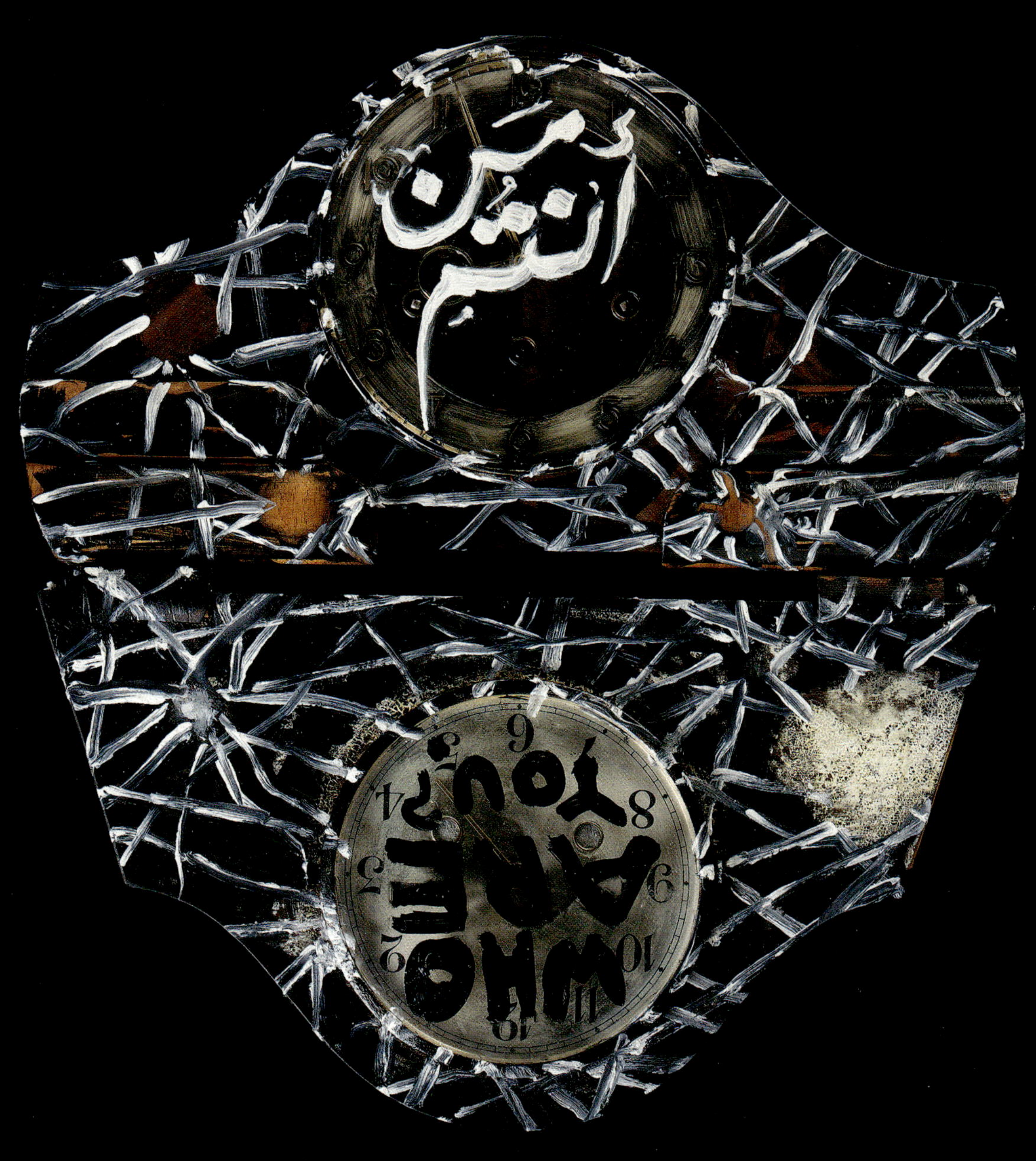

Wrong Way Time 2012–15 (details)

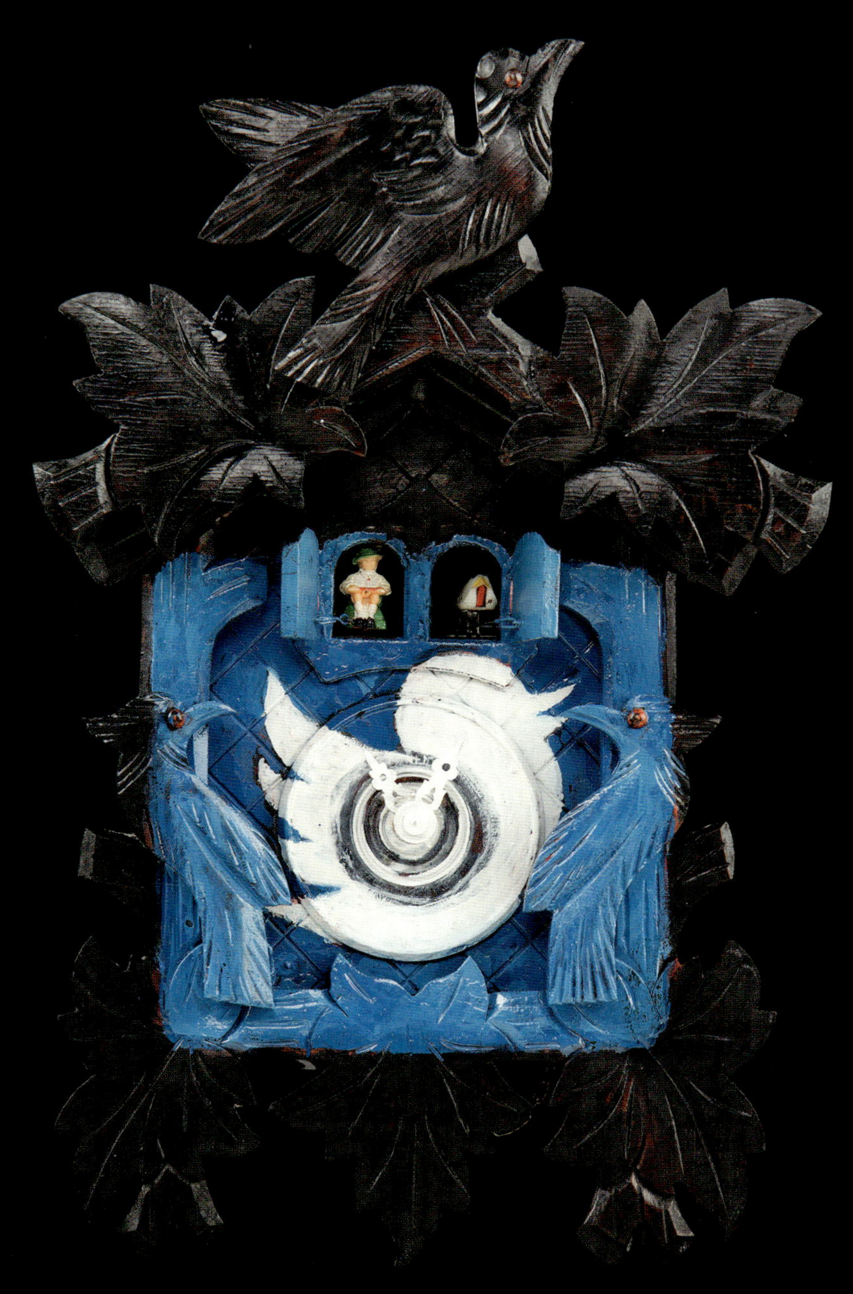

Wrong Way Time 2012–15 (detail)

List of Works

This list is correct at the time of printing. Titles of works in progress are designated 'Untitled' without italics.

Works are ordered by date then alphabetically.

Measurements are height before width before depth.

All works are courtesy of Fiona Hall and Roslyn Oxley9 Gallery, Sydney, unless otherwise stated.

Fiona Hall
Quercus robur; English oak
from the series *Paradisus Terrestris*
1990–2005
aluminium sardine tin
25 x 16.3 x 2.5 cm
Collection of the artist; on loan to Art Gallery of South Australia, Adelaide

Tender 2003–06
US dollars, wire, vitrines, vinyl lettering
86 nests, ranging from approx. 5 x 10 (diam.) cm to 108 x 17 x 13 cm; 2 vitrines, each 220 x 360 x 150 cm overall
Collection: Queensland Art Gallery
Purchased 2006. The Queensland Government's Gallery of Modern Art Acquisitions Fund
Fiona Hall: Wrong Way Time includes the nests and vinyl lettering only.

When My Boat Comes In 2003–
gouache on banknotes
installation dimensions variable

Holdfast (Macrocystis angustifolia; giant kelp*)* 2007
aluminium fish tin
25 x 16.3 x 2.5 cm

Fleet 2012
enamel paint, aluminium fish tins
12 parts, 20 x 24 cm, 24 x 14 cm, 22 x 13 cm, 25 x 19 cm, 22 x 12 cm, 25 x 11 cm, 26 x 24 cm, 25 x 10 cm, 25 x 20 cm, 25 x 19 cm, 34 x 10 cm, 25 x 19 cm

Wrong Way Time 2012–15
installation of longcase clocks, cuckoo clocks, mantle clocks, a banjo clock, and crow recordings; enamel and oil on clocks, wooden walking stick, model aeroplane, alarm clock set into volumes of British Museum's *General Catalogue of Printed books: Ten-year Supplement, 1956–1965*
8 longcase clocks, ranging from approx. 137 x 31 x 18 cm to 220 x 40 x 23 cm; 18 cuckoo clocks, ranging from approx. 30 x 24 x 15 cm to 74 x 36 x 19 cm, not including chimes; 12 mantle clocks, ranging from 22 x 32 x 13 cm to 57 x 36.5 x 13 cm; 1 banjo clock, 104 x 32 x 11 cm
installation dimensions variable

Amnesiac's Cartography (Narrow Road, Deep Chasm) 2014
bronze
2 parts, each 16 x 42 x 40.5 cm

Kuka Irititja (Animals from Another Time)
2014
installation of sculptures made from Tjanpi grasses (wild-harvested grasses including minarri grass), synthetic polymer yarn, wool, raffia, wire, camouflage military garment fabric, cotton and linen thread, buttons, ininti seeds, bamboo, emu and bush turkey feathers, buttons and camel teeth, on billy cans and burnt volumes of the British Museum's *General Catalogue of Printed Books: Ten-year Supplement, 1956–1965*

Works by Roma Butler, Yangi Yangi Fox, Rene Kulitja, Niningka Lewis, Yvonne Lewis, Molly Miller, Angkaliya Nelson, Mary Pan, Sandra Peterman, Tjawina Roberts and Nyanu Watson courtesy of Tjanpi Desert Weavers and the NPY Women's Council

Commissioned by TarraWarra Museum of Art for the TarraWarra Biennial 2014: Whisper in My Mask

Burnt books added only for Fiona Hall's installation in Venice

Roma Butler
Tjuwalpi (Lesser Stick-nest Rat;
Leporillus apicalis*)* 2014
14 x 11 x 28 cm

Yangi Yangi Fox
Mala (Rufous Hare-wallaby;
Lagorchestes hirsutus*)* 2014
39 x 38 x 45 cm

Tjilkamata (Echidna;
Tachyglossus aculeatus*)* 2014
14 x 17 x 37 cm

Walpuṯi (Numbat;
Myrmecobius fasciatus*)* 2014
33 x 21 x 85 cm

Fiona Hall
Mamu and Frog / Mamu munu ngaaṉngi
2014
55 x 36 x 36 cm; tin 29 x 27 cm diam

*Willy Wagtail (*Rhipidura leucophrys*) / Tjintir-tjintirpa maṟangka* 2014
17 x 43 x 28 cm; tin 19.5 x 18 cm diam

Aeroplane with Black Cockatoo and Bone / Irupulaina, kaki maru munu tarka
2014
133 x 70 x 80 cm

Helicopter and Sandhill Dunnart (Sminthopsis psammophila) /
Ilikapatura munu mingkiri 2014
100 x 50 x 50 cm

Spider and Bat Bomb / Warka munu Pinytjantjara pumpa bomb 2014
110 x 85 x 40 cm

*Mamu and Western Quoll (*Dasyurus geoffroii*) / Mamu munu Partjata* 2014
39 x 39 x 28 cm; tin 36 x 30 (diam.) cm

Rene Kulitja
Mulyamaru (Black-headed Monitor; Varanus tristis*)* 2014
32 x 26 x 43 cm

Tjilkamata (Echidna; Tachyglossus aculeatus*)* 2014
18 x 23 x 46 cm

Ngaya (Feral Cat; Felis catus*)* 2014
42 x 48 x 78 cm

Niningka Lewis
Walputi (Numbat; Myrmecobius fasciastus*)* 2014
26 x 19 x 86 cm

Waru (Black-footed Rock Wallaby; Petrogale lateralis*)* 2014
29 x 20 x 68 cm

Mala (Rufous Hare-wallaby; Lagorchestes hirsutus*)* 2014
46 x 20 x 44 cm

Ngaya (Feral Cat; Felis catus*)* 2014
24 x 23 x 78 cm

Yvonne Lewis
Yirtarrutju (Marsupial Mole; Notoryctes typhlops*)* 2014
10 x 7 x 32 cm

Tjuwalpi (Lesser Stick-nest Rat; Leporillus apicalis*)* 2014
19 x 19 x 50 cm

Molly Miller
Mitika *(Burrowing Bettong* Bettongia lesueur*)* 2014
33 x 19 x 44 cm

Tjakura (Great Desert Skink; Egernia kintorei*)* 2014
14 x 20 x 76 cm

Tjuwalpi (Lesser Stick-nest Rat; Leporillus apicalis*)* 2014
11 x 10 x 41 cm

Piiwi (Tawny Frogmouth; Podargus strigoides*)* 2014
29 x 27 x 58 cm

Angkaliya Nelson
Kamula (Feral Camel; Camelus dromedariius*)* 2014
20 x 13 x 46 cm

Ngiyari (Thorny Devil; Moloch horridus*)* 2014
20 x 13 x 46 cm

Ninu (Bilby; Macrotis lagotis*)* 2014
32 x 30 x 66 cm

Ngaya (Feral Cat; Felis catus*)* 2014
30 x 22 x 63 cm

Tjuni Kaputu (Helicopter) 2014
20 x14 x 41 cm

Mirilyirilyi (Rufous-crowned Emu-wren; Stipiturus ruficeps*)* 2014
23 x 25 x 34 cm

Piiwi Kulunypa (Tawny Frogmouth Chick; Podargus strigoides*)* 2014
23 x 25 x 34 cm

Mary Pan
Partjata (Western Quoll: Dasyurus geoffroii*)* 2014
32 x 24 x 96 cm

Partjata (Western Quoll: Dasyurus geoffroii*)* 2014
25 x 213 x 87 cm

Sandra Peterman
Ngaya (Feral Cat; Felis catus*)* 2014
36 x 24 x 58 cm

Tjawina Roberts
Yirtarrutju (Marsupial Mole; Notoryctes typhlops*)* 2014
6 x 13 x 23 cm

Partuta (Ghost Bat; Macroderma gigas*)* 2014
13 x 38 x 26 cm

Mitika (Burrowing Bettong; Bettongia lesueur*)* 2014
23 x 19 x 77 cm

Yirtarrutju (Marsupial Mole; Notoryctes typhlops*)* 2014
18 x 22 x 37 cm

Nyanu Watson
Tjulily-tjulilypa (Night Parrot; Pezoporus occidentalis*)* 2014
21 x 26 x 58 cm

Mala (Rufous Hare Wallaby; Lagorchestes hirsutus*)* 2014
31 x 15 x 101 cm

Tjakura (Great Desert Skink; Egernia kintorei*)* 2014
22 x 41 x 114 cm

Platonic Underground 2014
lead
5 parts, each approx. 10 x 10 x 10 cm

Untitled 2014 (detail)
aluminium, burnt volume from the British Museum's *General Catalogue of Printed Books: Ten-year Supplement, 1956–1965*
approx. 35 x 25 x 35 cm
Williams Sinclair Collection

Untitled 2014
enamel on carburettor, deer teeth
20 × 15 × 8.5 cm

Untitled 2014
enamel on light switch, driftwood
62 x 15.5 x 27.5 cm

Untitled 2014
enamel on plastic ornament and metal model tank
25 × 19 × 24 cm
Private collection, Melbourne

Untitled 2014
pool balls, deer teeth, wooden ornaments, enamel
22 × 18 × 11 cm
Private collection, Queensland

Untitled 2014
pool balls, zebra hoof, radiator hose
30 x 30 x 23.5 cm
Collection: Dr A. Dekker, Melbourne

Untitled 2014
bronze
approx. 40cm high

Untitled 2014
paper-wasp nests, books
3 nests, 5 x 9 x 9 cm, 5 x 11 x 8 cm,
4 x 10.5 x 11.5 cm
3 books, 25.5 x 17.2 x 2 cm,
23.5 x 20 x 1 cm, 26 x 18 x 1.5 cm:
Leonard L. Barton, *The Desert Harassers*, Astor Publications, Mosman, NSW, 1991; Theodore Shabad (ed.), *Soviet Geography: Review and Translation*, American Geographical Society, New York, 1976; *Dominion Atlas*, George Philip and Son, London.

Untitled 2014
lead; with found objects including wooden Shiva, plastic RMS *Titanic*, mobile phone, wooden branch, model of spine, credit card, dugong bone, metal spike, plastic Madonna, car light
11 parts, installation dimensions variable

All The King's Men 2014–15
knitted military uniforms; wire; animal bone, horns and teeth; dice; glass; leather boxing gloves; pool ball
20 parts, ranging from 102 x 58 x 31 cm to 190 x 45 x 42 cm
installation dimensions variable

Hack 2014–15
aluminium, LED lights, electrical circuitry, wood, viewing lens
23.5 x 23.5 x 160 cm

Manuhiri (Travellers) 2014–15
collection of driftwood from Waiapu River, Aotearoa New Zealand
installation dimensions variable

Spill 2014–15
collection of banknotes
installation dimensions variable

Triumph of the Damned 2014–15
collection of banknotes
installation dimensions variable

Untitled 2014–15
bronze
10 parts; 17.5 x 22 x 19 cm, 27 x 17 x 16 cm, 15.5 x 24 x 18 cm, 28 x 18 x 22 cm, 24 x 22 x 18.5 cm, 19 x 24.5 x 22.5 cm, 27 x 17 x 16 cm, 14 x 24 x 22 cm, 25 x 30 x 18 cm, 20 x 27 x 25 cm

Untitled 2014–15
bronze and newsprint
installation dimensions variable

Untitled 2014–15
collection of banknotes
installation dimensions variable

Vaporised 2014–15
enamel on perfume bottles, mobile phone
installation dimensions variable

Untitled 2015
bread and atlases
28 atlases, installation dimensions variable

Untitled 2015
coal, aluminium
coal: 30 x 40 x 50 cm

Untitled 2015
installation of Chinese cork dioramas, spiders, spider webs
39 dioramas, ranging from 7 x 7 x 2 cm to 28.5 x 59.5 x 11 cm

Untitled 2015
synthetic polymer paint on window, plastic car headlamp casings
installation dimensions variable

Where the Wind Blows 2015
gouache on banknotes
installation dimensions variable

Biography

Fiona Hall
Born 1953 Sydney, Australia. Lives in Adelaide, Australia.

1972–1975
Diploma of Painting, East Sydney Technical College, Sydney

1977–1978
Photographic Assistant to Fay Godwin, London, United Kingdom

1979–1982
Master of Fine Arts (Photography), the Visual Studies Workshop, Rochester, United States

1987
Artist in Residence, Tasmanian School of Art, University of Tasmania, Hobart

1983–1997
Lecturer in Photo Studies, South Australian School of Art, University of South Australia, Adelaide

1990
Artist in Residence, Phillip Institute of Technology, Melbourne

1997
Artist in Residence, Mount Coot-tha Botanic Gardens, Brisbane, in collaboration with Institute of Modern Art, Brisbane

Creative Arts Fellow, Canberra School of Art, Australian National University, Canberra

1998
Australia Council for the Arts Studio Residency, Acme Studios, London, United Kingdom

Appointed to Advisory Council, Centre for the Mind, Australian National University, Canberra

1999
Appointed to the Visual Arts/Crafts Board, Australia Council

Asialink Residency at the Lunuganga Estate, Colombo, Sri Lanka (an extended residency completed in 2009)

Lowenstein Sharp Arts 21 Fellowship, Melbourne

2007
Artist in Residence, Elam International Artist in Residence Program, Elam School of Fine Arts, University of Auckland, New Zealand

Selected Solo Exhibitions

2014, 2011, 2005, 2002, 1999, 1996, and 1995
Solo exhibitions at Roslyn Oxley9 Gallery, Sydney

2013
Big Game Hunting, Heide Museum of Modern Art, Melbourne
Veneer, Two Rooms, Auckland, New Zealand

2008
Fiona Hall: Force Field, Museum of Contemporary Art, Sydney; City Gallery Wellington, Wellington, New Zealand; Christchurch Art Gallery Te Puna o Waiwhetu, New Zealand; Newcastle Art Gallery, Newcastle

2005
Fiona Hall, Queensland Art Gallery, Brisbane; Art Gallery of South Australia, Adelaide

1999
A Transit through Paradise, Gallery 706, Colombo, Sri Lanka

1998
Cash Crop, Institute of Modern Art, Brisbane

1997
Canberra School of Art, Australian National University, Canberra

1995
Subject to Change, Experimental Art Foundation, Adelaide

1994
Garden of Earthly Delights, National Gallery of Australia, Canberra; National Gallery of Victoria, Melbourne; Art Gallery of New South Wales, Sydney; Plimsoll Gallery, Hobart; Art Gallery of Western Australia, Perth; Brisbane City Hall, Brisbane

1990
Fiona Hall: Words, Contemporary Art Centre of South Australia, Adelaide

1989
Illustration to Dante's 'Divine Comedy', Australian Centre for Photography, Sydney; Australian Centre for Contemporary Art, Melbourne; Experimental Art Foundation, Adelaide

1987
Selections from 14 Years: Fiona Hall, Experimental Art Foundation, Adelaide

1986
III III II: A Survey of Twelve Years' Work, Australian Centre for Photography, Sydney

1983
Fiona Hall: Recent Photographs, The Developed Image Gallery, Adelaide; Australian Centre for Photography, Sydney; Visibility Gallery, Melbourne

Fiona Hall: Recent Work, Australian Centre for Photography, Sydney

1982
Fiona Hall, Australian Centre for Photography, Sydney

1981
The Antipodean Suite, Tasmanian School of Art Gallery, Hobart

Recent Works, Australian Centre for Photography, Sydney

1978
Church Street Photography Centre, Melbourne

1977
Creative Camera Gallery, London, United Kingdom

Public Commissions

2009
Native Rockery Garden, Heide Museum of Modern Art, Melbourne

2007
Out of Mind, Queensland Brain Institute, Brisbane

2000
A Folly for Mrs Macquarie, commissioned by City of Sydney, Sydney Sculpture Walk, Royal Botanic Gardens, Sydney

1999
Bloodline, Sydney Organising Committee for the Olympic Games, Olympic limited edition print and poster commission

1998
Fern Garden, National Gallery of Australia, Canberra

1995
Occupied Territory, commission for the opening of the Museum of Sydney, Sydney

1989, 1987, 1986
Polaroid 20 x 24 commissions, Camera Project, New York, United States

1984–1986
Parliament House Construction Project, Canberra

1983
CSR Photography Project Collection, Tumut, NSW

Selected Group Exhibitions

2014
Kochi-Muziris Biennale 2014, Kochi, Kerala, India

TarraWarra Biennial 2014: Whisper in My Mask, TarraWarra Museum of Art, Healesville, Vic

2014 Adelaide Biennial of Australian Art: Dark Heart, Art Gallery of South Australia, Adelaide

2013
Australia, Royal Academy of Arts, London, United Kingdom

Future Primitive, Heide Museum of Modern Art, Melbourne

2012
ANIMAL/HUMAN, University of Queensland Art Museum, Brisbane

Contemporary Australia: Women, Queensland Art Gallery | Gallery of Modern Art, Brisbane

Kermadec: Nine Artists Explore the South Pacific, Tauranga Art Gallery, New Zealand, and national tour

dOCUMENTA (13), Kassel, Germany (*Fall Prey*)

Reconfiguring the Feminine, Gallery OED, Kochi, Kerala, India

Theatre of the World, Museum of Old and New Art, Hobart

2011
Djalkiri: We are Standing on Their Names: Blue Mud Bay, Nomad Art Productions, Darwin, and interstate tour

Monanisms, Museum of Old and New Art, Hobart

2010
21st Century: Art in the First Decade, Queensland Art Gallery | Gallery of Modern Art, Brisbane

The 17th Biennale of Sydney: The Beauty of Distance: Songs of Survival in a Precarious Age, Royal Botanic Gardens, Sydney (*Barbarians at the Gate*)

2009
The Third Moscow Biennale of Contemporary Art, Moscow, Russia

2008
Uneasy: Recent South Australian Art, Anne & Gordon Samstag Museum of Art, Adelaide

2007
The 3rd Auckland Triennial: Turbulence, Auckland, New Zealand

Port Arthur Project: Re-interpreting Port Arthur Historic Site through contemporary visual art, Port Arthur Historic Site, Tasmania (*Breeding Ground*)

DeOverkant/Downunder: Contemporary Sculpture from Australia and the Netherlands, The Hague Sculpture Foundation, The Netherlands

New Nature, Govett-Brewster Art Gallery, New Plymouth, New Zealand (*Mown*, garden installation)

2006
2006 Contemporary Commonwealth, National Gallery of Victoria and Australian Centre for the Moving Image, Melbourne

Multiplicity: Prints and Multiples from the Collections of the MCA and the University of Wollongong, Museum of Contemporary Art, Sydney and interstate tour

Prism: Contemporary Australian Art, Bridgestone Museum, Tokyo, Japan

Replant: A New Generation of Botanical Art, Nomad Art Productions, Darwin

2005
MCA Collection: New Acquisitions in Context, Museum of Contemporary Art, Sydney

Strangely Familiar, with Fiona MacDonald, University of Technology Sydney Gallery, Sydney

2004
Living Together is Easy, Contemporary Art Centre, Art Tower Mito, Mito Arts Foundation, Mito-shi, Japan; National Gallery of Victoria, Melbourne

More Easily Imagined: Crossings of the Blue Mountains, Bathurst Regional Art Gallery, Bathurst, NSW

2003
Face Up: Contemporary Art from Australia, Museum for the Present, Nationalgalerie im Hamburger Bahnhof, Berlin, Germany

Flagship: Australian Art in the National Gallery of Victoria, 1790–2000, National Gallery of Victoria, Melbourne

Nature and Nation: Vaster than Empires, Hastings Museum & Art Gallery, East Sussex, United Kingdom

2002
2nd Sight: Australian Photography in the National Gallery of Victoria, National Gallery of Victoria, Melbourne

Converge: where art + science meet, Adelaide Biennale, Art Gallery of South Australia, Adelaide

Fieldwork: Australian Art 1968–2002, National Gallery of Victoria, Melbourne

The First Twenty Years: Roslyn Oxley9 Gallery, Roslyn Oxley9 Gallery, Sydney

2001
The Art of Transformation, National Gallery of Australia, Canberra

Federation: Australian Art and Society 1901–2001, National Gallery of Australia, Canberra

Unpacking Europe, Museum Boijmans Van Beuningen, Rotterdam, The Netherlands; Haus de Kulturen de Welt, Berlin, Germany

2000
The 12th Biennale of Sydney (2000), Art Gallery of New South Wales, Sydney (Gene Pool)

Chemistry: Art in South Australia 1990–2000, Art Gallery of South Australia, Adelaide

Mirror with a Memory: A History of the Photographic Portrait in Australia, National Portrait Gallery, Canberra

Terra Mirabilis/Wonderful Land, Centre for Visual Arts, Cardiff, Wales

1999
Clemenger Art Award, Heide Museum of Modern Art, Melbourne

New Republics: Contemporary Art from Australia, Canada and South Africa, Canada House Gallery, London and tour to Canada and Australia

Signature Works, Australian Centre for Photography, Sydney

1998
Global Liquidity (with Nalini Malani), Gallery Chemould, Bombay, India; Roslyn Oxley9 Gallery, Sydney

1997
Archives and the Everyday, Canberra School of Art Gallery, Australian National University, Canberra

Contempora5 Art Award, National Gallery of Victoria, Melbourne (winner inaugural Contempora5 Art Award)

The Enigmatic Object, Art Gallery of New South Wales, Sydney

Australian Perspecta 1997: Between Art and Nature, Art Gallery of New South Wales, Sydney

1996
Art Across Oceans (Container '96), Copenhagen, Denmark

Art Cologne Internationaler Kunstmarkt, Messe- und Ausstellungs-Gesellschaft m.b.H., Köln, Germany

Asia Pacific Triennial of Contemporary Art, Queensland Art Gallery, Brisbane

Colonial Post Colonial, Museum of Modern Art at Heide, Melbourne

How Say You, Australian Centre for Contemporary Art, Melbourne

Photography is Dead! Long Live Photography! Museum of Contemporary Art, Sydney

The Power to Move: Aspects of Australian Photography, Queensland Art Gallery, Brisbane

1995
The Object of Existence, Australian Centre for Contemporary Art, Melbourne

1994
Adelaide Installations: Incorporating the 1994 Adelaide Biennial of Australian Art, Contemporary Art Centre of South Australia, Adelaide (*Biodata*)

Localities of Desire: Contemporary Art in an International World, Museum of Contemporary Art, Sydney

Sydney Photographed, Museum of Contemporary Art, Sydney

1992
Adelaide Festival Artists' Projects, Festival Centre, Adelaide

The Temple of Flora, Waverley City Gallery, Melbourne

1991
Australian Perspecta 1991, Art Gallery of New South Wales, Sydney

The Corporeal Body, Drill Hall Gallery, Australian National University, Canberra

Photodeath, Australian National Gallery, Canberra

Second Nature, P3 Art and Environment, Tokyo, Japan

Stranger than Fiction, Australian National Gallery, Canberra

1990
Adelaide Biennial of Australian Art, Art Gallery of South Australia, Adelaide

Art Dock: Exposition D'Art Contemporain Australien, Kowe Kara Melanesian Cultural Centre, Noumea, New Caledonia

Art from Australia: Eight Contemporary Views, Asialink travelling exhibition touring southeast Asia

Fragmentation and Fabrication: Recent Australian Photography, Art Gallery of South Australia, Adelaide

Harbour Hymns, City Songs: Visions of Sydney from the Collection, Art Gallery of New South Wales, Sydney

Photography: Recent Acquisitions, Australian National Gallery, Canberra

Terminal Garden, Experimental Art Foundation, Adelaide

Twenty Contemporary Australian Photographers, National Gallery of Victoria, Melbourne; Art Gallery of New South Wales, Sydney

1989
From the Sublime to the Sordid, Experimental Art Foundation, Adelaide

1988
Australian Photography: The 1980s, Australian National Gallery, Canberra, and interstate tour

Recent South Australian Art: New Acquisitions, Art Gallery of South Australia, Adelaide

South Australia Rephotographed, College Gallery, South Australian School of Art, Adelaide

1987
Constructed Images: Photographs of Parliament House, The Drill Hall Gallery, Canberra

Pure Invention, Parco Space 5, Tokyo, Japan; Contemporary Art Centre of South Australia, Adelaide; 200 Gertrude Street, Melbourne

Some Provincial Myths: Recent Art from Adelaide, Contemporary Art Centre of South Australia, Adelaide, and interstate tour

What is this thing called science, University Gallery, The University of Melbourne, Melbourne

1986
In Full View: An Exhibition of 20 x 24 Polaroid Photographs, Art Gallery of New South Wales, Sydney, and interstate tour

The Gothic, Perversity and its Pleasure, Institute of Modern Art, Brisbane; 200 Gertrude Street, Melbourne; Chameleon Galleries, Hobart

1985
Australian Perspecta 1985, Art Gallery of New South Wales, Sydney

1984
Interface: A Survey of Art and Technology, Centre Gallery, Adelaide

Time Present and Time Past, Australian Centre for Photography, Sydney

1983
A Decade of Australian Photography, Australian National Gallery, Canberra

1982
The 4th Biennale of Sydney: Vision in Disbelief, Art Gallery of New South Wales, Sydney

New American Photographs, California State College, San Bernardo, CA, United States

1981
Australian Perspecta 1981, Art Gallery of New South Wales, Sydney

By Arrangement, DBR Gallery, Cleveland, OH, United States

Project 38: Re-constructed Vision, Art Gallery of New South Wales, Sydney

1980
Fiona Hall, David Blount, Brian Thompson, Australian Centre for Photography, Sydney

1977
Creative Camera Gallery, London, United Kingdom

1975
Six Australian Women Photographers, Australian Centre for Photography, Sydney; National Gallery of Victoria, Melbourne

1974
Thoughts and Images: An Exploratory Exhibition of Australian Student Photography, Ewing and George Paton Galleries, Melbourne

Selected Public Collections

National Gallery of Australia, Canberra
Art Gallery of New South Wales, Sydney
National Gallery of Victoria, Melbourne
Queensland Art Gallery, Brisbane
Art Gallery of South Australia, Adelaide
Art Gallery of Western Australia, Perth
Museum of Contemporary Art, Sydney
Bendigo Art Gallery, Bendigo, Vic
Heide Museum of Modern Art, Melbourne
Latrobe Regional Gallery, Morwell, Vic
Newcastle Region Art Gallery, NSW
Tasmanian Museum and Art Gallery, Hobart
Museum of Old and New Art, Hobart
Olympic Fine Art Collection, SOCOG, Sydney

Further Reading

Texts by Fiona Hall

Hall, Fiona, *Subject to Change*, Experimental Art Foundation, Adelaide, and Piper Press, Sydney, 1995.

Hall, Fiona, 'Leaf Litter', in Suhanya Raffel (ed.), *Leaf Litter: An exhibition by Fiona Hall*, exh. cat., Asialink, Melbourne, and the Lunaganga Trust, Colombo, 2002, n.p.

Hall, Fiona, Text on Djambawa Marawili, *Djambawa Marawili*, exh. cat., Annandale Galleries, Sydney, 2011, pp. 6, 8.

Hall, Fiona, 'Listing to starboard', in Bronwen Golder and Greg O'Brien (eds), *Kermadec: Nine Artists Explore the South Pacific*, Unity Books, Auckland, 2011.

Hall, Fiona, 'Burning Bright', in Morgan, Kendrah (ed.), *Big Game Hunting*, exh. cat., Heide Museum of Modern Art, Melbourne, 2013, p. 71.

Interviews and documentaries

Hall, Fiona and Paula Savage, 'In conversation', *Fiona Hall: Force Field*, Museum of Contemporary Art, Sydney and City Gallery Wellington, Wellington, 2008, pp. 25–33.

Machan, Kim, *Art Rage: Artworks for Television*, video compilation for ABC TV (collaboration with Destiny Deacon), Brisbane, 1997 (VHS PAL).

Mead, Elizabeth, '*Further Shore*, 2002–5: Fiona Hall', interview with Fiona Hall, Sheba Chhachhi and Atul Dodiya, *Monanisms*, Museum of Old and New Art, Hobart, 2010, pp. 296–305.

Morrell, Timothy, 'Undermining the systems of a post-everything world: Timothy Morrell interviews Fiona Hall', *Art Monthly Australia*, no. 68, April 1994, pp. 8–11.

Morrell, Timothy, 'Fiona Hall interviewed, Adelaide September 1999', in Suhanya Raffel, *A Transit Through Paradise: Sri Lanka 1999/Fiona Hall*, Asialink Centre, University of Melbourne, 1999, p. 9.

Morrell, Timothy and Jim Moss, 'Fiona Hall interviewed by Jim Moss and Tim Morrell', *Photofile*, Summer 1988–89, pp. 25–27.

Nichols, Catherine, 'Interview with Fiona Hall', *Face Up: Contemporary Art from Australia*, exh. cat., Museum for the Present, Nationalgalerie im Hamburger Bahnhof, Berlin, 2003, p. 93.

Monographs and solo exhibition catalogues

Carcenac de Torné, Brigitte, *Illustrations to Dante's Divine Comedy by Fiona Hall*, Australian Centre for Photography, Sydney; Australian Centre for Contemporary Art, Melbourne and Experimental Art Foundation, Adelaide, 1989.

Davidson, Kate, *Garden of Earthly Delights*, exh. cat., National Gallery of Australia, Canberra, 1992.

Ewington, Julie, *Cash Crop*, exh. cat., Institute of Modern Art, Brisbane, 1998.

Ewington, Julie, *Fiona Hall*, Piper Press, Sydney, 2005.

Fiona Hall: Force Field, exh. cat., Museum of Contemporary Art, Sydney and City Gallery Wellington, Wellington, 2008 (essays by Vivienne Webb and Gregory O'Brien).

Morgan, Kendrah (ed.), *Big Game Hunting*, exh. cat., Heide Museum of Modern Art, Melbourne, 2013 (essays by Kendrah Morgan, David Hansen, Gregory O'Brien and Manoj Nair).

Raffel, Suhanya, *A Transit Through Paradise: Sri Lanka 1999/Fiona Hall*, exh. cat., Asialink Centre, University of Melbourne, 1999.

Raffel, Suhanya, *Leaf Litter: An Exhibition by Fiona Hall*, exh. cat., Asialink, Melbourne and The Lunaganga Trust, Colombo, 2002.

Walker, Linda Marie, *Fiona Hall: Words*, Contemporary Art Centre of South Australia, Adelaide and Australian Centre for Photography, Sydney, 1990.

Books and exhibition catalogues

Art & Australia (ed.), *Current: Contemporary Art from Australia and New Zealand*, Dott Publishing, Sydney, NSW, 2008, p. 132.

Cooper, Linda, *Converge: where art + science meet: 2002 Adelaide Biennial of Australian Art*, exh. cat., Art Gallery of South Australia, Adelaide, 2002, pp. 38–39.

Crombie, Isobel (ed.), *Flagship: Australian Art in the National Gallery of Victoria, 1790–2000*, National Gallery of Victoria, Melbourne, 2003, pp. 67, 76.

Crombie, Isobel and Susan van Wyk, *2nd Sight: Australian Photography in the National Gallery of Victoria*, exh. cat., National Gallery of Victoria, Melbourne, 2002, p. 98.

Ewington, Julie, 'In the wild: nature, culture, gender in installation art', in Catriona Moore (ed.), *Dissonance: Feminism and the Arts 1970–90*, Artspace, Sydney and Allen and Unwin, Sydney, 1995, pp. 228–48.

Ewington, Julie, 'Fiona Hall: blooming taxonomist', in *Clemenger Contemporary Art Award 1999*, exh. cat., Museum of Modern Art at Heide, Melbourne, 1999, p. 20.

Ewington, Julie, 'Fiona Hall', in Melissa Chiu (ed.), *Selections from the University of Western Sydney Art Collection*, University of Western Sydney, Penrith, NSW, 2001, pp. 94–95.

Ewington, Julie, 'Cell culture', in Britta Schmitz (ed.), *Face Up: Contemporary Art from Australia*, exh. cat., Nationalgalerie im Hamburger Bahnhof, Berlin, 2003, pp. 94–95.

Hansen, David, 'Fiona Hall', in Nick Mitzevich (ed.), *2014 Adelaide Biennial of Australian Art: Dark Heart*, exh. cat., Art Gallery of South Australia, Adelaide, 2014, p. 98.

Lynn, Victoria and Shireen Gandhi, *Global Liquidity: A Joint Exhibition, Fiona Hall and Nalani Malani*, exh. cat., Gallery Chemould, Mumbai and Roslyn Oxley9 Gallery, Sydney, 1998.

Morrell, Timothy, *Uneasy: Recent South Australian Art*, exh. cat., Anne & Gordon Samstag Museum of Art, University of South Australia, Adelaide, 2008, pp. 32–33.

Mundine, Djon and Natalie King, 'Whisper in my mask', *TarraWarra Biennial: Whisper in My Mask 2014*, exh. cat., TarraWarra Museum of Art, Healesville, Vic, 2014, p. 7.

Newton, Gael, 'Fiona Hall', in *Australian Perspecta 1981: A Biennial Survey of Contemporary Australian Art*, exh. cat., Art Gallery of New South Wales, Sydney, 1981, p. 160.

Newton, Gael, 'Fiona Hall: retro-spect Leura's theme', in Stuart Koop (ed.), *A Small History of Photography*, Centre for Contemporary Photography, Melbourne, 1997, pp. 56–60.

Savage, Paula and Fiona Hall, 'Force Field', in *Volume One: MCA Collection*, Museum of Contemporary Art, Sydney, 2012, pp. 282–89.

Smith, Jason, 'Fiona Hall: dead in the water', in *Fieldwork: Australian Art 1968–2002*, exh. cat., National Gallery of Victoria, Melbourne, 2002, pp. 130–31.

Smith, Jason, 'Fiona Hall' in Charles Green (ed.), *2006 Contemporary Commonwealth*, exh. cat., National Gallery of Victoria and Australian Centre for the Moving Image, Melbourne, 2006, pp. 76–79.

Stephen, Ann, 'Taking cuttings: Fiona Hall's *Paradisus Terrestris*', in Juliana Engberg (ed.), *Colonial Post Colonial*, exh. cat., Museum of Modern Art at Heide, Melbourne, 1996, pp. 40–41.

Webb, Vivienne, *MCA Collection: New Acquisitions in Context*, exh. cat., Museum of Contemporary Art, Sydney, 2005, pp. 17, 32.

Periodicals and newspapers

Alexander, George, 'Rosemary Laing and Fiona Hall: remembering forwards', *Art Asia Pacific*, no. 46, Autumn 2005, pp. 48–53.

Davidson, Kate, 'The art of Fiona Hall', *Art & Australia*, vol. 43, no. 1, Spring 2005, pp. 14–15.

Edwards, Deborah, 'Transported/transplanted: Fiona Hall's *A Folly for Mrs Macquarie*', Art & Australia, vol. 39, no. 2, Summer 2001, p. 164.

Ennis, Helen, '*Garden of Earthly Delights*: the work of Fiona Hall', *Photofile*, exh. review, no. 38, 1993, pp. 37–38.

Ewington, Julie, 'Cash Crop', *Artlink*, vol. 19, no. 4, 1999, pp. 41–43.

Ewington, Julie and Fiona Hall, 'The unnatural art of Fiona Hall', *Object*, issue 46, May 2005, p. 28.

Forrest, Nicholas, 'Fiona Hall reveals the secrets of her Documenta hunter's den', *Art Info*, 4 July 2012, http://www.artinfo.com/news/story/812136/fiona-hall-reveals-the-secrets-of-her-documenta-hunters-den-1.

Fulton, Adam, 'Hall's career honoured with top national award', *Sydney Morning Herald*, 14 September 2011, p. 12.

Gilbert, Alan, 'Documenta 13's Art Laboratory', *Hyperallergic*, 30 June 2012, http://hyperallergic.com/53591/documenta-13s-art-laboratory/.

Hart, Deborah, 'Fertile interactions—Fiona Hall's garden', *Art & Australia*, vol. 36, no. 2, Summer 1998, pp. 202–11.

Hart, Deborah, 'Fiona Hall: *Leaf Litter*', *Artonview*, National Gallery of Australia, Winter 2003, pp. 23–26.

Harvey, Nicola, 'Review of Fiona Hall, City Gallery Wellington and Museum of Contemporary Art, Sydney', *Frieze*, November–December 2008, p. 205.

Higson, Rosalie, 'Magic under the surface', *The Australian*, 7 March 2008, Arts p. 10.

Hill, Peter, 'Critic's picks', *Sydney Morning Herald*, 8–14 November 2002, Metro p. 27.

Hurrell, John, 'Mixed commotions: *Turbulence*: the 3rd Auckland Triennial', *Art Monthly Australia*, no. 201, July 2007, pp. 24–28.

McDonald, John, 'Material logic', *Australian Financial Review Magazine*, March 2005, pp. 16–21.

McDonald, John, 'A force to be reckoned with', *Sydney Morning Herald*, 19–20 April 2008, pp. 16–17.

Miller, Carrie, 'Big game hunter: Fiona Hall', *Australian Art Collector*, issue 64, April–June 2013, pp. 64–66.

Morrell, Timothy, 'Picturing the apocalypse—the art of Fiona Hall', *Art & Australia*, vol. 25, no. 2, Summer 1987, pp. 235–39.

Morrell, Timothy, 'The art of Fiona Hall in Brisbane', *Art Monthly Australia*, no. 179, May 2005, p. 21.

Muhlberger, Emma, 'Ordering chaos: Fiona Hall', *Eyeline*, no. 58, Spring 2005, pp. 48–49.

Smee, Sebastian, 'Hall mark', *Sydney Morning Herald*, 18 August 1998, p. 11.

Smee, Sebastian, 'Concepts take root', *Sydney Morning Herald*, 5 Oct 1999, p. 15.

Turner, Brook, 'Intelligent design—remaking the world in her image', *Australian Financial Review*, 15 September 2011, p. 42.

Turner, Brook, 'Fiona Hall: the art alchemist', *Australian Financial Review Magazine*, 27 April 2012, pp. 40–43.

Acknowledgements

Major Partner

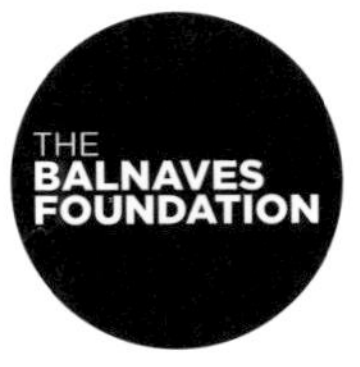

The Balnaves Foundation has supported Australia's representation at the Venice Biennale since 2007.

Founded in 2006 by Neil Balnaves AO, the Foundation disperses over $2 million per annum to organisations that aim to create a better Australia through education, medicine and the arts with a focus on young people, the disadvantaged, and Indigenous communities.

The Foundation has partnered with a number of key art organisations to produce exhibitions. These include the 'NEW' exhibition at the Australian Centre for Contemporary Art that features the work of young Australians, and a partnership with the Art Gallery of New South Wales to produce a program of contemporary exhibitions, named 'Balnaves Contemporary'. The Foundation also supports the production of Indigenous plays at Belvoir Street Theatre in Sydney.

The Foundation funds the main prize for Sculpture by the Sea, Bondi, and the McClelland Sculpture Survey at the McClelland Gallery and Sculpture Park in Melbourne. Financial support is provided for a free teenage program, Generationext, at the Museum of Contemporary Art Australia, and a children's program called START, at the Art Gallery of South Australia. The Foundation also supports Kaldor Public Art Projects and funds the free ferry at the Biennale of Sydney.

Support in the field of medicine includes grants to St Vincent's Hospital, Sydney, the Cerebral Palsy Foundation and the Children's Cancer Institute Australia. The Foundation has also made a long term commitment to the University of New South Wales to provide scholarships for Indigenous students studying medicine.

Supporting Partner

Maddocks provides premium legal services to corporations, businesses and governments throughout Australia and internationally. We advise national clients across education, government, infrastructure, healthcare, professional services and technology sectors from our Canberra, Melbourne and Sydney offices. With more than 500 people, we aim to work together to make a difference ... every day.

Maddocks is committed to supporting the contemporary arts. As the first Australian corporate sponsor for the Venice Biennale, the firm has supported Australian artists exhibiting at the world's premier contemporary art event since 2001.

We seek to have our partners and people engage with art in a way that brings our community closer together. Our vision as a firm is to be acknowledged for innovation, and as nurturing a culture of collaboration, respect and diversity.

The Maddocks Art Prize enables an emerging Australian artist to attend the Venice Biennale. The prize will be awarded to a recipient in both Sydney and Melbourne—accommodation and a stipend for a week in Venice. The winners of the 2015 Maddocks Art Prize will be announced in March.

Supporting Partner

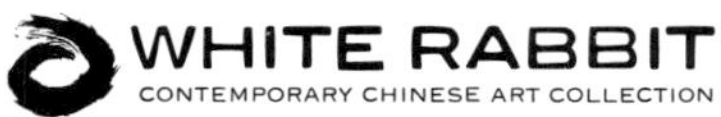

The White Rabbit Gallery is a not-for-profit private museum in Sydney, Australia. Opened to showcase Judith Neilson's vast collection of twenty-first-century Chinese contemporary art, the White Rabbit Gallery aims to make contemporary art accessible to all.

The Neilson Foundation and the White Rabbit Gallery are proud to support Australia's contribution to the 2015 Venice Biennale. With its unique position as the world's oldest Biennale, Venice is one of the most important locations for fresh, exciting contemporary art.

Supporting Partners

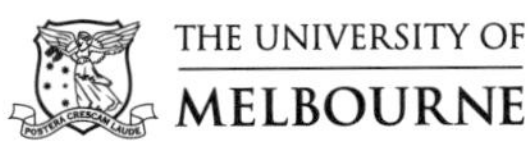

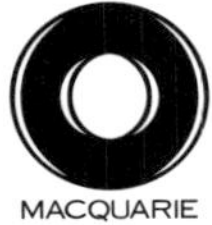

ERCO

Heide
Museum of
Modern Art

ANITA LUCA
BELGIORNO
NETTIS
FOUNDATION

COLLIDER

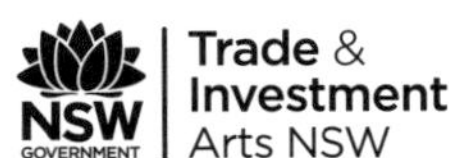

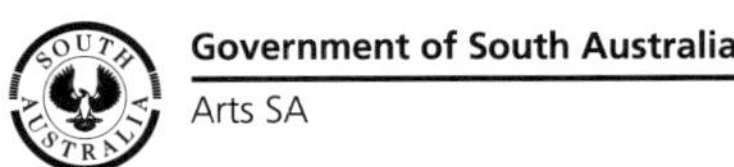

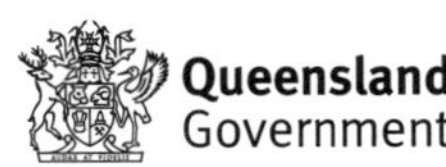

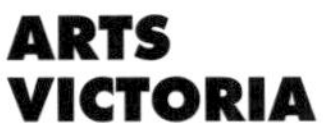

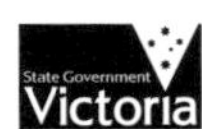

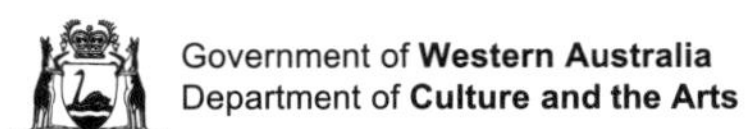

Donors & Champions

Victoria Alexander
Cathy Anderson and Anna Pianezze
Bernadette Archibald
Susan and Michael Armitage
Hamish Balnaves
Geoff and Jill Beadle
Anita Belgiorno-Nettis and
Luca Belgiorno-Nettis AM
Guido and Michelle Belgiorno-Nettis
John V. Beresford
Danielle and Daniel Besen
Brigid Brock
Lyndell Brown
Andrew Cameron AM and Cathy Cameron
Lisa Chung
Jan and Peter Clark
Jock Clough and Bobbie Salmon
Warren Coli
Melinda Conrad and David F. Jones
J. Andrew Cook, Dr Wendy Brown and Sophie Ullin
Phillip Cornwell and Cecilia Rice
Colin and Robyn Cowan
Anthony and Clare Cross
Fiorella and Phillip de Boos-Smith
Dr Paul Eliadis
Richard and Harriett England
Sally and Giles Everist
Adrian and Michela Fini
Barbara Flynn
William J. Forrest AM
Kiera Grant
Julian and Stephanie Grose
Kim Harding and Irene Miller
Michael and Janet Hayes
Mark Henry
Janet and Annabel Holt
Amanda and Steve Howe
Connie Kimberley and Chloe Podgornik
Vivien and Graham Knowles
Juliet Lockhart
James MacKean and Tee Beng Keng
Robyn Martin-Weber
Paul and Nikki McCullagh
David and Pam McKee
Jan Minchin
Angus Mordant
Simon Mordant AM and Catriona Mordant
Annabel and Rupert Myer
Dr Clinton Ng
John and Angela Nicolaides
Vicki Olsson
Judith O'Neil and Emily Brial
Roslyn Oxley OAM and Tony Oxley OAM
Mimi and Willy Packer
Lisa and Egil Paulsen
Frank Pollio
Veronique Ramen
Sue Rose and Alan Segal
Beverley Rowbotham and Francis Tomlinson
Jill Russell
Alan Schwartz AM and Carol Schwartz AM
Penelope Seidler AM
Eva and Michael Slancar
Thelma Taliangis and Elma Christopher
A. Tindale
Nick Tobias and Miranda Darling
Aida Tomescu
E. Tomlinson (TEWRR)
The University of Melbourne (represented by
Professor Charles Green)
Gwenyth and Stewart Wallis AO
Wesfarmers Arts
Jack and Cynthia Wynhoven
One anonymous

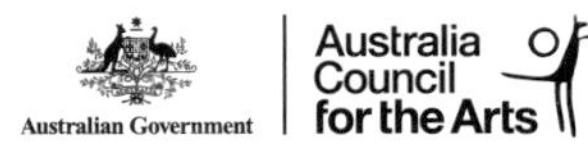

Commissioner

Simon Mordant AM

Artist

Fiona Hall AO

Curator

Linda Michael

Commissioner's Council

Simon Mordant AM, Commissioner
Professor Charles Green, Deputy Commissioner
Susan Armitage
Hamish Balnaves
Anita Belgiorno-Nettis
Dr Paul Eliadis
Adrian Fini
Mark Henry
Roslyn Oxley OAM
Lisa Paulsen
Nick Tobias

Australia Council for the Arts

Rupert Myer AM, Chair
Tony Grybowski, Chief Executive Officer
Danie Mellor, Chair of Visual Arts
Julie Lomax, Director, Visual Arts

Venice Biennale Project Team

Wendy Were, Executive Director, Arts Strategy
Elaine Chia, Director, International Signature Projects
Karen Hall, Manager, International Signature Projects
Bronwyn Papantonio, Projects Officer, International Signature Projects
Kate Murray, Producer, Publications and Marketing, Communications
Guy Betts, Project and Administration Coordinator, International Signature Projects
Diego Carpentiero, Australian Pavilion Supervisor
Elisa Torcutti, Venice Events Manager

Exhibition Installation Team

Adam Meredith
Andrew Moran
Philip Sticklen
Daniel Schutt

Emerging Curators

Pippa Milne
Megan Monte
Andrew Varano
Chantelle Woods

Australian Pavilion Exhibition Team Leaders

Jane Barlow
Ashleigh Campbell
Nadia Johnson
Niomi Sands
Eleanor Scicchitano
Katherine Wilkinson
Megan Williams

Australian Pavilion Exhibition Attendants

Mary Angove
Samuel Barbour
Lili-Belle Birchall
Philippa Brumby
Emma Buswell
Melinda Gagen
Anna Gore
Emma Hamilton
Thomas Hungerford
Patsy Killeen
Victoria Maxwell
Dan McCabe
Andrew Moran
Alyce Neal
Constantine Nikolakopoulos
Leanne Santoro
Marian Simpson
Ryan Sims
Annabella Snell
Diana Warnes
Olivia Welch

The University of Melbourne Intern

Jake Swinson

The Australia Council acknowledges the assistance provided by la Biennale di Venezia

Paolo Baratta, President
Okwui Enwezor, Director, 56th International Art Exhibition
Manuela Lucà-Dazio, Executive Manager, Visual Art and Architecture Department
Micol Saleri, Visual Arts and Architecture Department
Marco Truccolo, Visual Art and Architecture Department
Cristina Costanzo, Press Office

The Australia Council warmly thanks the following people for their contribution to the project:

Ettore Altomare, Toni Andon, Chiara Arceci, Susan Armitage, Michael Armitage, Mim Armour, Neil Balnaves AO and Diane Balnaves, William Barton, Toto Bergamo Rossi, Chelsea Beroza, Cassandra Bird, Desley Bischoff, Margaret Bishop, Andrea Bondi, Mitch Brown, Amanda Browne, Alison Buchbinder, Jaki Cammell, Christian Capurro, Diego Carpentiero, Jenni Carter, Giorgio Ceccato, Jude Chambers, Carolyn Christov-Bakargiev, Lisa Chung, Sam Creyton, Martina Cullen, Professor Glyn Davis AC, Fiorella and Phillip de Boos-Smith, Sandra Dear, Dr A. Dekker, Max Delany, John Denton, Vera Ding, Matthew Doyle, John Dunn, Nicole Durling, Hilary Ericksen, Joanna Foster, Elliott Foulkes, Lisa George, Michelle Glaser, Clayton Glen, Professor Charles Green, Mark Gumley, Katrina Hall, David Hansen, Mark Henry, Michael Hill, Anna Hyland, Naomi Iland, Associate Professor Alison Scott Inglis, Tony Kanellos, Rachel Kent, Natalie King, Jennifer Layther, Marita Leuver, Victoria Lynn, Clelia March Doeve OAM, Enzo Magris, Barrie Marshall, Dr Meredith Martin, Danie Mellor, Suzie Messner, Tony Mighell, Naomi Milgrom AO, Nick Mitzevich, Angus Mordant, Catriona Mordant, Simon Mordant AM, Kendrah Morgan, Aileen Muldoon, Djon Mundine, Djakapurra Munyarryun, Jane Murray, Peter McKay, Judith Neilson, Paris Neilson, Roslyn Oxley OAM, Tony Oxley OAM, Michele Paveggio, private collectors, Vicki Petrusevics, Simon Power, Andrew Purvis, Suhanya Raffel, The Hon Mike Rann CNZM, David Resnicow, Leigh Robb, Alex Robinson, Sarah Rosetta, Dr Philip Rylands, Luisa Saccotelli, Christopher Saines, Sean Semler, Clayton Sochacki, Jason Smith, Fraser Tanner, Elisa Torcutti, Doug Trappett, Andrew van der Westhuyzen, Riccardo Vanucci, Paul Westra, Sam Wild, Williams Sinclair Collection, Michelle Young.

Artist's acknowledgements

I would like to thank Linda Michael, curator; Simon Mordant, commissioner; Elaine Chia, Karen Hall and Bronwyn Papantonio from the Australia Council for the Arts; Clayton Glen, catalogue photographs; Mitch Brown, catalogue design; John Dunn, Piper Press; Philip Sticklen, cabinetry; Adam Meredith, lighting; Paul Westra, bronze casting; Hank Stegenga, clock specialist; Gary Warner, crow recordings; Ian du Rieu, LED circuitry design for *Hack*; Tony Rossiter, tunnel design for *Hack*; Graham Maslen from Spitting Image, pre-press; Daniel Schutt and Andrew Moran, installers; Kendrah Morgan and Michelle Nikou, installation assistants, Joanna Foster, Tjanpi Desert Weaver workshop coordinator; the Tjanpi Desert Weavers; Graeme Atkins and family, Natalie Robertson, custodians of Omaewa Beach, Aotearoa; and Roslyn Oxley9 Gallery, Sydney.

Curator's acknowledgements

I would like to thank Jason Smith, former director of Heide Museum of Modern Art, whose support allowed me the time to work on this project. Thanks also to other staff of Heide for their assistance, particularly Kendrah Morgan, Linda Short, Katarina Paseta, Sue Cramer, Lesley Harding and Kirsty Grant. My appreciation to Roslyn and Tony Oxley and the staff at Roslyn Oxley9 Gallery: Cassandra Bird, Anna Aspinall, Ruby Brown, Jessica Maurer, Ivan Buljan and Andrew Moran. I am grateful to Hilary Ericksen for editing my essay and Mitch Brown from Collider for his catalogue design. Thanks also to Andrew van der Westhuyzen and Naomi Iland from Collider; Rebecca Coates; John Denton; John Dunn; Joanna Foster; Elizabeth Gertsakis; Clayton Glen; Katrina Hall; David Hansen; Victoria Lynn and Mim Armour from TarraWarra Museum of Art; Adam Meredith; Djon Mundine; Linda Rive; Phil Sticklen; and Michelle Young and Karina Menkhorst from Tjanpi Desert Weavers for their assistance. Warm thanks to the extended team who has enabled the project's realisation, in particular Elaine Chia, Karen Hall, and Bronwyn Papantonio from the Australia Council for the Arts. It has been a privilege to work with Fiona Hall, whose unwavering focus and generosity have made the job a pleasure.

Contributors

Linda Michael is Deputy Director / Senior Curator at Heide Museum of Modern Art, Melbourne.

Dr David Hansen is Associate Professor, Centre for Art History and Art Theory, ANU School of Art, The Australian National University, Canberra.

Tjanpi Desert Weavers is a social arts enterprise established in 1995 by the Ngaanyatjarra Pitjantjatjara Yankunytjatjara (NPY) Women's Council to provide an income source for Aboriginal women living in desert communities. Over four hundred women across the Central and Western Desert region create an array of fibre art from locally collected grasses, sharing stories of culture, community and country.

Fiona Hall is represented by Roslyn Oxley9 Gallery, Sydney, Australia